'MEET ME IN THE ROKER END'

A Revealing Look at Sunderland's Footballing History

First published in the United Kingdom in 2004 by Vertical Editions,
7 Bell Busk, Skipton North Yorkshire BD23 4DT

ISBN 1-904091-07-5

Jacket design and typeset by HBA, York

Printed and bound by the Cromwell Press, Trowbridge

CONTENTS

Foreword   Page 5

1. A Club of Two Halves   Page 7

2. Teams of All Talents   Page 15

3. Magna Carter   Page 42

4. 'Peanuts – tanner a bag!'   Page 71

5. 'When we win promotion...'   Page 89

6. Fairy Tales Really Do Come True!   Page 134

7. How Are the Mighty Fallen!   Page 150

8. Seesaw Seasons   Page 163

9. Money, Money, Money   Page 177

10. Here Today, Gone Tomorrow   Page 194

11. Extra Time   Page 219

FOREWORD BY CHARLIE HURLEY

I spent 12 years with Sunderland and I can categorically state that there isn't a club in the land with a better set of supporters. It is 40 years now since the team I captained finally won promotion to what was then the First Division, and it meant so much to the fans, the players, the management and the entire town that people still want to talk to me about it. It was an honour for me to play for Sunderland and indeed just as big an honour to be voted 'Player of the Century' by the fans.

I signed for Sunderland in 1957 for £18,000 and received the grand sum of £10 as a signing-on fee. Alan Brown had not been in charge for very long and the club was clearly undergoing a period of change. We were relegated at the end of my first season but I can remember promising that I would do my utmost to lead the club back into the top flight. It took until 1964 to achieve that goal and I can assure you that there was a great deal of blood, sweat and tears shed before we eventually made it.

The Sunderland fans have always recognised honest players who give their all for the cause. That's because they are as knowledgeable as they are passionate. Shipyard workers and miners with pieces of coal engrained beneath the skin of their hands would ask to shake me by the hand and tell me what an honour it was to meet me. I would always tell them that the honour was all mine.

Sunderland supporters have not always had an easy ride, but I can say this with the utmost belief. If they had seen their club achieve what the likes of Manchester United and Arsenal have achieved in recent times, then you would not be able to build a stadium big enough to accommodate them.

For someone born in Cork and raised in Essex, I suppose you could say I am an adopted Wearsider. This is my club and will remain so until the day I die. The day I signed for Sunderland, I received a telegram from a beautiful young lady. Eighteen months later Joan and I were married. We have two lovely daughters Tracy and Joanne, who are married to Gary and Simon respectively, and five grandchildren James,

Mathew, Emma, Katherine and Charlotte. I love them all to bits.

And so joining Sunderland served me well. I married the love of my life and met the best fans in football. I was delighted to be asked to write the foreword for 'Meet Me in the Roker End', and I hope you enjoy reading the stories – some funny, some sad – many of which have been recalled by good friends of mine.

Charlie Hurley
September 2004

1

A CLUB OF TWO HALVES

A chill autumn wind cut through the thin frame of 17-year-old Raich Carter as he left Sunderland Football Club's Roker Park ground clutching what he regarded as a small fortune. Carter, later to be immortalised as one of the greatest players ever to don one of the club's famous red-and-white striped shirts, could hardly believe his luck. He had been born in the Hendon area of Sunderland, yet it had looked unlikely at one stage that he would have the opportunity to play for his home-town club.

But everything had changed in November 1931 when, still a month short of his 18th birthday, he was summoned to Sunderland's boardroom by manager Johnny Cochrane. Carter had been playing for the reserves as an amateur, having being rejected by Leicester City, and had initially been refused professional terms by the club. But now there was renewed hope because Cochrane had started to realise that he had someone with star potential on his doorstep. To borrow the title of a cult North-East based film, it had been time for him to 'Get Carter'. On the boardroom table was a professional contract which offered the youthful Carter £3 a week and an extra £1 when he played for the reserves. In addition, he watched in amazement as Cochrane handed him a huge £10 signing-on bonus. Carter, who was to rise from his humble beginnings in Hendon to scale football's greatest heights, later recalled in his book *Footballer's Progress*:

> I had never known so much money. I walked through the streets with the notes clutched tightly in my hand and went into a cinema for the matinee to celebrate the momentous occasion. Still holding on to the money like grim death – I dare not put it in my pocket and let go of it – I sat through the performance and then went home in triumph to my mother. I was now the family breadwinner. Each week I gave my mother all my wages except 10 shillings [50p], of which five went into the savings bank and five were my pocket money. Football to me was now the serious business of earning a living.

Less than six years on from what Carter called 'that red-letter day in my calendar – 12 November 1931', he would become the first player to captain Sunderland to an FA Cup final victory. But for now, he was concentrating on earning a living so that he could look after his widowed mother, Clara, and the rest of their family. Young Raich had been initially disappointed with his terms, but his Uncle Ted, who had accompanied him on that momentous trip to Roker Park, had ensured that common sense prevailed. Carter said:

> My uncle was doing the talking on my behalf and he accepted, so I picked up the pen and signed the professional forms with great pride and excitement. I remember thinking particularly of Charlie Buchan, perhaps the greatest of Sunderland's football stars, who would have been signing on in the same room – perhaps sitting in the same chair as I was – some years before. If I could make good on only half the scale that he had done, I should feel satisfied. Johnny Cochrane counted out ten £1 notes – my signing-on bonus.

It was a heart-warming tale that was typical of football in the early part of the 20th century. In those days an assortment of characters – such as ex-soldiers, pitmen, dockers, shipbuilders, apprentice electricians and labourers – were regularly rescued by the fast-growing sport that would eventually turn into one of the biggest industries in the world. In those days football gave them hope and provided an escape route from the harsh reality of the human condition in the aftermath of the Depression. In those days it was also the salvation for thousands of adoring fans who also needed an antidote to austerity. And Sunderland were a football club at the heart of it all. They had provided inspiration and a badly needed foil for the often-harsh North-East winters and the equally harsh industrial climate. When, for example, Carter held aloft the FA Cup for the first time in the club's history, it coincided with a period when unemployment in the area was reckoned to be two and a half times the national rate.

Carter, though, was never one for forgetting his roots. It shone through in his family loyalty and the memory of his boyhood idol, Charlie Buchan, who had occasionally visited the Ocean Queen, the Carters' pub in the docklands of Sunderland. Carter had had to show great resolve to make the grade with Sunderland, but so too had Buchan. When Buchan joined the club as a 19-year-old in 1911, he had to endure a baptism of fire. He was barracked by the fans in his early days at Roker Park and became homesick. And it is said that Buchan, a Londoner by birth whose name was to be enshrined in folklore for generations after he founded his own football magazine, immediately spent money on an overcoat to counteract the severity of the North-East climate. But he exorcised his personal demons to become Sunderland's leading League marksman of all time, with 209 goals, and would stay at Roker Park for 14 years.

Becoming a footballing hero with Sunderland was as character-forming as the unyielding aspects of the area's industrial landscape and bleak midwinters. The locals believed in working hard, and expected their footballers to do likewise. But if the footballers proved their worth, they were given due respect and adulation and treated as heroes in a way that few other areas could match. From the outset there was to be a close bond between the players and their public. For many years, though, the players were more or less on a par with their public in one sense because they were subject to a maximum wage. They were equally down to earth, and it was their performances rather than their pay packets that put them on a pedestal in those days. One of Carter's great contemporaries and colleagues, the self-effacing Bobby Gurney, who was born at Silksworth, did not turn up for home games in a flash car – instead he first walked a mile to the nearest tram and then travelled to the ground alongside the fans who idolised him. It did him little harm, though, because he became Sunderland's leading marksman of all time, with 228 League and Cup goals, and repaid the fans' appreciation of him by serving the club for 22 years as a player and, briefly, as a coach.

It was, though, all a far cry from the more sedate and comfortable beginnings of the club. It was founded by a group of schoolteachers, the chief of whom was James Allan, a Scot who had left Glasgow University to be the second assistant master at Hendon Board School in the town. The club began life in October 1879 under the unwieldy title of Sunderland & District Teachers' Association Football Club, following a meeting at the Adults' School in Sunderland's Norfolk Street at which Robert Singleton was chosen as the first captain with Allan as his vice-captain. A year later, however, the club had to open its doors to people outside the teaching profession, becoming just plain Sunderland AFC. Football was played more as a form of amusement at that time and had a certain novelty value about it. The few clubs in the county of Durham were affiliated to the neighbouring Northumberland federation, but gradually football's popularity grew. More clubs sprang up in different parts of the county and it became possible to establish Durham County Football Association with Sunderland and Darlington two of their main supporters.

Sunderland, who played mostly in blue in those days and did not adopt red and white shirts until 1888, progressed via various grounds to participate in the FA Cup for the first time in 1884/85. On 8 November 1884, they visited Redcar and lost 3–1, with their founder Allan on the left wing and John Grayston, the club's first secretary, at centre-forward. Right-winger Don McColl had the satisfaction of scoring the club's first goal in the competition, but it was scarcely a good career move because two months later Sunderland lost 11–1 at home to Port Glasgow – and he was in goal!

In 1887 Robert Thompson, a major shipbuilder and a magistrate, took an active interest in the club and was elected as their president. A management committee was formed with James Marr as the chairman and Samuel Tyzack as the treasurer, but it was a year of change in another sense. In December 1887 Middlesbrough lodged a complaint after Sunderland had beaten them in the FA Cup, claiming that three of their imported Scots had technically been professionals. Sunderland were thrown out of the competition, prompting Allan to depart following the club's annual meeting at the Workmen's Hall in Monkwearmouth in May 1888. Allan then formed Sunderland Albion and took several players with him, but it was hardly a good footballing career move for him. Sunderland went from strength to strength: Sunderland Albion, who ironically were disqualified from the FA Cup themselves in 1889/90, folded in 1892.

The progress made by Sunderland, who were now playing at their Newcastle Road ground, included admission to the Football League at its annual meeting in Manchester's Douglas Hotel on 2 May 1890, when the club's delegation included schoolteacher Lynn Marr, one of their founders. The bottom three clubs in the 12-strong League of 1889/90 – Notts County, Burnley and Stoke – had to seek re-election. Those wanting to join were Sunderland, Sunderland Albion, Grimsby Town, Newton Heath and Darwen. Notts County and Burnley were re-elected, but Sunderland got the nod over Stoke to become the only newcomers for 1890/91.

The Football League had been formed only in 1888/89, when Preston North End set the precedent for Arsenal in 2003/04 by remaining undefeated throughout their programme. They and Everton dominated the early seasons, but then Sunderland dramatically intervened. They emulated Preston by winning the League in two successive seasons, as Aston Villa also emerged as a force. But Sunderland were becoming the side to beat, winning the League three times in four seasons and becoming known as the Team of All Talents.

In 1895 Sunderland became a limited company and two years later one of the most influential figures in the club's history, the Cambridge-educated Fred Taylor, became a director for the first time. He retired from the board two years later, but in 1904 he began a nine-year stewardship as chairman. Taylor stayed on as a director until just before his death in 1947 and became known as 'Mr Sunderland'. He bred dogs and tropical birds and in an early cartoon was pictured reaching out to stroke a black cat perched on a football. And there is a tale that Raich Carter was once pictured holding a black cat after Sunderland had beaten Middlesbrough. This suggests that the club's nickname of the

'Black Cats' was not just dreamed up for the ground move from Roker Park to the Stadium of Light in 1997. It was revived then as an alternative to the 'Wearsiders' or the 'Rokerites', but in reality it had been around a long time. Perhaps one origin of the nickname was a black cat which was said to inhabit Sunderland's club offices at one time. Perhaps another origin had been handed down from the days of the Napoleonic Wars, when the silhouettes of the cannons strategically placed at the mouth of the River Wear for defence purposes resembled black cats.

On the pitch Sunderland continued to purr, and by the outbreak of the 1914–18 war they had won the League title five times and had been runners-up on three occasions. They had also finished third in the First Division three times and reached two FA Cup semi-finals and one final. Sunderland also remained a powerful influence in League football in the period between the two world wars, but it was not until the 1930s that they clinched the First Division title for a sixth time, winning the FA Cup a year later for the first time.

Sunderland had become firmly established as a big club and their evolution as a successful one meant that the area naturally developed into a hotbed of football. Having relied heavily on Scottish imports in their triumphant early years, they gradually produced a conveyor belt of talent from their own acres. Three of Charlie Buchan's best-known team-mates – George Holley, Jackie Mordue and Frank Cuggy – were originally from the North-East, for instance. But while some of the promising players joined Sunderland, others went elsewhere while still proclaiming an allegiance to their home region. Centre-forward Billy 'Ginger' Richardson, for example, played once for England in 1935 while with West Bromwich Albion, but he was from Framwellgate Moor, near Durham. He claimed, in fact, that he had never heard of Albion when he was asked to join them from Hartlepools United in the summer of 1929. Instead he insisted that he was 'all Sunderland' and that his father was 'a worshipper at the shrine of Charles Buchan and George Holley'.

Neither was the impact of joining a club of Sunderland's standing lost on outsiders. Eddie Burbanks, a slim, will-o'-the-wisp winger, was from Bentley, near Doncaster, and scored for Sunderland in the FA Cup final in 1937, as did Carter and Gurney. Carter later signed him twice when he was the manager of Hull City and then Leeds United, but in February 1935 Burbanks, then a 21-year-old clerk who had been playing as a part-time professional with non-League Denaby United, was well aware of the significance of his move to Sunderland. Accompanied by his father Henry and Denaby's manager Percy Harrison, he travelled north by train from Doncaster to York to meet the same Johnny Cochrane who had secured Carter's services more than three years earlier. Burbanks recalled:

Mr Cochrane was a cheery personality and knew all about me, but then the business started. It was six o'clock when Mr Cochrane, Percy Harrison and father first started talking. I sat tight and said nothing. I had a job to keep myself from yawning and it was 10 o'clock before everything was settled. We then went to Mr Cochrane's hotel just outside the station and I signed the forms. Yet on my return home that night I just felt that I had been dreaming. It seemed unbelievable that I was going from the clerk's desk to a famous First Division club, where I would be mingling with some of the biggest stars in football.

Sunderland's triumphs before the 1939–45 war left a lasting legacy, and the club's passionate fans now expected success as part of their yearly football diet. What they suffered instead was a severe bout of indigestion. The first half of Sunderland's League history had brought success, fame and high expectations from their adoring public. The second half brought frustration, anticlimax and inconsistency. There were many great players, yet the trophies largely dried up. Sunderland promised much, but delivered little. By 1958 they were the only club in the Football League never to have played outside the top flight, but then they were relegated. They eventually bounced back, only to be relegated again and enter a yo-yo existence. They managed to win the FA Cup again in 1973, but the club's fortunes reached a nadir when they dropped into the old Third Division for the first time in 1987.

All along there was a tendency to attract big names and pay big wages, but the big prizes generally remained out of reach. All along there were heroes and all along there were characters, but the talent of the individuals seldom gelled to bring silverware as a team. All along there was a tendency to flatter to deceive in marked contrast with the heady successes of those early days. Sunderland outwardly became a big club in name only. The fans' stomachs were by now grumbling for success on a regular basis, but the recipe for it had largely gone missing. There was still a voracious appetite for success, but there was very little success itself. The irony of it all was probably best summed up by the fact that Sunderland signed an all-time great before their first relegation in 1958. Charlie Hurley, born in Cork and brought up in Essex, was a towering centre-half who became one of Sunderland's greatest heroes. As with Buchan, he wondered what he had let himself in for when he left Millwall for the North-East. But, as with Carter, he came to respect the harsh working traditions of the area once he had settled in it:

I can remember driving up to Sunderland in my first car, a Ford Consul, and wondering just how far north I had to go. I thought I was driving to the end of the world. It was town after town and there were no motorways then. But all the time I was at Sunderland, big tough miners would shake my hands – men with actual pieces of coal ingrained under their skin. All they wanted to do whenever they saw me in the town was to shake hands. But it was I who was proud to shake their hands. I've always tried to be a very modest man, but that is how the people felt about me. And to have their love will suit me just fine until the day I die.

The empathy between exceptional players and expectant public has remained a thread throughout Sunderland's history. Whether they were hard men and natural leaders such as Charlie Hurley or extravagant entertainers or controversial characters such as Len Shackleton, there was a need for heroes. The fans still had their favourites despite the anticlimax of the post-war years.

And, as with Billy Richardson, there were still plenty of players who made the grade away from their native North-East despite being steeped in Sunderland's traditions. Ralph Coates, a forward from Hetton-le-Hole who left the area in 1961 and became an England international while with Burnley and Tottenham Hotspur, could never forget his affection for his roots when he offered his home thoughts from abroad:

I was Sunderland-crazy as a kid. They were the only team for me. But going to Burnley was my big chance and I couldn't afford to miss it. As far as I was concerned, Len Shackleton and Charlie Hurley were the greatest and I would have done anything to join them. I had always wanted to be a professional and, as a kid, I used to rush straight from school matches to watch Sunderland on Saturdays. All the kids at school were Sunderland-mad and just watching Shack made my day. He was a great ball artist: he could almost make the ball talk. He was a born entertainer with a wonderful repertoire of tricks and he had the confidence to carry them out.

The fervour for football was ingrained in the North-East heartland every bit as powerfully as the traces of coal were inlaid in the hands of the miners that Hurley so willingly shook in mutual respect. Micky Horswill, the ginger-haired midfield player who was the youngest member of Sunderland's FA Cup-winning team of 1973, recognised it as soon as he knew that manager Alan Brown wanted to sign him. It was 1968, and he recalled:

I would have died for Alan Brown. Everybody went to the club when they joined Sunderland, but he came to my house and signed me. I'd heard that Sunderland were going to watch me in a cup final for Stanley Boys against Newcastle Boys. I went over to take a throw-in and saw Alan Brown, who threw me the ball. He then walked round the ground and straight out, so I thought I'd blown my chance. But Sunderland's scout Charlie Ferguson saw me and said, 'Alan Brown's coming to the house tonight. I've heard of you and we've had reports about you.' I hurried home to Stanley and was waiting two or three hours for Alan Brown to come, but then he arrived and went round the back of the house. He came in and offered me £8 a week and said, 'You do as you're told now.' And then he turned to my dad Eric and said, 'You've just lost a son because I'm his father from now on.' I was just a scruffy lad from Annfield Plain who wanted to play football, but I practised and practised and I think I was just in the right place at the right time.

Maybe Sunderland tried almost too hard to regain former glories in the post-war years. Maybe the frustrations of the forces inside and outside the club took a stranglehold that could not be easily broken. Maybe the striving of the later years might never have needed to be so excessive if the triumphs of the early ones had not been etched so deeply in thousands of memories. The Sunderland area may have naturally developed into a hotbed of football, but that in itself guaranteed nothing. It always brought hope and expectation, but it made matters worse if instead there were disappointment and despair.

Put simply, the first half of Sunderland's history is more illustrious than the second half. The statistics reveal a tale of two Sunderlands. They were the second most successful Football League club of the 1920s, behind Liverpool. They were third behind Arsenal and Derby County in the 1930s. But they had dropped to 11th by the 1940s, 14th by the 1950s, 24th by the 1960s and 27th by the 1970s.

But pride and passion have remained integral parts of Sunderland football throughout the trials and tribulations. They stretched from the day in May 1888 when club founder James Allan defected to the day in May 2004 when Gerry Steinberg, the Labour MP for the City of Durham, tabled a motion in the House of Commons deploring the standard of refereeing and calling on the football authorities to introduce instant playback facilities in the wake of Sunderland's exit from the First Division play-offs. Through the peaks and troughs, the ups and downs, the highs and lows, it has above all been essential for those dedicated followers of Sunderland's fortunes to show how deeply and devotedly they cared. It was forever innate.

2

TEAMS OF ALL TALENTS

It is entirely appropriate that Sunderland should have been founded by a Scotsman, James Allan, because their astonishing early success was founded upon players from north of the border. The North-East of England has traditionally been regarded as one of football's heartlands, but Sunderland established a formidable reputation on the strength of an influx of Scots early in their League history. And when they joined the Football League in 1890/91, their reliance on Scots proved to be eminently successful.

They had had Scots playing for them in their FA Cup days before they attained League status. There was, for example, a forward called John Brackenridge who scored three times in two FA Cup appearances in 1888/89 (and later collapsed and died on a tram in Sunderland). But he never played for the club once they joined the League, and neither did three other Scots – Monaghan, Hastings and Richardson – who had been responsible for the club being thrown out of the FA Cup in 1887/88.

Squabbles still abounded in 19th-century football, so it is scarcely surprising that another one involving a Scot led to Sunderland making a disastrous start to their life in the League. Initially it surrounded the performances of goalkeeper Bill Kirtley. On 13 September 1890, Sunderland lost their inaugural League game 3–2 against Burnley at Newcastle Road, where they had played since 1886, and in their next match were beaten 4–3 by Wolverhampton Wanderers, having taken a 3–0 lead. Kirtley, the only remaining amateur from the club's pre-League days, played in both games, but was then dropped. His replacement was Edward 'Ned' Doig, who was signed from Arbroath and was already a Scottish international. But his registration was deemed to have been improper because he had played one game for Blackburn Rovers in November 1889. Doig was adjudged to have been ineligible when he made his Sunderland debut at West Bromwich Albion because the Football League had not approved his registration. It was Sunderland's first-ever League victory, but the punishment for Doig's appearance included a two-point deduction, the first occasion on which such a penalty was imposed. As a result, Sunderland were still without a point from their first three League games even though they had won one of them!

Kirtley never played another game for Sunderland because he was transferred to Sunderland Albion later in the month; he did not disappear from view entirely, because he was in charge of the billiards room in the offices at Roker Park into the 1930s. But Doig, who had been a right-winger as a teenager, soon progressed from club villain to hero. He became a fixture in goal, not missing a League or Cup game until January 1894, and was Sunderland's first Scottish international along the way, collecting a further three caps, all against England. Doig, who was just short of his 24th birthday when he was signed, was an ever-present in seven seasons and for a long time he headed Sunderland's leading appearances' list with 456. When he moved on in 1904, he had played for them in four First Division championship-winning seasons – a feat that only one other player, Scottish inside-forward Jimmy Millar, was to emulate. Doig, who became known as the 'Prince of Goalkeepers', was sensitive about his baldness and on one occasion was said to have been more concerned about retrieving his cap than the ball after he had lost both in a goalmouth scramble!

Millar was also with Sunderland from 1890 to 1904, but clocked up just 260 appearances because he had two spells with the club with a four-year stint at Glasgow Rangers in between. Yet he played in Sunderland's first League game against Burnley and scored 123 goals for them. He was also the first player to score five goals in a match for the club when they beat non-League Fairfield 11–1 in the first round of the FA Cup in February 1895 – still their biggest-ever win in a competitive match. He had previously scored four in a 7–1 win over Derby County, and in all he notched ten hat-tricks for Sunderland, but his three international appearances for Scotland came during his Rangers days.

Sunderland's Scottish evolution had been gathering momentum before they achieved League status in 1890. And some Scots – including left-half William Gibson, centre-half John Auld, winger John Harvey, inside-forward John Smith and centre-forward Johnny Campbell – stayed with the club from the non-League days into the League. Gibson, Auld and Campbell, in fact, were also in the side beaten by Burnley in that first League game.

Gibson, who had been signed in 1888, had a fair bit in common with Millar. He also had two spells at Sunderland broken by a stint at Glasgow Rangers, and the two were to become brothers-in-law. They also died quite young – Gibson at the age of 43 and Millar just short of his 37th birthday after having been struck down by tuberculosis while on Chelsea's coaching staff. Auld, who had represented Glasgow against Sheffield in an inter-city match in 1887, had previously had two spells with both Third Lanark and Queen's Park. He had also been capped three times by Scotland before joining Sunderland, for whom he made 116 appearances spread over six seasons, in 1889. He then earned himself a place in the club's history when he became their first player to join local rivals Newcastle United after asking to be reinstated as an amateur in 1896. The following year, when he retired as a player, he promptly became a Newcastle director! Curiously enough, Harvey and Campbell, both of whom had joined Sunderland in 1889, also moved to Newcastle as players in a joint deal in 1897 a month before Auld joined the board. They had also joined Sunderland together from Renton, the Scottish FA Cup winners in 1885 and 1888. But the pint-sized Harvey, who was the supply line for many of Campbell's goals, also set the trend for Gibson and Millar by having two spells at Sunderland with a return to Scotland in between – in his case a period with Clyde.

Campbell's goals were central to Sunderland's early success. He was said to have cut a nonchalant figure at times, but he was ruthless enough about his goalscoring. In 1891/92 Campbell scored the first League hat-trick in Sunderland's history, netting four times in a 5–2 win against Bolton Wanderers. The following season he scored 25 goals in 29 games, including four in a 6–1 victory over Blackburn and three other hat-tricks. And in their second title-winning season he was on the mark 31 times in 30 games with four more hat-tricks. Campbell then scored 21 times in the 1894/95 title-winning season, and finished his Sunderland career with 150 goals in 215 appearances. It made him the first of the club's great goalscorers, and he remains their fifth highest of all time.

Another Scot who was a member of Sunderland's first League side in the 3–2 defeat against Burnley did not last much longer than Kirtley – John Spence, who had been signed from then non-League Kilmarnock. He scored both goals against Burnley, but played in only five games for the club, while Campbell became one of the club's earliest heroes.

John Smith, signed from Kilmarnock a year before Spence, struggled to become a Sunderland regular although he did win a medal for his contribution to the their first championship-winning season of 1891/92. He too switched routinely between Scotland and the North-East of England, with two spells at Kilmarnock and a brief stay with Newcastle East End. East End developed via mergers into Newcastle

United, and Smith duly joined them in 1894 –not directly from Sunderland, but via Liverpool and Sheffield Wednesday.

John Scott, one of the other players who often supplied the goalscoring ammunition for Campbell and Millar, also had a Scottish background and spent six years with Sunderland after joining them in 1890 from the club then known as Coatbridge Albion Rovers. He chipped in with 34 goals of his own in 110 games for the club, but was not always a regular even though at times he formed a vital left-wing partnership with winger David Hannah.

Hannah was not a Scot by birth – he originated from County Down in Ireland – but he had lived in Scotland since he was a youngster and, as did Harvey and Campbell, he joined Sunderland from Renton during the summer of 1889. He was an ever-present in their first League season and contributed 25 goals from 89 games for the club before having spells with Liverpool and Woolwich Arsenal and ending his career back at Renton.

Wing-half John Murray arrived from Vale of Leven, where he had been in the side beaten in the Scottish FA Cup final of 1889/90, in time for Sunderland's first League season. Already a Scottish international, he was once described as 'one of the best runners and jumpers' in the country. But his stay with Sunderland lasted just two years before he moved on to Blackburn, for whom his son Robert subsequently played.

Winger James Gillespie, on the other hand, earned his only Scotland cap in 1898, six years after leaving Sunderland, whom he had rejoined in readiness for their League baptism. In fact, he was on the mark in their first home game in the First Division when they lost 4–3 to Wolves, and went on to score 51 goals in 149 appearances for the club. Signed from Morton, he followed the early pattern of two spells with Sunderland, with a year in between spent with neighbours Sunderland Albion. Gillespie moved to Albion having been overlooked after his debut against Wolves, but he established himself on his return to Newcastle Road and played an integral part in Sunderland's history at a crucial time in 1896/97. The club was faced with relegation and had to play a series of what were known as Test matches, to preserve their First Division status. They finally beat Newton Heath 2–0 to do so, becoming the club with the longest unbroken run in League football's top flight, and Gillespie scored both vital goals. It was Gillespie's last appearance for the club because he then moved to Third Lanark, for whom several of Sunderland's early Scots played. It was also indicative of the club's preoccupation with Scottish links in the 1890s that they signed full-back John Gillespie from Morton two years after signing James Gillespie from Morton.

And it took a Scot to keep them all together on the pitch – skipper Hugh 'Lalty' Wilson. As with several of his contemporaries at Sunderland, he came originally from Ayrshire and had spells with Third Lanark and Kilmarnock. But he started his career with his home-town club, Mauchline, and then moved a little further north to Newmilns, with whom he earned his first Scotland cap. But it was at Sunderland, whom he joined as part of the exodus from Scotland in the summer of 1890, that his career blossomed as he became one of the club's early heroes. He scored 45 goals in 258 games for them, but the figures tell only part of the story. A half-back, Wilson was known for his legendary one-handed long throws and was said to have been responsible for a change in the law that insisted on all throw-ins being two-handed. He was the only player to have appeared in Sunderland's first League game in 1890 and their first League game at Roker Park eight years later. He was also the first Sunderland player to be sent off in a League game – in a 5–0 defeat at Stoke in March 1896. Wilson was also versatile, capable of playing in goal in an emergency, as a full-back and as a forward, scoring a hat-trick in a 3–0 home win over Bury in October 1898. And although he gained two of his paltry four Scottish caps while with Sunderland, he led the club to three First Division titles in four seasons and two FA Cup semi-finals.

A horde of Scots came south to accumulate a hoard of medals, and Englishmen were almost excluded in those early years in the League. But full-back Tom Porteous was an exception. He was born in Newcastle, but he joined Sunderland in 1889 after spells with Scottish clubs Heart of Midlothian and then Kilmarnock. He stayed to make 93 appearances for the club in five years, beginning with their first League game a year later. Porteous was also the first Sunderland player to win an England cap, and fittingly it came in a 4–1 win over Wales in March 1991 – at Newcastle Road.

The unfortunate Bill Kirtley also hailed from the North-East, while there was one genuinely local lad who played in Sunderland's first League game and was briefly a member of what became known as the Team of All Talents – left-back John 'Dowk' Oliver. He came from Southwick and had been with the club from 1886, but he enjoyed just two seasons of League football with them before moving to Middlesbrough Ironopolis after a dispute over terms.

There was nothing particularly great about Sunderland's first season in the League. They had replaced Stoke, the bottom club in 1889/90, and finished seventh in a 12-team, one-division Football League, although they had also reached the semi-finals of the FA Cup. Only 31 clubs participated in it that season, after Old Westminsters had scratched, and Sunderland began with a 3–0 home win over Everton, who were to become League champions, before winning 2–0 at Darwen and beating Nottingham Forest 4–0 at home. Their semi-final opponents were Notts County, who had beaten Stoke 1–0 at the quarter-final stage in a controversial tie that ultimately brought the introduction of penalties by the FA in September 1891. The first semi-final ended 3–3, but County won the replay 2–0.

But Sunderland's modest start to League life merely disguised what was to follow. Manager Tom Watson, who had been appointed as the club's match secretary and manager before the start of the 1889/90 season, continued to assemble the Team of All Talents with a further helping of Scots. Watson had managed in Newcastle, where he was born, but found greater ambition at Sunderland. He immediately maximised the possibilities and, William McGregor who was one of the Football League's founders, is supposed to have given Sunderland their tag when he said after they had beaten his club Aston Villa 7–2 in a friendly in April 1890: 'They have a talented man in every position.' And youngsters in the North-East were even taught to recite a poem about the most successful side in Sunderland's history. It went:

> The team of all talent
> The cream of all the land
> The best of forwards, halves and defence
> Picked by a master's hand
> The League is at their mercy
> Should one team make a slip
> And surely now can nothing
> Stand 'twixt cup and lip.

Full-back Don Gow and wingers James 'Blood' Hannah and James Logan all arrived in 1891/92, when Watson led Sunderland spectacularly to the championship of the 14-strong League. The team scored 93 goals in their 26 matches, winning 13 games in a row between November 1891 and April 1892 and finishing five points clear of runners-up Preston. The mould had been made, and the Football League held their annual meeting in Sunderland in 1892 to mark the triumphant title win.

Gow, who finished up as a referee, fitted into Sunderland's developing Scottish tradition if only because he had two spells with the club, sandwiched around a second stint with Glasgow Rangers, from whom he had initially been signed. He came from the relatively remote Blair Atholl in Perthshire, and his representative honours were especially notable. He is thought to have been the first Scot to be chosen to represent the Football League in England and had made just one international appearance for Scotland when he captained the side at the age of 20. Hannah, a Glaswegian, had also made just one appearance for Scotland and spent two periods with Third Lanark, but Sunderland signed him from Sunderland Albion and he stayed for six years. He did not immediately establish himself as a first-teamer, but would give sterling service with 77 goals in 172 appearances, scoring a hat-trick in the 11–1 FA Cup defeat of Fairfield. Logan, from Troon, also made one appearance for Scotland, but did not last long at Sunderland, soon returning to Ayr, from whom they had signed him. In fact, he made his name in English football by becoming only the second player to score a hat-trick in an FA Cup final when Notts County beat Bolton 4–1 in 1893/94. He died young after catching pneumonia when Loughborough's kit failed to turn up for a Second Division game against Newton Heath, and he played in heavy rain in his own clothes, which he had to wear afterwards.

The Scottish invasion did not meet with universal approval and winger Arnie Davison, who died young in the workhouse in Sunderland, was viewed as one of the unfortunate victims of it. In fact, a poet wrote at the time:

> Who played right well in former days
> For love of play and honour's praise
> Before the dawn of the Scottish craze?
> 'Twas Arnie!

But the Scots made Sunderland successful, because the Team of All Talents retained the League championship in 1892/93 even more emphatically. Preston were again the runners-up, but finished 11 points in arrears as Sunderland scored 100 goals in their 30 games in the 16-strong First Division – there was also a Second Division of 12 clubs – and had the best defensive record, conceding just 36.

More Scots joined the cause in 1892 – wing-half William Dunlop and full-backs Robert Smellie and John Gillespie. Dunlop made 144 appearances in seven years and, as with Jimmy Millar, was signed from his home-town club of Annbank to where he returned at the end of his career. He made more of a mark in the 1894/95 title-winning side and was not the only William Dunlop to serve Sunderland. Amazingly, the other one was also from Ayrshire and played for Annbank, although he came originally from Hurlford, near Kilmarnock. He was a Liverpool player in his thirties when he won his only cap for Scotland, and his link with Sunderland was only as a member of their coaching staff from 1922. Neither Smellie, an amateur who returned to Queen's Park, where he eventually became club president, nor John Gillespie, who soon switched to Sunderland Albion, lasted very long, but they did make contributions to the championship season.

Sunderland's Team of All Talents had started to dominate English domestic football but soon discovered that Aston Villa were becoming their first bogey side. Villa had beaten them 4–1 in the semi-finals of the FA Cup in 1891/92 to deprive them of the Double, but then they pipped them for the 1893/94 title by six points and again knocked them out of the FA Cup, defeating them 3–1 in the second round after a 2–2 draw. It was also during 1893/94 that Sunderland lost at home to Blackburn midway through the season – their first League defeat at Newcastle Road in an amazing 45-game run since September 1890. But Sunderland regained the title in 1894/95 – their third in four seasons with the runners-up spot in-between – although Villa popped up to overcome them 2–1 in the FA Cup semi-finals to rob them of the Double again. Whether Sunderland had by now put a curse on Villa is not known, but in September 1895 the FA Cup was stolen from the window of boot-and-shoe manufacturer William Shillcock and melted down for counterfeit half-crowns. Villa's carelessness cost them a £25 fine, which was used to buy a replacement trophy!

Sunderland had become temporarily more cosmopolitan by signing a Canadian winger called James Dalton, but there was a fresh flurry of Scots who helped them to regain the title in 1894/95, when they finished five points clear of second-placed Everton. Defender Peter Meechan had arrived in 1893, and full-back Robert McNeill, centre-half Andy McCreadie, half-back Harry Johnston and inside-forward Tom Hyslop were signed the following year. Meechan and Hyslop both stayed for just two years. Meechan (whose name also appears in the records as Meehan and Meecham) was signed from Hibernian and then joined Glasgow Celtic, immediately helping them to the Scottish championship. In 1896 he won his sole Scottish cap, and later became an FA Cup finalist with Everton and Southampton. McNeill gave Sunderland greater service at full-back, staying seven years, eventually becoming skipper and making 157 appearances. He was a Glaswegian who was signed from Clyde, while Johnston was a Glaswegian who went to Clyde after four years with Sunderland. McCreadie, signed in exchange for Gibson when he first left Sunderland, was small for a centre-half, but contributed some useful goals in the 1894/95 title-winning side. He came from the Ayrshire town of Girvan and had twice been capped by Scotland; he returned to Rangers when Gibson returned to Sunderland. Hyslop did not stay long but scored 10 goals in 18 games. As with Wilson, he was from Mauchline and later alternated between Stoke and Glasgow Rangers, winning two Scottish caps.

The Scots, who had formed the backbone of the Team of All Talents, regularly travelled to and fro between their homeland and Sunderland during the club's early years. Another 50 Scots played for the club in the years before the 1914–18 war. In fact, Sunderland signed at least one Scot in every year leading up to it. Many came from Glasgow, Ayrshire and Lanarkshire – in keeping with the earlier trend – but occasionally others would turn up from elsewhere in Scotland. Some stayed a while and served the club well; others came and went comparatively fleetingly. But they had put Sunderland well and truly on the footballing map, and they often appeared for the Anglo-Scots against the Home Scots in the international trial matches of the day. But, above all, they left a legacy that was going to be hard for future generations to uphold because of their stunning success in winning three First Division titles in four years so early in the club's evolution.

As it was, Sunderland were never again to be as spectacularly successful, and they had two seasons when they dropped to fifth and then, in 1896/97, to 15th place out of 16. They had to play in the Test matches to ensure their First Division survival, facing fellow strugglers Burnley and the Second Division's top two, Notts County and Newton Heath (the forerunner of Manchester United). The games were played on a round-robin basis, and Notts County and Sunderland finished as the top two to take their places in the First Division the following season. Old rivals Aston Villa had been the champions and FA Cup winners and they added two more League titles, in 1898/99 and 1899/1900. Sunderland were second behind Sheffield United in 1897/98, third in 1899/1900 and second in 1900/01, when Liverpool pipped them for the title by two points even though they had the best defensive record in the division. In addition, there was trouble at St James' Park on Good Friday that season: the derby with Newcastle had to be called off before the start when the pitch became waterlogged, fighting broke out among the fans and goalposts and corner-flags were smashed.

Above all, there was an immense irony in the outcome of the 1900/01 season because Liverpool's manager when they won the League championship for the first time was Tom Watson, who had produced Sunderland's Team of All Talents. Watson had left Sunderland in 1896 to take over at Anfield because he received a better offer, even though he had had the added income from his own tobacconist's shop in Monkwearmouth railway station for the previous two years. His successor was Johnny Campbell's brother, Robert, who had mixed fortunes – Sunderland lost all of his first eight games in charge. Oddly enough, the run ended when they beat Watson's Liverpool 4–3. Trainer Tommy Dodds left after six years when he had a row with chairman James Henderson in February 1897, and Campbell moved on in 1899 to take charge of Bristol City, whom he helped into the Football League two years later. He then had a spell as Bradford City's manager before returning to Scotland to become a lecturer in football. Campbell had been succeeded by another Scot, Alex Mackie, an administrator who had never played professionally, but he built up Sunderland again and led them to their fourth League championship.

The club had some diverse characters on their books in the late 1890s. There was full-back Phil Bach, who played one game for England in 1899 but was subsequently better known as a football administrator. He followed Campbell to Bristol City, but was closely linked with Middlesbrough as a player and had two spells as their chairman. Bach was also an FA councillor for 12 years, serving on their international selection committee; he was a member of the Football League's management committee, president of the North-Eastern League and a vice-president of the North Riding FA. Sunderland met Middlesbrough on New Year's Day, 1938 – two days after Bach's death – and two minutes' silence was observed in his memory. Full-back Peter Boyle played in his native Republic of Ireland, for whom he won just five international caps after being selected 13 times, and in Scotland and England, but had greater success when he left Sunderland to join Sheffield United. Then there was Lancastrian winger Tom Bradshaw, who played briefly for a host of clubs – in 1897/98 in Sunderland's case – and was guilty of training misdemeanours in addition to having a conviction for wife-beating, a stint as a beggar and a spell as Harrow's cricket coach!

Sunderland were involved in some extraordinary episodes themselves in the early years. In 1892/93 a League game against Bolton was delayed for 20 minutes when one of the crossbars snapped. The opening match of the title-winning 1894/95 season at home to Derby was 45 minutes old before the referee arrived. He then insisted on playing the full 90 minutes and restarted the game, enabling Sunderland to record an 8–0 win. And in September 1908 it was found at half-time that the first half of Sunderland's 2–1 home win over Nottingham Forest had been two minutes short. When play resumed the two minutes were made up before the two teams changed ends and played the second half.

Alex Mackie, meanwhile, had utilised a further batch of Scots to help Sunderland to their fourth League title in 1901/02, the last season before the introduction of the traditional six-yard box instead of semi-circular marked areas in front of goals. Doig and Millar were still around as they finished three points clear of runners-up Everton, but some influential new Scots – defenders Andy McCombie and Jimmy Watson, wing-half Matthew Ferguson, centre-half Sandy McAllister, half-back Billy Farquhar, inside-forward Jimmy Gemmell and winger Colin McLatchie – emerged to play vital roles in the success.

McCombie, signed from Inverness Thistle, was an ever-present in his first full season with the club and went on to make 164 appearances for them. His consistency eventually won him four Scottish caps, but the financial aspects of his move to Newcastle brought about a court case, an FA inquiry and a three-month ban for Mackie. McCombie had further title and FA Cup success at St James' Park and then served the Magpies on their backroom staff for 42 years before retiring in 1950, two years before his death. Curiously, the last of McCombie's six goals for Sunderland came two months before he left – on New Year's Day 1904 against Newcastle at Roker Park. And when he returned to Sunderland with Newcastle the following Christmas, he was on the mark again – this time with an own goal!

Watson was another Scot who hailed from Lanarkshire and was signed from Clyde. He had a fair bit in common with McCombie: he too was consistent, a full-back, capped by Scotland – six times in his case – and left Sunderland to join a North-East club as a player and then a coach – Middlesbrough in his case. Watson ended up becoming involved in Canadian football after emigrating, but made 225 appearances for Sunderland, missing only one game during the title-winning campaign.

Ferguson, a Glaswegian signed from Mossend Brigade in 1896, was still a Sunderland player at the time of his sudden death at 29 in June 1902, having just helped them to win the title. He had been an ever-present in his first season with the club and a first-team regular consistently, clocking up a total of 182 appearances for them.

McAllister, signed from his home-town club Kilmarnock, was the only ever-present in the 1901/02 title-winning side. He and Ferguson had both arrived at Sunderland in 1896, made their reputations in the 1896/97 Test Matches and died young. McAllister was 39 when he contracted food poisoning while serving with the Northumberland Fusiliers in France in 1918. He had made 225 appearances for the club and was so popular with the supporters that they presented him with a piano and a gold watch when he scored his first goal for the club in 1901!

Farquhar was by no means a regular in the 1901/02 title-winning side, not establishing himself fully until later, but he was versatile and gave Sunderland substantial service for nine years after joining them from his home-town club Elgin City in 1898, amassing 195 appearances.

McLatchie, well built and with a fierce left-foot shot, also arrived at Sunderland in 1898 and his career soon blossomed. As in the case of McAllister, he had been a miner in his native Ayrshire and had played for Kilmarnock, but he was snapped up from Preston. He stayed for five years and scored 29 times in 130 games for Sunderland.

Gemmell served Sunderland well for 12 years from 1900, albeit in two spells with them. A Glaswegian signed originally from Clyde, he was the joint top goalscorer with Billy Hogg with 10 goals in the 1901/02 championship-winning season. In the end he scored 46 goals in 227 appearances for Sunderland.

But there were also notable English influences in Sunderland's title-winning side of 1902 – wing-half Dickie Jackson and forwards Bobby Hogg and Billy Hogg. All three of them were born in the North-East – Jackson in Middlesbrough, Bobby Hogg at Whitburn and Billy Hogg in Newcastle. In fact, Jackson and Billy Hogg shared a benefit in 1904 in recognition of their staunch service. Jackson, who had won the FA Amateur Cup with Middlesbrough as a centre-half, played in 169 games in a seven-year stay with Sunderland from 1898. Curiously, he later managed Darlington in non-League football, and Durham City, where he guided future England international Sammy Crooks from nearby Bearpark, in the League. Ironically, Crooks, another one-time miner, was later to partner one of Sunderland's all-time greats, Raich Carter, in forward lines with England and Derby County. Bobby Hogg played in only 73 games for Sunderland in a three-year stay from 1899, but he scored 19 goals and made his mark during the championship-winning season, when he was a regular. The speedy Billy Hogg, in contrast, scored 85 goals in 302 appearances for Sunderland in 10 years with the club from 1899 and played three times for England. He was the top goalscorer in the title-winning campaign and totally defied previous Sunderland logic by being an Englishman who moved to Scotland. Newcastle-born Hogg joined Glasgow Rangers and won three Scottish League titles with them, but eventually returned to

Roker to help out on Sunderland's coaching staff for seven years from 1927.

Sunderland then slipped into a relatively ordinary patch of First Division form for the first time in their League history. They were third in 1902/03 as they and their old rivals Aston Villa finished just one point behind the Sheffield team then known simply as The Wednesday. And in March 1903 there was further crowd trouble when Sunderland crucially lost 1–0 to The Wednesday at Roker Park and a number of spectators stoned the referee as he left the ground, which was closed for a week as a punishment. Manager Mackie, meanwhile, was involved in a dispute with McCombie and banned for three months after an FA inquiry found irregularities in the club's books. In 1904 he sold centre-forward Alf Common to Middlesbrough for £1,000, the first-ever four-figure deal, and soon afterwards followed him to Ayresome Park.

This time Sunderland turned to an Irishman, Bob Kyle, who became their secretary-manager in August 1905. Originally from Belfast, he had been Distillery's secretary, but he was to become Sunderland's longest-serving manager, staying at the helm for 23 years. By the club's previous high standards, there were some modest seasons in the early part of the 20th century and only two third places in 1908/09 and 1910/11 held out hope of a return to past glories.

But there were some memorable moments, including two in derbies with Newcastle. At the start of September 1906, Sunderland began the season with a visit to St James' Park for a game that attracted a record crowd of 56,375 and what was then the record temperature for an English League game – 91 degrees Fahrenheit at pitch level. Sunderland's Jimmy Watson fainted in the heat, while Newcastle's players wore sun-caps with their peaks reversed – presumably setting what has now become the strange modern trend – as protection against sunstroke. And in December 1908 the scene was again St. James' Park, where Sunderland set the record for the biggest away win in the top flight of English League football. They thrashed Newcastle 9–1, eight of their goals coming in a 28-minute period and the last five arriving in just eight minutes. The goalscorers in what remains Sunderland's biggest-ever League victory were Billy Hogg and George Holley with hat-tricks, Arthur Bridgett with two and Jackie Mordue with one. There were also the bad times in this phase of Sunderland's history because they went down 8–0 against The Wednesday on Boxing Day 1911, then the heaviest defeat in their history, although it has since been equalled twice. But the most disappointing factor was that they were not winning silverware as they had in their inaugural League seasons.

There were still some Scots who gave Sunderland valuable service, with wing-half Tommy Tait leading the way. Although signed from Bristol Rovers in 1906, he was originally from Carluke in Lanarkshire and stayed at Roker Park for six years, making 194 appearances. And he earned his only Scottish cap at the age of 31 while with Sunderland. Gavin Jarvie, like Tait, was a wing-half from Lanarkshire. He had also played for Airdrieonians and Bristol Rovers and made 103 appearances in five years for Sunderland, while full-back Willie Agnew stayed at Roker Park only briefly, but played three times for Scotland and became the first player to represent the North-East's big three because he had previously had two-year spells with Newcastle and then Middlesbrough.

In international terms however, Sunderland were becoming more cosmopolitan in the early part of the 20th century. There were, for example, two Northern Ireland internationals and two Welsh internationals with the club. Belfast-born left-winger Harold Buckle scored 15 times in 46 appearances in four years from 1902 and made the first of his two Northern Ireland appearances when they lost 3–1 to England in March 1904. The ironically named wing-half English McConnell made four of his 12 Northern Ireland appearances while with Sunderland between 1905 and 1908, even though he played in only 45 games for the club. Welsh international goalkeeper Leigh Roose was a popular amateur who gained the last nine of his 24 caps while with Sunderland and played 99 games for the club between 1908 and 1911, gaining a reputation for positively punching crosses and dashing out of his penalty area to kick clear. He also took free-kicks outside his penalty area and had been known to bounce the ball to the halfway line before the law was changed. He also received an illuminated address, for which supporters subscribed, for his part in saving Sunderland from relegation soon after joining them in 1907/08. Roose was the son of a Presbyterian minister and was so wealthy that at one point in his career he hired his own train to take him to a game. The fact that Sunderland were refused permission to stage a testimonial match for him because he was an amateur would not exactly have troubled him financially. He was also known as a practical joker; sadly, he was killed in action at the Battle of the Somme. Centre-forward Walter 'Mark' Watkins played just 16 games for Sunderland during the 1904/05 season, but scored eight goals, four of them in his first two appearances. He won three of his ten Welsh caps in the brief time that he was at Roker Park.

Sunderland also fielded four England internationals in the early 1900s – Robert Brebner, Arthur 'Boy' Brown, John 'Tim' Coleman and Arthur Bridgett. As with Roose, Brebner was an amateur goalkeeper.

He had studied at Edinburgh University and played in just two games for Sunderland in December 1905, but was notable later in his career for saving three penalties in a game while with Stockton and earning a gold medal at the 1912 Olympic Games in Stockholm when Great Britain beat Denmark in the final. Brown had won the first of his two England caps as an 18-year-old inside-forward before costing Sunderland a £1,600 fee from Sheffield United in 1908. He scored a respectable 23 goals in 55 games in two seasons for them, but never really fulfilled his early potential. Coleman, also an inside-forward, had won one England cap while at Woolwich Arsenal, but spent just the 1910/11 season at Roker Park. It was a prolific one, though, because he amassed 20 goals in 33 appearances. But Bridgett, a goalscoring left-winger, was a Sunderland stalwart, staying with the club from early 1903 to 1912, during which time he won his 11 England caps, and scored 119 times in 347 appearances. The tally might have been even higher if he had not been a lay preacher and refused to play on Christmas Days and Good Fridays. As a public speaker, he once gave a discourse on 'the game of life'. Maybe, though, it all helped a touch to prolong his career because he made a comeback in League football with Port Vale in his native Staffordshire at the age of 41. Bridgett had a penchant for goalscoring feats, scoring in nine consecutive League games for Sunderland in 1907. He was one of three forwards to score twice in three days for England in two games against Austria in Vienna in June 1908, and he scored only a minute into his League comeback as a 41-year-old.

There were other notable characters who represented Sunderland in the early 1900s – a barren period by their earlier standards. Alf Common had a relatively average record in his two spells with his home-town club Sunderland, but played three times for England while elsewhere and twice moved for record transfer fees. Another centre-forward, Jack Foster, scored three times in his eight appearances for Sunderland in 1907/08, but became prolific as a centre-half when he joined Huddersfield Town, whom he then helped to the First Division title as assistant manager to the famed Herbert Chapman. Two full-backs, Ephraim 'Dusty' Rhodes and Henry Forster, gave valuable service during the quiet phase of the early 20th century, both coming originally from the North-East and clocking up more than 100 appearances for the club, but there was a growing clamour for a return to the previous successes.

The experience of goalkeeper Walter 'Buns' Scott in the early part of the 1912/13 season illustrated the frustration. Scott, who had saved three penalties in a match for Grimsby Town, cost Sunderland £750 from Everton in the summer of 1911 and made a disastrous start to the season. He had appeared in 34 games in 1911/12, but then he conceded 11 goals in the first four matches of the following campaign and never played for the club again. He was sacked by the directors, fell out with the fans and soon moved on to Irish club Shelbourne. In fact, it was the storm before the quiet: Sunderland were running into smoother waters and Bob Kyle had carefully assembled a squad who were capable of providing the most successful season in the club's history.

As Sunderland took only two points out of 14 from the first seven matches of the 1912/13 season, Kyle signed the players who would be the final pieces in his jigsaw for another Team of All Talents. Naturally he needed a goalkeeper after Scott's difficulties, so he snapped up former miner Joe Butler from Glossop North End. Butler, too, had had his controversial moments because he had been suspended for the whole of 1911/12 following an incident in a game against Chelsea. Butler made his Sunderland debut in the last game of the bad start to 1912/13 – oddly enough at Chelsea – but never looked back and became a consistent and reliable performer. Kyle then signed full-back Charlie Gladwin from Blackpool, and Sunderland won their next five games. Gladwin was often said to be a bag of nerves before matches, but he was an influential figure who was renowned for his physical presence on the pitch. Apparently he also had a physical presence off it. He once overheard a sceptic hint at how much he might have been paid when the ball skidded in off his foot to give Newcastle a late equaliser in a cup-tie. It is said that Gladwin at once threw the malcontent off the tram they were sharing!

Sunderland lost only two of their final 23 League games from the start of December 1912 and went on to win the First Division championship for the fifth time. It had hardly looked likely in the early weeks of the campaign, but Kyle had brought together some of the greatest players in Sunderland's history, and everything fell neatly into place once he had made his adjustments. They included replacing full-back Billy Troughear early in the season after he had completed 108 appearances for the club and bringing in Jimmy Richardson in the close season to provide competition for Tom Hall.

At the crux of the success of Sunderland's latest multi-talented team was inside-forward Charlie Buchan, who scored 224 goals in 413 appearances for them between 1911 and 1925 and was always reckoned to have been unlucky to have won a paltry six England caps, the bizarre argument usually having been that he was often too subtle for his team-mates. But his ingenuity and mastery of the glancing header might have been welcomed elsewhere – perhaps, say, in Scottish football. And nowadays he would probably have won a bundle of caps for Scotland under present-day qualification rulings. After all, Buchan was born in London of Scottish parents from Aberdeen, his father having been a sergeant in the Highland Regiment. Instead he had to be content with the irony of having skippered England against Scotland on his final international appearance in 1924.

Buchan grew up in Woolwich and first kicked a football on Plumstead Common. He began as a wing-half, but became an inside-forward after scoring five goals in a schoolboy game. In those days he spent his time watching Woolwich Arsenal at Manor Field, but he could not afford the 3d (1p) admission into the ground and had to wait until 10 minutes from the end to gain entry for nothing when the gates were opened. In 1909/10 Buchan played a handful of games as an amateur with Woolwich Arsenal's reserves, but had an argument about expenses when manager George Morrell refused to pay him 11 shillings (53p), and that ended his link with the club – until they signed him from Sunderland 16 years later! But that dispute gave Buchan the idea of turning professional, which he did with Leyton in preference to Fulham and Bury in March 1910 after a short but successful spell with Gravesend & Northfleet. Buchan initially wanted to become a schoolteacher, but the lure of football was too much and he served a year's apprenticeship with Leyton before being transferred to Sunderland for a £1,200 record fee after competition from Everton. He received a signing-on fee of £10, which he promptly spent on an overcoat to combat the biting North-East weather.

Buchan's gangling frame began to fill out after he moved to Roker Park, and his skills accordingly blossomed as he was afforded help and advice from fellow inside-forward George Holley. Buchan struck up a formidable right-wing partnership with winger Jackie Mordue, who had had a spell with Arsenal himself, and wing-half Frank Cuggy. They helped Sunderland to the First Division title in 1912/13 as they finished four points clear of Aston Villa, whom they then met in the FA Cup final. But Villa won 1–0 – after their inside-forward Clem Stephenson, an England international who was originally from the North-East himself, had told Buchan at a throw-in in the early stages that he had had a dream about the game. Buchan did not believe Stephenson when he proclaimed that Villa would win by the only goal and that it would be scored by their wing-half Tom Barber with a header, but that was just what happened. But some of the action had been less predictable. Villa's right-ringer Charlie Wallace missed a penalty and they were reduced to 10 men for 10 minutes because of an injury to their England goalkeeper, Sam Hardy. Sunderland's revenge, meanwhile, was to make sure of the title by beating Villa at Villa Park four days later.

It had been hard enough to reach the FA Cup final in the first place. Sunderland disposed of Clapton Orient, Manchester City and Norwich City in the first three rounds, but then there were three ties against Newcastle United – a 0–0 draw at home, a 2–2 draw and then a conclusive 3–0 victory. At the semi-final stage they drew 0–0 with Burnley at Bramall Lane, Sheffield, and then won the replay 3–2 at St Andrew's, Birmingham. The defeat in the final robbed Sunderland of the League and Cup Double, but it was still the most successful season in their history. And although they finished strongly to take 19 points out of the last 20, taking the title had hardly looked likely when they took just two points from their first seven League outings.

Buchan was the brains behind another supremely talented Sunderland team and became their leading marksman every season from the title triumph of 1912/13 to 1923/24. In addition, he was the first Sunderland player to score five goals in a League game, in a 7–0 home win over Liverpool in December 1912, and was the First Division's top goalscorer overall in 1922/23. But it might have been very different when the Roker crowd barracked him in the early stages of his Sunderland career, questioning his commitment. Buchan, though, filling out as he began to put on weight, received welcome support from trainer Billy Williams and eventually became the subject of local youngsters' street songs. Even so, a homesick Buchan had returned to the South at one point, but was then talked out of leaving the North-East after Sunderland's manager Bob Kyle had travelled to London specifically to plead with him to turn again.

George Holley was a local from Seaham Harbour and scored 154 goals, including nine hat-tricks, in 315 appearances for Sunderland after joining them in the autumn of 1904. An inside-left or left-winger, he is the club's fourth-highest marksman of all time, twice scoring four in a game. He was famous for his skills and artistry and he greatly influenced the burgeoning Buchan, who was almost six years his junior. Formerly a ship's plater, Holley was so forceful that on one occasion he tussled with The Wednesday's goalkeeper Jack Lyall and left him swinging upside down with one foot caught high in the netting! His England career was fruitful, too, with eight goals in ten internationals. His son Tom was also a colourful character. He played for Barnsley and Leeds United, worked for the *Sunday People* and became a restaurateur on a remote Yorkshire peninsula.

Harry Low was a versatile half-back and occasional inside-forward who was an ever-present in 1912/13 and maintained the Scottish tradition. He was signed from his home-city club Aberdeen in 1907 and scored 38 goals, including one hat-trick, in 228 appearances for Sunderland. There was a certain pathos about Low, whose brother Wilf was with Newcastle and had already played for Scotland, because he missed out on international recognition in March 1913 to play for Sunderland in a cup replay. The tie – against Newcastle – took place two days after Scotland had met Ireland in an international for which Harry had been called up. Harry Low, who also died young, never received a second chance with Scotland.

Another Scot, Charlie B. Thomson, was an important member of Sunderland's title-winning half-back line. Signed, just short of his 30th birthday, in May 1908 from Heart of Midlothian, where he had been a big success, Thomson played 265 games for Sunderland in seven years with the club. He became captain and provided experience, backbone and strength: in fact, his tussles with the equally rugged England and Aston Villa centre-forward Harry Hampton in 1912/13 earned them both suspensions at the start of the following season. Thomson won nine of his 21 Scottish caps while with Sunderland, sustaining his longevity at the highest level.

Right-winger Jackie Mordue, who also arrived in May 1908, was a local lad, but came home via Barnsley and then Arsenal, where he been a team-mate of England goalkeeper Jimmy Ashcroft, his brother-in-law. He scored 83 goals, many of them from the penalty spot, in 299 appearances for Sunderland and made two England appearances, in 1912 and 1913 – alongside Holley the first time and Buchan the second.

Full-back Albert Milton arrived directly from Barnsley in May 1908 – a seminal month for important signings who played major roles in the success of 1912/13. Milton, who was killed in action during the 1914–18 war, made 143 appearances for Sunderland, but missed the final two ties of Sunderland's FA Cup run in 1912/13 when he was replaced by fellow Yorkshireman Harry Ness. Apart from that change, the same side played in all ten games in the cup run, but Milton's absence enabled Ness, who had been the first-choice left-back at the start of the season, to qualify for a championship medal. Ness, who played 101 games for Sunderland, was signed in 1911, but also came from Barnsley, with whom he had already won a loser's medal in the 1909/10 FA Cup final against Newcastle.

In March 1909 Sunderland snapped up right-half Frank Cuggy from Willington Athletic. Originally from the Walker area of Newcastle, he made 190 appearances for the club and also played twice for England. It was fitting that he played alongside Mordue and Buchan on his international debut in February 1913 because they had developed a great understanding of each other's play that proved to be crucial in

Sunderland's success that season.

It was equally apt that Cuggy, who later coached noted Spanish club Celta Vigo, played alongside his Sunderland team-mate Harry Martin when he won his other England cap a year later. It was the only international appearance of Martin's career, but he was an ever-present during Sunderland's title-winning season of 1912/13. A left-winger from Nottinghamshire, Martin was signed from Sutton Junction in 1912 and played in 231 games, scoring 24 goals. He scored on his Easter debut for the club – in a 2–1 defeat at Liverpool when Arthur Bridgett dropped out on religious grounds – and was also on the mark the following day when they beat Everton 4–0 at home.

The centre-forward spot was largely shared by Tom Hall and Jimmy Richardson in 1912/13. Hall, from the Newburn area of Newcastle, was signed in early 1909 after being a regular goalscorer in junior football. He is best remembered, though, for scoring twice at Roker Park on his debut for Newcastle after joining them from Sunderland! Richardson, a Glaswegian signed from Huddersfield at the start of the 1912/13 season, was the more prolific marksman for Sunderland with 30 goals in 46 appearances, but his family struggled to settle in the North-East.

In 1912/13 Sunderland briefly used other players such as goalkeeper George Anderson and winger Bobby Best, both of whom were signed from Mickley Colliery – in the area that was the birthplace of Bob Stokoe, later a Sunderland managerial legend. Best had a respectable scoring record of 25 goals in 94 games. There were also contributions from half-back Billy Cringan, another son of Ayrshire who later became a Scottish international. Full-back Bert Hobson, signed from Crook Town in 1912, made 172 appearances for Sunderland, but did not become a first-team regular until 1913/14; and inside-forward Billy Moore, signed as an amateur in late 1912, eventually played once for England during his lengthy service for West Ham United. Utility player Bobby Coverdale, meanwhile, bucked the Scottish trend a little when he was signed from Rutherglen Glencairn –he was born down the road from Sunderland, in West Hartlepool. The extra irony was that he had become a Scottish junior international before it was confirmed that he was an Englishman!

Sunderland had two modest seasons after winning the First Division title again in 1912/13, so maybe it was not the dawn of a new era of success. Time would have told, of course, but the 1914–18 war intervened. At the end of it Sunderland played 14 games against their North-East rivals in the Victory League in the early part of 1919, but many of the players from 1912/13 were no longer with the club when hostilities ended. Equally significant was the fact that most of them lost vital years at the prime of their football careers when the so-called Great War broke out.

Sunderland were hardly roaring in the 1920s. Although there was a huge amount of talent again at their disposal, at best this was an era of 'so near and yet so far'. They still had a host of good individual players, but could win no more silverware – a state of affairs that would be part and parcel of their future. There would be no return to those early years of trophies, titles, medals and dominance. For a while Sunderland hinted at success in the mid-1920s – finishing as the First Division runners-up in 1922/23 and third in 1923/24, 1925/26 and 1926/27 – but also flirted with disaster when they dropped to 15th in 1927/28.

Some of the pre-war regulars were still around – Mordue, Cuggy, Ness, Best, Martin, Hobson, goalkeeper Leslie Scott and Buchan. Others found that their careers suffered as a result of the missing wartime years, Scotsman George Philip being a prime example. Converted from a centre-half to an inside-forward, he scored 22 goals in 38 appearances for Sunderland in 1914/15, but never reappeared for them when the war was over.

The first loyal servants in the post-war years were led by right-footed left-back Ernie England. He cost Sunderland £100 from Shirebrook as an 18-year-old in 1919, appeared in 351 games and then moved briefly to West Ham in 1930. For much of the time England was partnered in defence by centre-half Charlie Parker, a local lad signed for £3,300 from Stoke as a 29-year-old in 1920. Although small for a centre-half, Parker showed great consistency, made 256 appearances for Sunderland, took over the captaincy when Buchan moved on and stayed until 1929 to underline his longevity in the game. Jack Poole was another half-back who gradually became a Sunderland regular from 1919. He made 152 appearances after manager Bob Kyle was said to have spotted him playing wartime beach football for the Sherwood Foresters at Roker. Left-half Arthur Andrews was another local lad who was known for his consistency, making 244 appearances between 1922 and 1931.

But Sunderland's most noteworthy home-grown defender from the 1920s was the cultured full-back Warneford Cresswell, who came from a footballing family: his younger brother Frank also played briefly for the club, and his son Corbett was an England amateur international. The brothers were from South Shields, from where Sunderland signed Warney for £5,500 in 1922 after Aston Villa and Tottenham Hotspur had shown interest. Already an England international, he won five more caps during his Sunderland days, during which he chalked up 190 appearances. He then left for Everton, with whom he won two First

Division titles, the FA Cup and one more England cap in 1927.

Goalkeeper Albert McInroy had a fair bit in common with Warney Cresswell – a respected technician, a lengthy career, an England international and an FA Cup winner after leaving Sunderland. A Lancastrian who had been a schoolboy left-winger, he first joined Sunderland from Leyland in 1923, played in 227 games and won an England cap alongside Cresswell in October 1926. In 1929 McInroy moved to Newcastle, with whom he won the FA Cup three years later, for £2,750 and amassed a total of 496 League appearances in his career, but failed to add to his Sunderland tally when he returned to the club for the 1934/35 season.

Other England internationals who played for Sunderland in the 1920s were of varying import in the club's history. Inside-forward Bill Marsden, from Silksworth, scored in two of only three appearances for the club between 1920 and 1924, but later won three England caps while with Sheffield Wednesday. Inside-forward Bob Kelly, another Lancastrian, cost £6,500 from Burnley as a 32-year-old in 1925. Like Buchan, whom he effectively replaced, he was noted for his body swerve, but he played in just 55 games for Sunderland. He won only one of his 14 England caps while at Roker Park for 14 months, but played on in League football into his forties. Another Silksworth lad, centre-forward Bobby Gurney, arrived in 1925 and was, in effect, a parting gift from Buchan when the latter joined Arsenal. Buchan recommended Gurney to Sunderland after spotting him playing for Bishop Auckland, and the gesture was repaid in full. Gurney went on to become an all-time great at Roker Park – as a loyal servant and prolific goalscorer – but, surprisingly and shamefully, he won only one official England cap when he faced Scotland in April 1935.

The influx of Scots continued after the 1914–18 war, with three of them – centre-half Michael 'Rubberneck' Gilhooley, winger Alex Donaldson and centre-forward John 'Jock' Paterson, all of whom were internationals – arriving at Roker Park in March 1922. Gilhooley, who had won his only Scottish cap a month before he cost Sunderland £5,250 from Hull City, was hampered by knee trouble at Roker Park. Similarly, Donaldson, who had made six international appearances, had had a serious injury before joining Sunderland from Bolton Wanderers in a £2,100 deal. Paterson provided longer service, though, and scored 40 goals in 77 appearances. Wounded several times during the 1914–18 war, he had won his one international cap with Leicester City, who sold him to Sunderland for £3,790. Paterson had a particularly fruitful season in 1922/23 and stayed until October 1924. But wing-half Billy Clunas was the one Scottish international who became an imposing fixture in Sunderland sides of the 1920s. He cost £2,500 from St Mirren in October 1923 and stayed until 1931, clocking up 272 appearances. Clunas also contributed 44 goals, most of them from the penalty spot, and won his two international caps after moving to Roker Park.

Sunderland were also given devoted service by some of their forwards of the early 1920s. Left-winger Billy Ellis arrived from local football in the West Midlands in 1919 and stayed until late 1927, scoring 31 times in 202 games. Inside-forward Bobby Marshall arrived from non-League football in the East Midlands in 1920 and stayed until 1928, scoring scored 73 goals in 205 appearances. Marshall outlasted local lad James Hogg, who scored eight times in nine games before departing because of a personality clash between the two. Little more was heard of Hogg, while Marshall, in contrast, eventually left for Manchester City, with whom he won the First Division title and the FA Cup. Inside-forward Arthur 'Tricky' Hawes, a son of Norfolk, established a formidable left-wing partnership with Ellis after joining Sunderland for £1,750 from South Shields in 1921. Known for his habit of carrying a handkerchief in his left hand during games, Hawes stayed until 1927 and chipped in with 39 goals in his 147 appearances.

Ellis, who was said to have provided regular 'dandy crosses' for Buchan, recalled how the public had taken him to their hearts:

> The 1920s were great days at Sunderland. And, even after I'd left the club, I discovered that the fans never forgot you. I couldn't walk anywhere in the town without being stopped by people asking me how I was. We trained on a diet of a glass of sherry with a raw egg in it because it was supposed to give you energy. And some players would have one before games, too.

As with most of his contemporaries, Ellis lived in a club house within walking distance of Roker Park. He recalled:

> We lived in Stranton Terrace – just a couple of minutes' walk from the ground. But all the players walked to training and to home matches then. We didn't have cars for a start, so you were encouraged to remain within touching distance of the ground. Travelling to away games was different, though. The club had their own railway carriage, which used to be kept at Monkwearmouth Station. It would be hitched up to the main-line trains when we were travelling and we would remain in our

own luxurious surroundings, playing cribbage on green-baize tables. Then we would take up the same positions at our tables upon returning the following day. And, if we had won, there would be a packet of 10 cigarettes set out at everyone's individual place. That was an extra bonus for winning.

But packets of cigarettes weren't the only bonuses being picked up by Sunderland's players of the 1920s. Ellis recalled: 'There would be a £2 bonus for each of us after a victory – and £2 was a lot of money!'

Amid it all, though, Sunderland could not produce a blend to repeat the success of the early years. The 1920s were associated with constant anticlimax, with the exception of the 1927/28 season when the First Division programme produced an amazing climax. Sunderland had diced with relegation death in 1896/97 when they had to participate in the end-of-season Test matches, but they had been identified much more with success than failure. In fact, they were long noted for the longest run in top-flight English football – 68 years – until their first relegation in 1957/58, but they went dangerously close again in 1927/28.

At the top of the table, Dixie Dean helped Everton to the title with his record 60 goals, but it was crazy at the other end. At one stage eight teams were level on points at the bottom and 12 teams were still in danger of relegation with a fortnight of the season left. By the day of the final round of fixtures – 5 May 1928 – four teams were level on points at the bottom and five could still go down – and Sunderland were one of them. They began the day in 21st spot on 37 points with only Manchester United below them, and were visiting Teesside rivals Middlesbrough, who were just one place above them. Boro had been promoted a year earlier thanks to a prolific marksman of their own – George Camsell – but were missing him sorely in the latter stages of 1927/28 when he was sidelined by a broken rib. As it was, they gambled on his fitness on the final day, but Sunderland were comfortable 3–0 winners and shot up six places to finish 15th. And the name of the scorer of Sunderland's final goal was left-winger Billy De'ath, a Yorkshireman, in what was his final League appearance for the club! Middlesbrough and Tottenham Hotspur, who had already departed for a continental tour after completing their fixtures in midweek, went down, but the closeness of it all was incredible. In the final League table only two points separated the bottom nine and only seven separated the bottom 19 behind Everton, Huddersfield and Leicester.

What made it all the more ironic was the fact that two of

Sunderland's greatest-ever goalscorers were at the club that season, the emerging Gurney and another Scotsman, centre-forward David Halliday, but they seldom played together. Gurney might have been hard done by in terms of international recognition, but the same applied to Halliday, who was never capped by Scotland even though his phenomenal facts and figures with Sunderland spoke for themselves. He scored twice in his first two games for the club, at home to Birmingham City and Blackburn, and then hit hat-tricks in the next two against West Bromwich and Sheffield United to take his tally to 10 from his first four appearances. In that difficult 1927/28 campaign Halliday scored in the each of the opening eight League matches – 12 goals in all – and registered 15 hat-tricks for the club in total, including four goals in games against Manchester United, Portsmouth and Sheffield United. His totals of League goals in his four full seasons at Sunderland were 38 in 1925/26, 35 in 1926/27, 33 in 1927/28 and a club record of 43 in 1928/29. Halliday finished with 162 goals from his 175 games for the club and an amazing career record of 347 goals from 464 League appearances. Originally from Dumfries, Halliday had drifted round the Scottish scene until Sunderland paid Dundee £3,500 for him in April 1925. It was a testimony to his goalscoring craft that they sold him to Arsenal for £6,500 in late 1929 when he was just short of his 32nd birthday. What is more, he returned to Roker Park to score a hat-trick in eight minutes for Manchester City against Sunderland in a 5–2 win in January 1932. During his time with Sunderland he was one of their most popular players, and the Roker Park crowd even gave him a standing ovation on one occasion when he was sent off against Arsenal!

Another Scot who was to have an influential effect on Sunderland's fortunes arrived in 1927, full-back Billy Murray. He and inside-forward David Wright cost £8,000 from Cowdenbeath in a double deal. Wright, who would return home to his native Kirkcaldy every summer to look after his bakery business, did not stay too long, but Murray stayed much longer – until 1957, in fact. The unlucky Jimmy Oakley had to vie first with Warney Cresswell and then with Murray, who had trained as a shipping engineer, for the right-back berth. But Murray established himself, became a regular and stayed at Roker Park as a player for nearly ten years. He then moved to St. Mirren before starting an 18-year stint, interrupted by the 1939–45 war, as Sunderland's manager.

The disappointing 1927/28 season, though, culminated in the departures of manager Bob Kyle and trainer Billy Williams. Kyle's 23-year spell in charge meant that he remains Sunderland's longest-serving manager. Williams had been at the club even longer – since 1897. Sunderland's directors looked again to a Scot as Kyle's successor when they opted for Johnny Cochrane, who had been a player and secretary with St Johnstone before becoming manager of St Mirren, with whom he had won the Scottish FA Cup two years earlier. Cochrane's arrival, along with trainer Andy Reid, brought about an immediate improvement in Sunderland's fortunes, and they finished fourth in the First Division in 1928/29. But then they slipped back and did not finish in the top six again until 1933/34. And, not surprisingly in view of Sunderland's football heritage, Cochrane's appointment heralded the arrival of a number of Scottish internationals at Roker Park.

Three of them – inside-forward Tommy McInally, left-winger Adam McLean and inside-forward Bobby McKay – arrived in 1928 soon after Cochrane had taken over, but none of them lasted very long. McInally, who had previously won two Scottish caps while with Celtic, was known for his exceptional pace, but was reputed to be inconsistent even though he was made Sunderland's captain at one stage, and moved on after 18 months. McLean was also signed from Celtic, but left them after a pay dispute surrounding a summer tour. He had by then been capped four times by Scotland and went on to make 70 appearances for Sunderland. The diminutive McKay moved to Roker Park from Newcastle in exchange for left-back Bob Thomson and scored twice in a 5–3 defeat at Manchester City on his debut. It was something of an anticlimax, though, because he had hit a hat-trick on his Newcastle debut, but he was on the mark 17 times in 51 games for Sunderland. He and Thomson, who later played in France, were both capped once by Scotland – in different internationals.

Centre-half John 'Jock' McDougall served Sunderland much longer and made 184 appearances after joining them from Airdrieonians in 1929. A Glaswegian, he captained Sunderland, and also Leeds after he left for Elland Road in 1934. McDougall had won only one Scottish cap earlier in his career, while his younger brother, Jimmy, earned two. Goalkeeper Bob Middleton had won his only Scottish cap while with Cowdenbeath not long before he left them to join Sunderland in 1930. Similarly, inside-forward Benny Yorston had won his only cap for Scotland with Aberdeen before venturing south to Roker Park early in 1932. In fact, it was something of a family trait because his nephew Harry was also capped just once by Scotland while with Aberdeen.

Benny Yorston was one of several Sunderland players of the day who scored regularly for the club without hanging around at Roker Park for too long. Yorston's record was 26 goals from 52 appearances, while the services rendered to Sunderland by centre-forward Evelyn Morrison, inside-forward James 'Hookey' Leonard and wingers Gordon Gunson and Jimmy Temple might best be described as short but sweet in each case. Morrison and Leonard were Scots whose stays at Roker Park were brief for very different reasons. Morrison, who cost £6,500 from Falkirk, had business interests in his native Lanarkshire and was reluctant to journey south on a regular basis, while Leonard left Sunderland after a breach of discipline.

Cochrane also signed some notable Englishmen as the 1920s ended and the next decade began, many Sunderland fans having forgotten what it was like for their club to be successful. Winger Tommy Urwin arrived in February 1930, making his debut three days after his 34th birthday and completing the rare treble of playing for each of the North-East's big three. He had won four England caps during his spells with Middlesbrough and then Newcastle, with whom he had won the First Division title in 1926/27, but struggled to become a regular first-teamer at Sunderland, although he did later serve the club as their youth coach for a while. Left-back Harold Shaw also arrived in February 1930 and cost £7,100 from Wolves. He went on to play 217 times for Sunderland, scoring the only five goals in his lengthy career for the club. And in November 1930 Cochrane signed a young inside-forward, who had had an unsuccessful trial with Leicester, on amateur forms. He was a local lad, named Horatio Stratton Carter, and was destined to become one of Sunderland's all-time heroes.

Bobby Gurney and Raich Carter were to become integral parts of Sunderland's success as the 1930s unfolded, but Cochrane's next batch of Scots was going to be equally instrumental. Soon after he had taken over as manager he ensured that promising inside-forward Patsy Gallacher turned professional in 1928, and the following year he signed full-back Alex Hall. Left-winger Jimmy Connor and wing-halves Alex Hastings, Charlie M. Thomson and Sandy McNab then climbed onto the latest Scottish conveyor belt to Sunderland and won international honours. Sammy Blyth, who died quite young in the 1950s while scouting for Carter when he was Leeds' manager, was responsible for sending Scots such as Thomson, McNab and Gallacher to Sunderland And he believed that Scottish football would never recover its greatness until the country was swept by unemployment: 'Just like the boxers, all the good footballers came out of hungry homes.' But the backbone of a successful Sunderland side was slowly forming again at long last. For years Sunderland had had teams of talented players, but Cochrane was slowly moulding a squad with the collective drive to provide the success that had inspired the early years. The club's footballing wheel had come full circle to the extent that, with some notable exceptions, they were grateful for the profound Scottish influence again.

3

MAGNA CARTER

Johnny Cochrane was not the Sunderland board's first choice to replace the long-serving Bob Kyle as manager in 1928. Their initial target was George Jobey, who had been in charge at Derby County for three years at that stage. But they were unable to get him, and he ended up managing the Rams for 16 years in all. Next on the directors' hit list was Major Frank Buckley, who was then manager of Wolverhampton Wanderers – where Jobey had been in charge between 1922 and 1924. Buckley had taken over from Fred Scotchbrook at Molineux in 1927 and ended up staying there for 17 years. Sunderland then turned their attention to Cochrane, who became the fourth Scottish manager out of five up to that time.

In the early part of their history Sunderland were never known as a sacking club. They gave their managers plenty of time, and the policy paid dividends in Cochrane's case. The 1920s had been a disheartening decade because the club had been unable to recapture their former glories, despite doing well in the League in four seasons out of five, but the directors stuck to their guns and bit by bit Cochrane repaid them by producing a side which not only won the First Division title again, but also the FA Cup for the first time.

Sunderland had been close to the League and Cup Double in 1912/13, but fell at the last hurdle in the FA Cup. Having won the League title on five occasions, it had become annoying that winning the FA Cup should prove elusive. They had reached one final and two semi-finals before Cochrane's era, and there was further frustration in 1930/31.

Sunderland beat Southampton 2–0 at home with goals from Billy Eden and Tommy Urwin in the third round, and then overcame Bolton Wanderers 3–1 after a 1–1 draw at Burnden Park. A crowd of 63,016 then watched them defeat Sheffield United 2–1 at Roker Park in the fifth round. Perversely, Sunderland managed only a 1–1 draw at home to mid-table Third Division South side Exeter City in the quarter-finals in the first ever meeting between the clubs, and had to rely on a 4–2 victory in the replay at St James' Park to progress further. Jimmy Connor had scored six times in four consecutive ties, but the goals dried up in the semi-final when Sunderland lost 2–0 to Birmingham City at Elland Road, Leeds, despite applying plenty of pressure.

The importance of the FA Cup remained – a fact that was further underlined when Sunderland reached the last eight in 1932/33. In the quarter-finals they drew 4–4 against Derby at the Baseball Ground before losing the replay 1–0 to a header by Peter Ramage. But the second meeting attracted the biggest home attendance in Sunderland's history when 75,118 spectators packed into Roker Park. Raich Carter later observed:

> Outside the ground were a dense mob through whom we had to fight our way to the entrance. Inside was pandemonium. The spectators spawned out from the stands over the cinder track and across the touchlines on to the pitch itself. We did not know how and where we were going to play. I do not think that the match should ever have started. Players could not be expected to do themselves justice in such conditions although there would probably have been a riot if the game had been called off.

The public, though, would by this time have welcomed success from anywhere as a return to the good old days. But it was again a case of 'if only...' in the First Division in 1934/35 as Cochrane gradually inspired progress. For the fifth time in their history Sunderland finished second in the League, this time as Arsenal won their fourth title in five seasons. Sunderland began well and even beat Everton, who had pipped the Gunners for the 1931/32 championship by two points, 7–0 at Roker Park on Boxing Day 1934 – a day after losing 6–2 to them at Goodison Park! Sunderland also lost 6–4 at Everton in the FA Cup, and it was all far too typical of the inconsistency that finally got the better of them when they won only two of their last eight League games and their chance went as Arsenal finished four points clear at the top. Equally infuriatingly, Sunderland took three points out of four against the Gunners that season, beating them 2–1 at home and then setting what remains the crowd record of 73,295 for a game at Highbury when they drew 0–0 in the return meeting in March 1935.

Fortunately, though, the best was yet to come for Cochrane's side, because he was bringing back the good times. Sunderland promptly went one better in 1935/36 to win the First Division title for the sixth time and then finally won the FA Cup the following season. And their League success coincided with the relegation of both Aston Villa and Blackburn Rovers, which left Sunderland with the immense distinction of being the only club never to have played outside the First Division.

There was a touch of déjà vu about the start of the Sunderland's First Division programme in 1935/36, because they lost 3–1 away to Arsenal on the opening day. That aside, this was a team which was almost capable of scoring at will even on their many off-days. Thanks to their free-scoring forward line, they won the championship in style. They set the club record of 109 League goals in a season – and it hardly mattered that they also conceded 74. This was the worst defensive record in the top half of the division, and even Liverpool, who finished 19th, gave away only 64. The contrary side of Sunderland's nature surfaced when they lost 4–0 at Grimsby Town and 6–0 at Middlesbrough, two sides which ended up in the bottom half of the table. But Raich Carter insisted: 'We decided on a deliberate policy of going all out to attack at the risk of conceding goals. We were confident that we could score more goals than we yielded.' Sunderland still won 25 of their 42 League games and clinched the title with eight points to spare. And they had three games left after they had secured the title with an away win at Birmingham, after which it was reported that 'In the drawing-room of the Midland Hotel in Birmingham the winning of the championship was duly celebrated in the time-honoured fashion.' Skipper Alex Hastings made a speech, and Sunderland even received a congratulatory telegram from Arsenal's manager, George Allison, in which he said, 'The ex-champions hail you as the champions of the season and wish you prosperity and good luck.' In fact, four of Sunderland's last five games were away, and they fielded a slightly below-strength side in their final League match when they lost 4–0 away to runners-up Derby. The situation was not helped by suspensions for Carter and Bert Davis, who had both been sent off in the Middlesbrough mauling.

The significant factor was the majestic way in which Sunderland swept aside opponents with a torrent of goals: three times they scored seven in a game, beating both Blackburn and Bolton 7–2 at home, and winning 7–2 at Birmingham to clinch the championship with further games remaining. They also put six past West Bromwich Albion and beat Arsenal 5–4 at Roker Park. The fans had never had it so good in terms of entertainment. The way forward had been with the forwards. Only two of the 109 goals did not come from the forward line – one by wing-half Charlie M. Thomson and an own goal early in the season at Manchester City.

While Cochrane had drafted in a further bevy of Scots, many of whom had by coincidence trained as engineers, to help Sunderland to win the title, two local lads, Raich Carter and Bobby Gurney, emphatically topped the goalscoring charts, both scoring 31 goals in 39 League appearances in 1935/36. Carter led the way in the first half of the season with four against West Bromwich, and 12 in a run in which he scored in eight consecutive games. Gurney missed three games in the first part of the season – when his 31-year-old replacement George Goddard chipped in with two goals – but caught up with five in the demolition of Bolton and four at Birmingham as the title race reached its climax.

Carter, in the meantime, was on his way to becoming one of football's greats in addition to being an all-time Sunderland hero. He came from the town's Hendon area, but his early career did not always run smoothly. It is fitting that from 1918 he had attended Hendon Board School, where the club's founder, James Allan, had taught on his arrival from Scotland. It is fitting too that he was known for taking football into new spheres, because his great-great-great-uncle was James Cook, the famous explorer. Raich came from a footballing family: his father, Robert, who was known as 'Toddler', had been a winger with Burslem Port Vale, Fulham and Southampton before returning to Hendon, where he became the licensee of the Ocean Queen in Tower Street. The pub was occasionally visited by Charlie Buchan, who was to become Raich's early footballing hero. Robert Carter seldom discussed football with Raich – who did, however, take heed of one piece of advice from him. The young Raich once returned from a game and said to his father that his team had played well despite losing. Robert is said to have told him, 'I fail to see how any losing team can be said to be the better side. The objective of the game is to score goals, so, however achieved, the team scoring more must be the better one.'

Carter also turned one piece of perceived adversity to his advantage. He hated his name Horatio – one that he shared with Jimmy Thorpe, Sunderland's goalkeeper of the 1930s – and ensured that his own son was christened Raich. Horatio was his mother Clara's father's name, and one of Sunderland's grounds in their pre-Football League days had curiously been in Horatio Street. Carter said:

I might never have become a footballer without the name Horatio. It was useless to point out to the kids at school that my Christian name was the same as Nelson's. To them Horatio sounded cissyish and I quickly realised that the only thing that might save me from a very rough passage through schooldays was to excel at sport.

Raich was naturally left-footed, and began his football career as a left-half. He said: 'I continually practised with my right foot and by the time that I was 12 I could kick with either foot with equal force and accuracy. You have two feet, so why halve your efficiency by being content to kick with only one?' He went on to represent England at schoolboy level, playing first for the North against the South in trial matches. The North won one of them 4–2 at Bournemouth. Carter recalled: 'It was after this game that I received money for the first time. A spectator gave me half-a-crown for playing a good game!'

Carter then went on trial to Leicester City, which, according to his mother Clara, had been arranged since he was three when their next-door neighbour, former South Shields centre-half George Metcalfe, saw him play in his backyard. Metcalfe arranged the trial, which took place just after Carter's 17th birthday. He travelled back with the Leicester party after they had won 5–2 at Roker Park on Christmas Day, 1930, and played for their reserves. But the game did not go well for him, and he had another obstacle to overcome: Leicester's manager Willie Orr told him, 'You're too small to play football. You want to go home and build yourself up physically. Get some brawn and weight on you and gain some experience of the game.' It was not, of course, the first time that a Scot from Lanarkshire with an international pedigree had done Sunderland a big favour!

The deflated Carter, who became known to his team-mates as Raichy, signed as an amateur for Sunderland, served his apprenticeship as an electrician, and played non-League football locally for Esh Winning. But then he inadvertently got himself into trouble by wrongly agreeing to accept Huddersfield Town's offer of a trial while still on Sunderland's books. Cochrane refused to cancel the registration. Carter recalled: 'Johnny was a little fellow, but he had twice as much fire to make up for his size. I knew that there were far healthier places in the world than Johnny Cochrane's office and I left quickly while the going was good.' The outcome was that Carter was offered a trial in Sunderland's reserves, and then a professional contract. Carter's second wife, Pat, said:

> Sunderland was close to his heart because it was where he played as a kid. He was always excited about the time he played for them because he started just after the dark days of the Depression. He always respected how the supporters raised the money to get to games, so he felt that the players had to give performances in return. But he didn't like pubs because he could see the sawdust and spittoons from his bedroom and they represented a life when you didn't work.

Carter paid tribute to the advice given to him by Joe Devine and Tommy Urwin as he gained reserve experience. He made sufficient progress to make his Sunderland debut as an 18-year-old in October 1932 at Sheffield Wednesday, when Patsy Gallacher was injured and Gurney was ill. His first goal followed a fortnight later on his home debut in a 7–4 win over Bolton. Carter soon established himself in the side and never looked back. He was in the first team to stay, and it is noteworthy that once he had fought his way into prominence, the forward line that eventually brought the First Division championship back to Roker Park remained intact for much of the remainder of the 1932/33 season. Carter's importance as a piece in Cochrane's jigsaw for success cannot be underrated. In addition, he was a full England international by 1934 and ultimately he took over the captaincy at Sunderland on occasions when Alex Hastings was missing, but it was not until 1936/37 that he assumed the role regularly.

The fact that Carter was capped only 13 times by England should not diminish his importance. It is true that his career was interrupted by the 1939–45 war, when he should have been in his footballing prime, but his prowess should surely have earned him much greater international recognition, despite suggestions that he was too inconsistent. There is a distinct parallel, in fact, with Buchan, who lost much of his League career to the 1914–18 war when he too was in his mid-twenties. It is a stark fact that Carter and Buchan mustered just a total of 19 England caps between them. Carter won six England caps during his pre-war Sunderland days, making his debut in a 3–0 win over Scotland at Wembley in April 1934, but he played in only one international during the season in which he was a leading light in the club's title effort. His international career blossomed a touch more in his post-war days at Derby, especially when he hit a hat-trick in an 8–2 victory over Holland.

Carter became an imposing figure, which made the claims of inconsistency at international level all the more surprising, and it was largely the improvement in his personal tally of goals that provided the extra dimension that won the title in 1935/36. Carter went on to score 118 times in 245 League appearances for Sunderland, but he did not return to the club after the 1939–45 war. As he contemplated his Roker Park future, his main concern was a financial one:

All in all, I wanted to recoup some of the losses of the war years, so I wrote to Sunderland asking if they would be able to meet the requests that I set out. In addition, I wanted them to sign me on for ten years so that I would qualify for two more benefits. I did not think I was asking for the moon. Without any false modesty, I had done a lot for Sunderland and I thought they would meet me. They agreed instead to place me on the transfer list.

Pat Carter added, 'He'd have been happy staying at Sunderland, but they didn't offer him terms.'

Carter joined Derby, had a spell as Hull City player-manager, and also took charge of Leeds United, Mansfield Town and Middlesbrough. There was also a stint in Ireland, and he was consistently successful elsewhere, although, as his daughter Jane said, 'Football was all a stage act for him because he was performing once he got on to the field. Everybody liked to talk about football with him and I think he missed it when he wasn't directly involved in it.'

Carter eventually settled in Willerby, three miles west of Hull. His wife Pat said:

> He was a great family man, but he wouldn't let his family get in the way of his job. He had that willpower and he was dedicated. But there was a public figure and a private one. The telephone was always ringing with people asking him for his opinions. They often asked him if he could remember such-and-such a goal and they were always amazed that he could remember in detail how he scored them all. But at home he was the opposite of what he had to be as a footballer. He was quiet, witty and very easy to live with.

And Jane Carter added: 'He was very sensitive. He was a kind, soft man who would give away his money to tramps and helped other footballers.' Team-mate Patsy Gallacher was one recipient of Raich's help when he came upon hard times late in life.

The Carter family, though, were naturally upset by a newspaper article that erroneously suggested that Raich had to sell his football memorabilia to finance some medical treatment. At least those items eventually found their way to his native Sunderland, where his football genius might be readily recalled. Raich Carter died in October 1994, at which time one of his protégés, David Coates, was Sunderland's chief scout during Mick Buxton's time as manager. Coates, who was from Silksworth and had played for Carter at Hull and Mansfield, reflected:

> He was easily the most outstanding personality that I have met in the game. He was outstanding to look at because, even though he was not all that tall, he gave the impression of being a big man. He had an aura about him and he knew it. Raich had a wicked sense of humour and the ability to make a point firmly, but also

humorously. He always coated his criticism with a touch of humour and he was always very generous with the people he played with.

And the renowned playwright Alan Plater, who was born in the North-East himself, beautifully summed up the essential Raich: 'He was the greatest of his kind and he knew it. He reinvented the game as he went along. He didn't just play it: he presided over it.'

Carter's name will always be remembered in football circles as an all-time great. He even featured on a postage stamp for the Republic of Equatorial Guinea in strange circumstances when a set of stamps featuring eight top players was issued to commemorate the 1974 World Cup. Philatelists suggest that Eastern European countries in particular exploited the names of poorer countries for money-making ventures with stamps. In fact, it is unlikely that the Republic of Equatorial Guinea, a former Spanish colony, knew much about them. The stamps were rarely used and remain rare. A more lasting tribute has stood closer to home since the opening of the Raich Carter Sports Centre in Hendon on 5 October 2001.

Gurney was six years older than Carter, but immediately made him feel at home at Sunderland. Gurney's daughter, Dorothy, told how 'Dad and Raich were friends off the field from being young. In fact, the two families went on a camping holiday to Stratford-upon-Avon together.' As with Carter, Gurney had to overcome setbacks to establish himself in Sunderland's team. His son-in-law Michael Bates explained:

Bobby played for Silksworth School against Ford School, from Hylton, and they won 18–0. He'd scored nine goals when a master told him that it had gone a bit too far and moved him to full-back. He immediately gave away a penalty, which was missed, so he was moved back to centre-forward. He ended up scoring 13 goals and he thought that it was a schools' record. In September 1925 he scored nine for Sunderland Reserves against Hartlepools United Reserves in the North-Eastern League and never looked back. Bobby was very fast and incredibly brave, but he always played himself down in relation to Raich. And Bobby just missed out on becoming an England schoolboy international when he was 14. He played in a trial at York and apparently he played well in the second half, but some of those responsible for the teams had gone off somewhere at half-time. As a result, Bobby left school and went down the pits at Silksworth, but then he was notified that he had been picked for England in a schoolboy international against

Wales. But he couldn't play because he was no longer a schoolboy. When Bobby was 16, he went to Bishop Auckland and then he joined Sunderland when he was 17?. Charles Buchan had seen him playing and obviously rated what he had seen because he was instrumental in Sunderland finding him. In May 1925 Bobby signed for Sunderland for £5 a week and that's what he earned for the first three months without having kicked a football. It was more than his dad and brothers earned and he was so grateful for that because he had signed in the May and could help everybody out. Bob Kyle was Sunderland's manager then, but Johnny Cochrane released all his players except Bobby. At the same time he tried often enough and there were transfer negotiations with Liverpool at one stage.

Gurney also had to overcome further misfortune as a youngster because he broke his fibula in a reserve game at Workington as a 19-year-old. A doctor diagnosed it as 'just a badly bruised bone', but when the train jolted on the way home, he realised that it was more serious, and an X-ray the next day confirmed the real extent of the injury. He had just started to show signs of emerging as a force in Sunderland's first team, having made a goalscoring debut as an 18-year-old in a 3–2 defeat at West Ham United in April 1926. A week later he marked his home debut by scoring Sunderland's goals when they beat Arsenal 2–1. Gurney's first hat-trick was also against Arsenal, but he did not establish himself immediately as a first-team regular. It was only when David Halliday left for the Gunners towards the end of 1929 that Gurney took over his mantle with some authority, serving up a reminder of his ability when he scored four times in a 6–0 victory at Liverpool. After that, Gurney's goals kept coming. Michael Bates said:

> He was fast and had quite an eye for goal. He used to say that he scored some outlandish goals. He enjoyed scoring them so much that he would just have a go at times. He wasn't big-headed, but he was outstanding and, if he and players of his generation were playing now, I think that they'd be just as great.

Gurney came into his own in the 1930s and was Sunderland's leading goalscorer for seven successive seasons, though he and Carter finished level on 31 in 1935/36. Three times in that period Gurney reached the 30-goal mark in a season, reaching a personal peak with the five in the 7–2 win over Bolton at Roker Park in December 1935. And it emulated Buchan's feat of having scored five in the 7–0 demolition of Liverpool –

23 years earlier to the day!

It is remarkable that Gurney officially played only once for England – in a 2–0 defeat against Scotland at Hampden Park in April 1935. Thirteen months earlier he and Carter had played for the Rest against England in an international trial at Roker Park. The instructions for the team were relayed by FA international selection committee official Philip Bach, the Sunderland full-back from the 1890s. The Rest ran out 6–0 winners, with Carter scoring four and Gurney two. Gurney had also played for the Rest in a trial match 10 days before his debut, and yet Carter, who lined up against him in the England team, was not chosen to face Scotland. Gurney also played for England in an unofficial match against Scotland in 1935, and for the Probables against the Possibles in another trial match in October 1937 when his Sunderland team-mate Jimmy Gorman was a travelling reserve.

Gurney became an all-time great in Sunderland's history, and Dorothy Bates spoke of the hero status afforded to him by the public:

> Dad had to walk for about a mile from Middle Herrington to get a tram to Roker Park for matches. On one occasion there was a queue, and the conductor wouldn't let him on to the tram because he said it was full. But someone shouted at him, 'You've got to let him on because the game can't start without Bobby Gurney,' so he was allowed to get on!

Gurney, though, was an essentially modest person. Dorothy added:

> He just loved playing football. He liked all sports, but football was his great love. He didn't go to pubs and wasn't interested in living it up. He was a very quiet person and had a lovely sense of humour. He and Raich could be hilarious together. He was polite with people and liked meeting them. He loved reminiscing, but he could see the need for change and was always in favour of the Stadium of Light replacing Roker Park because he didn't want the club to slip behind the times. He would have loved it.

Gurney broke his leg twice, and on both occasions he was unaware that he had done it. In February 1939 it happened for the second time during the early exchanges of an FA Cup replay against Blackburn at Sheffield Wednesday's Hillsborough ground, but he went back onto the pitch without realising the seriousness of his injury. It heralded the end of his one-club League career, and there was a sour note to it after Billy Murray, once a Sunderland team-mate of Gurney, had replaced Johnny

Cochrane as manager. Michael Bates explained:

> Bobby was with the club from May 1925 to May 1946, but when
> he broke his leg in 1939 it finished him for that season. Then the
> war intervened, he joined the RAF and he was posted to Belgium.
> He played the odd wartime game, but when he came back after it,
> I think that Bill Murray wasn't comfortable with Bobby's
> reputation. There was a little feeling towards him in the last few
> months and it wasn't quite the same because they didn't make him
> welcome. Sunderland never gave him a benefit, and Bill Murray
> may have put the kibosh on it. It was an extraordinary oversight,
> but Bobby didn't have any side to him and he wouldn't be pushy.
> He never pulled rank or used his reputation to gain favours. He
> wasn't one to complain, but his wife Molly was a bit off about it.'

Dorothy Bates echoed the sentiment: 'In later years Dad did give interviews, but he never asked for a payment or a fee. He always wanted to pay for everything and hated asking for favours. But he never got a benefit match from Sunderland and that rankled more with my mother Molly.'

Gurney, whose League career consisted of 348 appearances, had a brief spell on Sunderland's coaching staff, but later moved into management. According to Dorothy, though, 'He was too nice a person to be a manager. He didn't have the driving ambition and wasn't cut-throat.' Instead he became a commercial traveller in confectionery and wines and spirits. Gurney died in 1994 – just six months before his great friend and colleague Raich Carter. But they had both graced a Football League ground for one last time. It happened at Boothferry Park when Hull City met Sunderland in October 1988, and the highlight of the pre-match entertainment came when Carter and Gurney kicked off from the centre spot, passed the ball from one to the other and planted it into the South Stand net. Ironically the ensuing game then finished gloomily as a goalless draw.

Patsy Gallacher, the other regular inside-forward in 1935/36, also helped out with his fair share of goals – 19 from 37 League appearances, including a hat-trick in the trouncing of Blackburn. And there were useful contributions from the wingers – 10 from Bert Davis in 25 games as he alternated on the right with Len Duns, who was on the mark five times in 17 appearances, and six from ever-present left-winger Jimmy Connor.

Gallacher and Connor formed the left-wing partnership and both came from Renfrewshire. Gallacher came from Bridge of Weir and joined Sunderland in 1927, turning professional the following year, after his 19th birthday. Known as the Mighty Atom, he did not make his first-team debut for another year, but he went on to make 307 appearances for the club, and bagged six hat-tricks in his 108 goals. Liverpool once offered £7,000 for Gallacher, who was said to be skilful rather than energetic, and that he was 'often taken for an Irishman and rarely denied it'. In fact, he earned himself one Scottish international cap before costing Stoke City £5,000 in 1938, and was also noted for guesting for 15 clubs during the 1939–45 war. Connor was from Renfrew itself and was just 82 days older than Gallacher. He was nearly 21 when he joined Sunderland from St Mirren for £5,000 in 1930. Known for his cultured left foot, Connor scored 61 times – including the winner in the 5–4 victory over Arsenal in 1935/36 – in 284 appearances for the club, and the total would have been greater if he had not had his injury troubles in later years. It was injury that led to his retirement towards the end of the 1938/39 season, but he did win four international caps with Scotland.

The diminutive Davis was 25 when he was signed from one of his home-city clubs, Bradford Park Avenue, in a £4,000 deal in 1932. He scored his only hat-trick for Sunderland in his 24th League appearance and was an ever-present during the 1933/34 and 1934/35 seasons. His run of 104 successive League games ended when he was sent off after scoring in a 4–3 win at Wolves; he was dismissed again five months later in the thrashing at Middlesbrough. Davis scored 40 goals in 163 appearances for Sunderland before moving to Leicester towards the end of 1936, after the rapidly developing Duns had mounted a sustained challenge for his place. It was so rapid, in fact, that Newcastle-born Duns joined Sunderland as an amateur when he was 17, turned professional when he was 18 and won a medal as a championship winner when he was 19! Equally spectacular was the ginger-haired Duns' introduction to League football with Sunderland: he made his debut a fortnight after Davis's first sending-off, and then scored twice in his first home appearance a week later in a 4–2 win over Preston North End. Duns, who had been signed from Newcastle West End, was basically there to stay – and he stayed until he retired in 1952. He scored 54 goals in 244 games, the last of which was in March 1952 when he was 35.

But there was also a considerable price to pay for Sunderland's title success of 1935/36 because they had to go through the pain of one of the clubs's worst tragedies almost two-thirds of the way through the season. Goalkeeper Jimmy Thorpe, a Jarrow lad, had made his debut for Sunderland in October 1930 a little more than a month after his 17th birthday. He had to vie first with Scotsman Bob Middleton and then with local lad Matt Middleton for the goalkeeper's jersey at Sunderland, but was an ever-present in the championship-winning season until tragedy struck him after the 26th game of the season – a 3–3 draw at home to Chelsea on 1 February 1936. Thorpe did not have the biggest build for a goalkeeper and was injured in a goalmouth scramble in the second half, but indicated that he was fit enough to carry on. Four days later, however, Thorpe, a diabetic who had to take regular insulin and lost a lot of weight in the previous two years, died.

Raich Carter later mused:

> Jimmy Thorpe was a good goalkeeper and his heart and soul were in the game. As far as he was concerned, the only thing that could keep him out of our 1935/36 championship team would be a loss of form, and Jimmy never suffered from that. But during that last season it was noticeable that he was losing weight rapidly: he seemed to be shrinking inside himself. In our match against Chelsea there was a lot of play in our goalmouth, and I heard that Jimmy had been bumped about a bit, although, being up the field, I never saw it myself. I remember most distinctly that when we left the ground, Jimmy appeared to be all right and made no complaint of feeling ill, so it was a terrible shock to us when we reported as usual for training on the following Tuesday and learned that he was dead.

It was believed that Thorpe had died in a diabetic coma, but a coroner's jury decided that 'the illness had been accelerated by rough usage of the goalkeeper'. The jury criticised the referee, who had not been called as a witness at the inquest, but an FA commission later vindicated him and insisted that he had acted 'totally in accordance with his instructions'. But the coroner's jury also urged referees to exert stricter control, and there is little doubt that goalkeepers became better protected as a result of the incident. An attacker was no longer permitted to raise his feet towards a goalkeeper who already had the ball in his hands, but it was a case of being wise after the event. Thorpe had died at just 22 after his 139th appearance for Sunderland. It was sufficient to earn him a championship-winner's medal posthumously, and it was duly presented to his family. Matt Middleton replaced him in goal for the next nine games before 19-year-old Johnny Mapson took over for the final seven games of the run-in to the title. Mapson was signed from Reading, where he had been the third-choice goalkeeper, in a £2,000 deal the month after Thorpe had died, and embarked on what was to be a substantial career with Sunderland. But it could perhaps have begun in less agonising circumstances.

The rest of Sunderland's title-winning defence were almost exclusively Scottish – full-backs Billy Murray, Tom Morrison and Alex Hall, and half-backs Charlie M. Thomson, Bert Johnston, Jimmy Clark, skipper Alex Hastings and Sandy McNab. It was once claimed that 'the back division conceded more goals than a championship defence ought', but they still lent crucial experience to the side as a whole.

The right-back spot was shared between Murray and Morrison, and both played in 21 League games. Murray, originally from Aberdeen, had served in the Gordon Highlanders, trained as a mining engineer and then concentrated on his football with Cowdenbeath, whom he had captained to promotion from the Scottish Second Division as runners-up to St Johnstone in 1923/24. He became a Sunderland regular after joining them in April 1927 and made 328 appearances for the club, but was approaching the end of his playing career when he left for St Mirren as a 35-year-old almost 10 years later. In contrast, Morrison, who was originally from Kilmarnock, had played for St Mirren before his time at Sunderland, whom he actually joined from Liverpool as a 32-year-old wing-half after the 1935/36 season had started. Eight years earlier he had won his only Scottish cap, but Morrison's contribution to Sunderland's history was quietly effective rather than celebrated. He played his 21 League games at right-back, helped them to title glory and then disappeared, curiously popping up with the pseudonym Anderson in Cambridgeshire football the following season before returning to his native Ayrshire.

Harold Shaw made the last of his appearances for Sunderland in the opening League game of the 1935/36 season at defending champions Arsenal and was then promptly replaced by Alex Hall for the next 39. Shaw and Hall, a Scot from Kirknewton, west of Edinburgh, had latterly been regular rivals for the left-back berth. Hall, a good sprinter who had two good feet and could play equally comfortably on the right and the left, had had to serve a long apprenticeship to establish himself after joining Sunderland from Dunfermline Athletic as a 20-year-old towards the end of the 1928/29 season. He had staying power, though, and clocked up 233 appearances for Sunderland, until the onset of the 1939–45 war.

Charlie M. Thomson, a Glaswegian, was the other ever-present during 1935/36. As with several other team-mates, he developed during the 1930s into a reliable, consistent wing-half who was reckoned to play 'with his head as well as with his feet'. He was constructive and skilful and was said to be able 'to manoeuvre the ball on the space of a sixpence'. Slight of build, Thomson joined Sunderland as a 20-year-old during the summer of 1931 and made only two isolated appearances for the club in his first season, but he did not look back after that and played in 147 consecutive League games at one point. He stayed with Sunderland, his only League club, until the end of the 1938/39 season, by which time he had played in 264 games, before announcing his retirement during the wartime hiatus. By then he had also been capped once by Scotland, in 1937.

Another Glaswegian, Jimmy Clark, played in two-thirds of Sunderland's League games at centre-half during the title-winning season, treading a similar path as some of his contemporaries. He joined Sunderland as a youngster during the summer of 1933 and had to learn his trade in the reserves, not being given a first-team opportunity until he had been at Roker Park for the best part of two seasons. He came to the fore during the 1935/36 season, but had made only 50 appearances for the club by the time he moved to Plymouth Argyle during the autumn of 1937. He later emigrated to South Africa, but never consistently upstaged fellow Scot Bert Johnston apart from in 1935/36. Falkirk-born Johnston was 19 when he joined Sunderland from Scottish junior football during the summer of 1929, after Cochrane had beaten Glasgow Rangers for his signature by 24 hours, and it was nearly two years before he was given his first-team chance. He first had to compete with 'Jock' McDougall for the centre-half berth, and then largely missed out to Clark during the title-winning season. But Johnston outlasted them both, played in 163 games for Sunderland and stayed at Roker Park on the coaching staff when Murray became manager. Johnston also emulated Thomson by winning his only Scottish international cap against Czechoslovakia in 1937.

There was also a sort of symmetry to the left-half spot in Sunderland's title-winning team because it was contested by two Scottish internationals – one from Falkirk and another Glaswegian. Alex Hastings had been a regular goalscorer in schoolboy football in Falkirk, but then established himself as a wing-half with Sunderland and Scotland, who capped him twice against Northern Ireland, in 1935 and 1937. And Hastings soon established himself after moving to Roker Park from Stenhousemuir as an 18-year-old during the summer of 1930. He matured more quickly than many of Cochrane's other young Scottish imports, earned a regular place in the first team a month after joining Sunderland and was soon made captain. He went on to play 300 games for the club – 31 of them in the League in the title-winning season – before the 1939–45 war ended his playing career. Hastings had had to face stiff competition from fellow Scot Sandy McNab, who was 20 when Sunderland signed him from Glasgow Pollok, where he had been a team-mate of Thomson, in May 1932. Ironically, the ginger-haired McNab then became a first-team regular in 1933/34 – at the expense of Thomson rather than Hastings – but ended up making only 112 appearances for the club, who received a handy £6,750 fee from West Bromwich when they sold him in 1938. He played 13 times during the championship-winning season and did win two Scottish international caps, the first while with Sunderland in 1937.

Curiously, Les McDowall made a rare appearance in the No. 6 shirt in the final game of 1935/36 at Derby. He was born in India, the son of a missionary from Scotland. Sunderland had arguably won the title again thanks to a healthy contribution from their Scottish imports, another of whom, Edinburgh-born inside-forward James Russell, made his debut as a teenager on the same afternoon. Russell later reflected on Cochrane's managerial style: 'He was laid-back and held very brief team talks. He would appear in the dressing-room just before the game with a cigar and a whisky glass.' Apparently Cochrane would then query the name of the opposition and, when told, would reply, 'Oh, we'll stuff them' before disappearing!

Cochrane's triumph in guiding Sunderland to the title was marred only by the team's performances in the FA Cup in 1935/36. They could only draw 2–2 at home to Port Vale in the third round and then lost 2–0 to them on a frozen pitch in the replay two days later. It led to Cochrane holding a post-match inquest that lasted into the early hours at the team's hotel. And while Sunderland carried on to taste First Division championship glory, their giant-killers Port Vale were relegated from the Second Division.

But when Sunderland failed to mount a serious challenge to retain their title in 1936/37 – they conceded 87 goals and only two First Division clubs conceded more – they were grateful for the relief provided by the FA Cup and they finally exorcised the ghost of 1912/13 when defeat in the final against Aston Villa had deprived them of the Double. Carter tried to put it all into context: 'The fact that Sunderland had never won the Cup was a terrible thing for the North. Every year was to be Sunderland's Cup year, and there was always great disappointment when they were knocked out.' But this time they went all the way for the first time in their history.

Sunderland finished only eighth in the League in 1936/37 despite winning five games in a row during the autumn following a 5–5 draw at Middlesbrough. They took 36 points out of a possible 42 at home – the same return as in their championship campaign – but conceded 63 goals in their 21 away games. Their contrary nature was also underlined in the second half of the season by a 6–4 defeat at West Bromwich, a 5–3 defeat at Stoke and a 6–0 defeat at Grimsby. Sunderland were more tailor-made for the occasional requirements of the FA Cup, but even then the road to Wembley was rocky because they had to play eight ties to get there.

Most of the players who had won the title a year earlier were still around, but two newcomers – full-back Jimmy Gorman and left-winger Eddie Burbanks – played significant roles in the Cup run. Another two – left-back George Collin and inside-forward Cecil Hornby – played in the first tie and then missed the rest. Clark and Hastings, who passed on the captaincy to Carter after he had been injured against Arsenal in January 1937, also managed just one appearance each in the FA Cup that season.

Gorman, a Liverpudlian who had played for Skelmersdale United and Burscough Rangers before making his name with Blackburn, was not even a Sunderland player when the FA Cup run began. He was signed for a £6,250 fee in January 1937 and made his debut for the club only a week before the fourth round. But he was quick and keen to overlap, and soon became a first-team regular until the 1939–45 war, making 99 appearances for the club. He also had to endure constant dressing-room reminders about his appearance for Blackburn against Sunderland in October 1932. Gallacher had outwitted Gorman to complete a hat-trick, and Raich Carter, who made his League debut a fortnight later, observed: 'It took Jimmy a long time to live down that goal!'

Burbanks, a Yorkshireman, was a right-footed left-winger who was signed from Midlands League club Denaby United for just £750 during the summer of 1934. He played just two League games in 1934/35 and then missed the whole of the title-winning season when Jimmy Connor was an ever-present. Burbanks, though, gradually displaced Connor as Sunderland's first-choice left-winger and made 152 appearances for the club, but he had wrestled with his conscience about a football career at one stage:

> I wanted to be a schoolteacher, but a long waiting-list for entry to a training college changed my plans and I found a job as a clerk in the electricity department of Doncaster Corporation. I lived just outside Doncaster and played football on Saturday afternoons to keep myself fit. I had the first big decision of my life to make at 19 when I had to choose between football and my job. I was playing for Thorne Town and had trials with Manchester City and Bolton Wanderers, but my boss said, 'The time has come when you've got to choose between working and playing football.' I did some quick thinking, chose the office job, explained the position to Bolton and carried on with Thorne Town. But a year later I had to face the football-versus-job problem again. I was playing for Denaby

United, I was a part-time professional and playing didn't interfere with my work. It lasted three weeks and then one day Percy Harrison, Denaby's secretary-manager, and my father called at the office where I was working and told me that a League club were after my signature. Percy wouldn't tell me which club, but their manager was to meet me at York railway station. I had heard that certain clubs, including Sheffield United, Norwich City and Notts County, had been watching me, but I really did not think that I would ever reach the standard required. After getting permission from the head clerk where I worked, I set off with father and Percy for Doncaster railway station. On the way a fourth man joined the party and he was introduced to me as a scout. Once in the railway carriage on the way to York, I sat back to think the thing out and let the other three talk football. The name Sunderland was used several times, the first indication I had had of the club who were interested in my future. I stared out of the window and thought over every argument for and against football as a full-time job. It was football versus a safe and progressive position, and this time football won. When we left the train at York, a fifth man came to meet us and he was introduced to me as Johnny Cochrane, so that puzzle was solved.

There were differing accounts as to why Cochrane was interested in Burbanks. One tale was that Sunderland were scouting in the Midlands to look at a full-back, who was given the runaround by Burbanks, so they signed him instead. Another tale was that Burbanks 'was recommended to Sunderland by a former Wearside League referee who used to reside in the Houghton district and is now at Denaby'. Cochrane himself said:

When playing for Denaby United, he was recommended to me by a friend who occasionally travelled with the team. At the first possible opportunity I had the rule run over him and eventually arranged that he should be brought to York, where an appointment was fixed. I well remember finding on reaching York that a pressman was at the hotel: whether by accident or design I do not know. It is perfectly true that Burbanks did not know which club was on his trail and he seemed more than surprised when I revealed to him that Sunderland proposed to engage his services. The signing was completed whereupon I called my pressman friend into the company, the first occasion on which one had actually been bang on the premises when I had been negotiating for a player in such circumstances.

Connor was said to have become a possible transfer target for Everton, but Burbanks, who had been linked with a £6,000 move to Bolton himself, was quick to praise his team-mate and rival:

> I found an air of friendliness about Sunderland players and officials, which soon made me feel at home, and Jimmy Connor was one of the friendliest of the bunch. From the first I became a big admirer of Jimmy's play and, if anyone had told me that I stood a chance of becoming the club's regular left-winger while he was on the books, I would have laughed politely. So great an impression did Jimmy make on my mind that I became resigned to being in the background for a long time. All the time, though, I was learning and, if Jimmy noticed a fault in my play, such as bad positioning, he would tell me about it in a friendly way and point out how I could put it right.

Burbanks later recalled his scoring debut in a 4–1 win at home to Portsmouth on 27 April 1935:

> In the dressing-room before the game Raich Carter came over to me and said, 'Don't worry, Eddie! Run into an open space and I'll do my best to put the ball in front of you.' Open spaces were made for me so often that afternoon that I might have had the playing-field to myself. I became quite confident and I began to hold onto the ball a bit longer. In the second half I ran into the middle to find out what the centre-forward's job was like when Bert Davis, our right-winger, centred. I obtained the ball and shot and it left my foot like a rocket. The next second John Gilfillan, the Portsmouth goalkeeper, was picking something from the back of the net. I rubbed my eyes and then felt someone slapping my back – I'd scored my first League goal.'

His wife Joyce added:

> Eddie always said that he had fond memories of his time at Sunderland, whose team had a lot of camaraderie. They all got on so well together and were really good mates. He was a good all-round sportsman and at one point it was thought that he would have been an even better cricketer, but football was his first love. Eddie never sought to be the centre of attention. He was very kind, caring and easy-going. He could tear a strip off somebody, but not loudly. He was helpful and a soft touch.

Sunderland's involvement in the 1936/37 FA Cup began with a third-round tie at lowly Second Division side Southampton and they went away to prepare for it with special training at Bushey Hall in Hertfordshire. The side included at left-back Collin, who had suffered a broken leg in the early part of his career and then given lengthy service to Derby before leaving for Roker Park during the summer of 1936, and at inside-right the versatile Hornby, who had been signed from Leeds for £1,000 11 months earlier and had scored twice when called up during the title run-in the previous season. On the morning of the match Carter had failed a fitness test – which amazingly consisted of running along the underground platform at Waterloo en route to Southampton – but Hornby was on the mark again as his deputy, as were Gurney and Gallacher in a 3–2 victory. Sunderland progressed, but Collin and Hornby had made their only FA Cup appearances for the club.

Sunderland then found the going tough against Third Division opposition Luton Town in the fourth round. To be fair, the Hatters, for whom centre-forward Joe Payne had scored a League record of ten goals in a game nine months earlier, scored 103 goals in winning the Third Division South title that season, but Sunderland, who brought in Gorman and Carter, needed two attempts to get past them. They drew 2–2 at Kenilworth Road, with goals by Duns and Connor, and only the brilliance of goalkeeper Mapson, who was given a standing ovation, kept their interest in the competition alive after they had been 2–0 down. In the replay, which attracted a crowd of 53,200, Sunderland won 3–1 with goals from Duns and Connor (again) and Carter, while Johnston emerged with great credit for the way he subdued Payne.

The fifth round threw up a home tie against Swansea Town, another side in the lower half of the Second Division, and Sunderland won 3–0 in front of a crowd of 48,500. Clark replaced Johnston and Burbanks took over from Connor, who against Luton had received a bad injury which eventually required surgery. Carter and Gurney were given some rough treatment on a windswept day, and Duns was again on the mark, this time following a corner by Burbanks. Gurney also scored, and an own goal by Tommy Caldwell completed the scoring in a 3–0 win. Sunderland were in the quarter-finals and had not yet met First Division opposition, but that was about to change.

They were drawn away to Wolves in the sixth round and again had special training at Bushey Hall. They needed it because a week earlier they had ventured into the West Midlands and lost 6–4 at West Bromwich in a match that also featured three penalties. Two were missed, including one by Carter, which was the fifth in a row spurned by Sunderland. But they had Johnston back in place of Clark for the cup-tie as a crowd of 57,751 saw them draw 1–1 at Molineux with another goal by Duns, who equalised after Welsh international Bryn Jones had scored for Wolves. The replay at Roker Park four days later attracted a gate of 61,796, and this time there was an epic 2–2 draw after extra-time. Wolves, who finished fifth in the First Division that season, led after 86 minutes with a low, left-footed shot from Tom Galley, but were foiled when Gurney scored a magnificent goal while lying on the ground in the 89th minute. Apparently 'muteness gave way to pandemonium', and Sunderland's fans were said to have marked their let-off with 'dances of delirium'. Duns was on the mark for the fifth time in a row after 95 minutes, but Wolves equalised with a goal by Harry Thompson two minutes later. The action then switched to Sheffield Wednesday's Hillsborough ground for the second replay the following Monday, and on this occasion Sunderland made no mistake. Gurney scored after nine minutes, Carter and Gallacher added two in two minutes just before half-time, and Thomson wrapped up a 4–0 win with a penalty.

As in 2003/04, Sunderland were then left to face Millwall in the semi-finals. The difference was that the two clubs were not then in the same division: Sunderland were a proud First Division outfit and Millwall were in the top half of the Third Division South. But the Lions had beaten Derby and Manchester City in the previous two rounds, after having accounted for Second Division Fulham and Chelsea earlier on as they became the first Third Division side to reach the last four of the FA Cup. Derby finished fourth in the First Division that season, Manchester City were the champions and Chelsea were a mid-table outfit, but all three had come a cropper at the Den. But the attention turned to Leeds Road, Huddersfield, on 10 April 1937, and an attendance of 62,813 for the semi-final. Hastings returned in place of the injured McNab, but Sunderland continued to live on a knife-edge in the competition as Millwall took the lead after 11 minutes with a goal by their captain Dave Mangnall. It took an equaliser by Gurney, who had missed an early chance, after 30 minutes, and a headed winner by Gallacher in the 70th minute to turn the game round and send Sunderland to Wembley for the first time. Their opponents were to be Preston, who were then a mid-table First Division side and had just beaten West Bromwich 4–1 in the other semi-final to take their goal tally to 17 in four rounds, having accounted for Newcastle United in the third round.

Sunderland prepared for the final by returning to Bushey Hall, travelling there straight from their final League game of the season – a 3–0 defeat at Leeds. But Carter and Gurney stopped off in the Derby area, where Carter married his first wife Rose (who was to die when she was only 39), and Gurney was his best man on the Monday. They then joined the others at Bushey Hall, which was favoured because it had a golf course, baths, a trainer's room with massage facilities, a cinder track and plenty of grassland for training – although Gorman and McNab plumped for croquet at one stage! Carter recalled:

> We took things easily and had a quiet time. The peace was solace to the nerves. In the mornings we did a bit of limbering up or played golf, we went for walks in the afternoons and in the evenings we went to the pictures. One day we were taken to Wembley to have a look round so that those who had never been there before could familiarise themselves with the ground.

At one stage manager Johnny Cochrane left trainer Andy Reid in temporary control during the build-up, but in midweek he too spoke about the preparations:

> My players have been out in the grounds in an unpleasant drizzle, endeavouring to develop certain moves which they may put into operation at Wembley on Saturday. It would not be fair to discuss the nature of any plans which we are making. In fact, the players themselves are pledged to secrecy. Pressmen are turning up from all quarters and practically sitting on the doorstep and we are button-holed whenever we appear in the lounge or outside the hotel. Telephone calls, too, are coming most persistently and I am afraid that I have had to tell the porters that I am on the golf course even if that is not always the case. Our 12 players are perfectly fit, but they are not yet discussing the match in the hotel. They endeavour to forget football in their moments of relaxation, which, however, is difficult for one reason only – the autograph hunters. Heavy packages with autograph books are coming by every post – we wish that they had contained tickets! Sometimes I think that a charge should be made for each autograph with the proceeds going to charity.

Cochrane insisted on calling the competition the Coronation Cup, and Carter was in bullish mood about the prospects during the build-up to the final:

> My team-mates and I have a profound respect for the calibre of our antagonists, Preston North End, but Sunderland will make no mistake about the FA Cup this time because they are the best

team in England. That may seem a rather tall claim to make, but I think our record is convincing proof of what I say. If I really receive the Cup – a cherished ambition since I, as a 12-year-old, used to watch Charles Buchan – it will be one of the biggest thrills of my life. It will be an immense source of gratification to Sunderland if at long last we win the cup of cups.

The tradition of staging the FA Cup final on the final Saturday of April was shelved in 1937 when it took place on May Day to mark the Coronation celebrations. In fact, King George VI and Queen Elizabeth were at Wembley to watch the final and were honoured by massed bands from Portsmouth, Chatham and the Irish Guards, and an RAF flypast in formation. In fact, the combined bands of the Royal Navy and the Welsh and Irish Guards prolonged the half-time break by three minutes.

Sunderland had needed eight games to reach the final – just as they were to do in 1973 when they won the FA Cup for the second time. They were at full strength. Thomson, an ever-present in the Cup run, had recovered from knee trouble, while McNab returned at Hastings' expense. Preston stuck with goalkeeper Mick Burns even though England international Harry Holdcroft, who had missed their semi-final win over West Bromwich, was fit again having suffered a broken finger. Their line-up also included Scottish internationals Andy Beattie and Bill Shankly, who were born within 22 days of each other and later became renowned as top managers, and Jimmy Milne, whose son Gordon played for England. In fact, Sunderland were outnumbered by Scots despite the great influence that they had always had on the club. Sunderland – without Hastings – fielded five but Preston included seven – Beattie, Shankly, Milne, James Dougall, brothers Frank and Hugh O'Donnell and Willie Fagan. Dougall and Frank O'Donnell were also internationals. There were other curious parallels between the two teams. Mapson had been a baker's boy in Swindon; Preston's centre-half Bill Tremelling, whose brother Dan played in goal for England, had been a baker in the East Midlands at the outset of his career. Gorman was a Lancastrian who had played down the road from Preston at Blackburn; Preston's goalkeeper Mick Burns was from Leeholme in County Durham and had played down the road from Sunderland at Newcastle. In addition, Burbanks and Preston's inside-right Joe Beresford both came from the Bentley area, near Doncaster. Curiously, Burbanks' rival left-winger in the semi-final, Millwall's Jack Thorogood, had also played in local football in the Doncaster area.

As the game got under way in front of a crowd of 93,495, who paid a total of £24,831 6s 0d, Gurney missed a chance, but then Frank

O'Donnell joined the select band of players to score in every round of the FA Cup when he beat Mapson with a powerful shot after 38 minutes after Dougall had set him up. It seemed ominous for Sunderland because the side scoring first in 12 of the previous 14 FA Cup finals at Wembley had gone on to win, but they drew level six minutes into the second half when Preston failed to clear a corner, which had been won and taken by Burbanks, and Gurney finally made sure with a header. Gallacher had a penalty appeal rejected, and Carter chose to pass when he might have shot and scored. But Gurney set up the chance for Carter to make amends in the 71st minute when he put them ahead, dribbling and swerving his way through before planting a low shot past Burns after leaving Tremelling in his wake. Sunderland then clinched victory in the 77th minute after a stoppage while the injured Gurney received treatment. Gurney and Gallacher combined after play restarted with a dropped ball, and Burbanks worked his way into a position to enable him to score with an angled drive. Gallacher received a blow to the head, but Sunderland, who had Johnston booked for a foul on Frank O'Donnell, held out comfortably for a 3–1 victory. Gorman was said to have been outstanding in defence, and there was praise for wing-halves Thomson and McNab, but Burbanks was generally acknowledged to have been Sunderland's man of the match. He said of his goal: 'When the ball hit the back of the net, I wasn't conscious of the great roar that follows a cup-final goal, but, as I turned round I had a picture of the whole of Wembley lifting up. Of course, it was the crowd jumping to their feet and waving their arms. I'll never forget that.' His wife Joyce added: 'Eddie said that it was great to meet *the King*, but he wasn't overawed by the occasion and scoring the last goal was the highlight of his career.'

Carter, meanwhile, described the feeling of being an FA Cup winner:

We filed up to the Royal Box, there was a din of applause and cheering that seemed to swamp your brain, and I was too excited to take in the scene in detail. It was a blur of visions. I recall the beaming smile of King Farouk of Egypt, and then the Queen was shaking hands with me and the King, standing at her side, was adding his congratulations. I remember the Queen saying as she handed me the Cup, 'That is a nice wedding present for you.' I had the Cup clutched to me with one arm and was holding the stand, which had come away from it, in the other hand while the Queen was still trying to hand me my cup-winner's medal. Fortunately, Alec Hall, who was immediately behind me, came to the rescue and relieved me of the stand. Those few minutes' breathing-space standing in front of the King and Queen were gone with a vengeance because making my way down the gangway was like running the gauntlet. The crowds were leaning over to try to touch the Cup and grabbing me by the arm, by the shirt and even by my hair. I was clutching the Cup to myself like mad to hold on to it. Once more on the field, my team-mates dived for my legs, hoisted me onto their shoulders and carried me off the field. It was a bumpy ride with the Cup even more precariously balanced than ever, and my heart was in my mouth in case I should drop it. In the dressing-room the directors filled the Cup with champagne and everybody was drinking out of it.

Sunderland had finally won the FA Cup. The trio of Carter, Gurney and Burbanks had provided Cochrane with three steps to heaven, and it was fitting that Charlie Buchan, one of the losers in the final 24 years and a world war earlier, was covering the game as a journalist for the *News Chronicle*. There was no lap of honour in those days – in fact, the National Anthem was played after the match – but twice Carter's colleagues hoisted him onto their shoulders to hold the FA Cup aloft. Sunderland's vice-chairman Duncan White commented: 'There was only one team in it after the interval and that team won. We opened badly, as we have done in several other cup-ties, but I felt quite happy once we got the equaliser.' And long-serving director Fred Taylor, the former chairman, added: 'We have won the Cup at long last. I cannot express in adequate terms how happy I am. Again Sunderland have shown how they fight back.'

Sunderland had not planned anything special as an after-match reception despite Carter's pre-match confidence, but Preston had. As a result, some of Sunderland's players accepted their invitations to join their rivals at their reception in London! Referee R. G. Rudd later visited the Sunderland team at London's Russell Hotel, where they autographed the match ball for him. He went on to describe Gurney as 'the finest fellow I have ever met on a football field' and insisted that Burbanks 'was worthy of two medals'. The trophy was also shown off at King's Cross as the squad set out on a special Pullman train decked out in the club's red-and-white colours for their return to the North in readiness for a civic reception at Sunderland Town Hall. On the way, well-wishers waved flags from houses and railway embankments from Darlington onwards before the Sunderland party stopped for 25 minutes at Newcastle Central station, which was packed with thousands of fans. More remarkable was the fact that a civic party, led by the Lord Mayor of Newcastle, Alderman John Grantham, welcomed the players and offered their congratulations. Members of the civic party even boarded the train and drank to the team's success from the Cup, while Newcastle City Police Band played for the duration of the stay in the city.

Further down the line, crowds had started to take up vantage points more than two hours before the Sunderland party arrived at Monkwearmouth station. Carter was one of the first off the train, grasping the Cup, but was at once ushered into temporary wireless headquarters to broadcast. The team then emerged from the station to a roar from the crowd as they began their tour of the town in four coaches. Carter, who had had to postpone his honeymoon, and his fellow inside-forwards, Gurney and Gallacher, sat at the front of the first coach. Tugs and vessels on the River Wear hooted in acknowledgement as the party crossed the Wearmouth Bridge, and cinemas ground to a halt in the middle of films. There were people 20 or 30 deep on both sides of Fawcett Street, where the nearly completed Coronation illuminations were later switched on for an hour as part of the celebrations, as the party approached the town hall. It was estimated that 250,000 people turned out to watch the procession and welcome home their heroes. The Mayor, Alderman Thomas Summerbell, welcomed them at the town hall before they moved on to the Wheatsheaf's reception room half a mile away. Speeches were relayed to the cheering crowd. Alderman Summerbell said that 'The players have put Sunderland on the international map of sport. Our football club are a fine trade advertisement for the town and we are proud that they have achieved one of the greatest ambitions in football.' There were also speeches from Carter, who congratulated his team-mates on the way they had rallied in the second half, and Gurney. Carter added: 'It is worth winning the Cup for this marvellous reception alone. I am sure we deserved to win for our play in the second half when all the boys struck a really wonderful game.'

The procession then moved on to Roker Park, where a crowd of about 20,000 had gathered, via Bridge Street, Roker Avenue and Brandling Street, and the team and the Cup were paraded round the ground. Johnny Cochrane and local boys Carter and Gurney placed the trophy in the centre of the pitch. In the boardroom Duncan White, who had to deputise because chairman Sir Walter Raine was ill, proposed a vote of thanks to the players, and it was seconded by former chairman Fred Taylor. It was fitting that the despair of 1913 and the joy of 1937 should be compared, and there was a special mention for assistant trainer Billy Dunlop, the only member of the backroom staff who was with the club for both finals.

It was also time to broach Sunderland's famed bottle of beer, which had been reserved at the Trade Union Club in the town's Frederick Street after the defeat in the 1913 final. Its manufacturers had promised to mark winning the Cup by sending the club another bottle of beer, which had been sealed in 1901 to celebrate the accession of King Edward VII. Apparently the contents of that original bottle of beer were duly drunk to mark the Cup triumph, and Carter put the achievement into perspective by remarking that they were as old as he was!

Carter said of the fans' reception:

> It was a never-to-be-forgotten sight. Sunderland had gone crazy. My arms ached from holding aloft the Cup. Every member of the team must have been moved, but to me it meant so much more. This was my home town and these were my own folk. I was the local boy who had led the team to victory and brought home the Cup for which they had been waiting for 50 years. What more could any man ask? My happiness could never be more complete.

The outcome of it all was that Sunderland had removed three trophies from Arsenal's boardroom in little more than a year. They had taken over from them as First Division champions in 1935/36, and as FA Cup holders in 1936/37, and also beaten them 2–1 in the Charity Shield at Roker Park in October 1936 when – 30 years before Geoff Hurst's famous World Cup final controversy at Wembley – Carter had been awarded a crucial goal at the Fulwell End after his shot had bounced down from the bar and been ruled to have crossed the line. Carter seemed to have perfected the technique because the same kind of dispute followed his winner against Birmingham at Roker Park in October 1937. And if Sunderland had made only a modest defence of their League title in 1936/37, then they did not relinquish their hold on the FA Cup easily.

In 1937/38 Sunderland reached the semi-finals with four successive 1–0 victories. Duns scored in the wins over Watford and Bradford Park Avenue in the third and fifth rounds respectively, Gurney was on the mark at Everton in the fourth round and Carter was the match-winner at Tottenham Hotspur in the quarter-final when another crowd record was set in North London – 75,038 at White Hart Lane. Burbanks was Sunderland's goalscorer at the semi-final stage, but they lost 3–1 to Huddersfield Town at Ewood Park, Blackburn, to end their run of 13 FA Cup ties without defeat. But Town were then beaten 1–0 in the final as Preston went one better than the previous season. Their line-up included goalkeeper Bob Hesford, whose son Iain was to play for Sunderland in the 1980s, and wing-half Ken Willingham, a top-class athlete who was to spend a brief post-war spell at Roker Park.

The majority of Sunderland's players who had brought success in successive seasons stayed with the club for the remainder of the 1930s, with occasional additions. Full-back John Feenan, who was capped twice by the Republic of Ireland in 1937, cost the club £2,000 from Belfast Celtic and made just 29 appearances. Half-backs Arthur Housam and Alec Lockie were two local lads whose careers were disrupted by the 1939–45 war, but played a handful of games both before and after it. Sunderland-born winger John Spuhler temporarily displaced Duns during the 1937/38 season, and John Smeaton was a Scottish inside-forward who established himself in Gallacher's place during the 1938/39 season. Centre-forward Bill Robinson, who was from Whitburn, scored 14 goals in 24 appearances, including four in a 5–2 home win over Manchester United in March 1939. But his feat coincided with the resignation of manager Johnny Cochrane and his assistant George Crow becoming secretary. Cochrane's successor was Billy Murray, the defender who had left the club two years earlier to see out his playing career with St Mirren.

Sunderland had become a mid-table First Division side towards the end of the 1930s despite the talent at their disposal, but the players were never to be given the chance to emulate their earlier successes because of the 1939–45 war. They played three games at the start of the 1939/40 season before it was aborted as hostilities began and football became fragmented. It became largely regionalised, Sunderland fielded numerous guest players and took part in the North League from 1941 and various cup competitions. They played in the FA Wartime Cup, the Tyne-Wear-Tees Cup, the Durham Professional Cup and the West Riding Cup, which they won in notable circumstances in 1942/43. In the final they beat Huddersfield 7–6 on aggregate, the first home leg being a personal triumph for centre-forward Cliff Whitelum. Sunderland won it 6–2 and Whitelum scored all six of their goals.

As an air of normality began to return after the war ended, a largely two-legged FA Cup competition was hastily arranged in 1945/46, but it was not until the following season that League football resumed. Many players had lost some of their best years to the conflict. Sunderland's own tragic wartime situation was perhaps summed up most poignantly by Percy Saunders, an inside-left who was with them between 1936 and 1939. He was born during the 1914–18 war and killed in action midway through the 1939–45 war – and his middle name had the military ring of Kitchener about it.

The conflict, in fact, turned out to be something of a watershed in Sunderland's history. They had had a lot of success before it, and were going to strive unsuccessfully for the most part after it to rekindle those previous glories. There were threads that bound the club before and after the 1939–45 war. Burbanks, for example, scored the club's last League goal before it, in a 5–2 defeat at Arsenal in the jettisoned 1939/40 season, the day before war was declared. And he was around to score the club's first League goal after it, in a 3–2 home win over Derby at the end of August 1946. But other aspects had changed significantly. After all, that Derby line-up included Carter, who had already earned the honour of being the only player to appear in FA Cup-winning sides before and after the 1939–45 war when they beat Charlton Athletic 4–1 in the 1945/46 final. One way or another, things were never going to be the same again for Sunderland.

4

'PEANUTS –
TANNER A BAG!'

Leonard Francis Shackleton was never short of the odd cutting quip. On one occasion, having walked a couple of hundred yards from his sea-front home to address dinner guests at Sunderland's Seaburn Hotel, Shack gave it to them straight: 'I've heard of selling dummies. But this club...well, they just keep on buying them!' he roared.

Len Shackleton, arguably *the* most famous player in Sunderland's history, never really gave twopence for what anyone thought of him. But then Shack could afford to think that way. As a maverick inside-forward, he remained one of the game's biggest draws until his retirement in 1957. His meagre five England caps would have been more like 95 if he had been around today. But Shack courted controversy both on and off the field. Most fans loved his individual wizardry on the ball – although, to be fair, there were those who believed he was never a team player, and therefore not the godlike figure he had swiftly become on Wearside. Indeed, if the England selectors had not thought along those lines, Shackleton would surely have gone on to become one of the world's leading football showmen of the 1950s.

Shack was as near to being a football genius as was possible during the immediate post-war years. He played one-twos off corner-flags and was not averse to sitting on the ball, never mind putting his foot on it! He was an entertainer whose passion for the unorthodox and eagerness to bewitch opponents totally was second to none. Shack was a natural – a footballer whose innate talents were special. And for one so richly blessed, it was perhaps inevitable that one of the country's wealthiest clubs should have snapped him up from arch rivals Newcastle United in February 1948. Sunderland, who would later become known as the game's Bank of England club, had broken the British transfer record to snap up Shackleton for £20,050. It was an enormous, yet astute investment that was to be paid back several times over as Shack's audacious skills played a major part in pulling in the fans. Dubbed the Clown Prince of Soccer – the title he used for his own controversial autobiography – Shack was never one for toeing the line. In fact, he was socking it to them right between the eyes when he was still at the height of his career. It was then that he published his book, one chapter of which sent shock waves reverberating throughout the game.

Chapter 9, entitled 'The average director's knowledge of football', attracted the most attention. In it, Len wrote...precisely nothing. Page 78 contained nothing below the chapter title apart from a publisher's note at the bottom which read: 'This chapter has deliberately been left blank in accordance with the author's wishes.' It was heady stuff for the times, but that was Shack. People either loved him or loathed him – although the majority seemed to favour the first option. He became a football writer following his retirement from the game and, naturally enough, his razor-sharp wit remained much in evidence. Reporting on a Sunderland home game, it would not be unusual for Shack to turn up such comments as 'This club is really going places – but who wants to go to Scunthorpe?' or 'Talk about running a football club, this lot couldn't run a Christmas club!' He described the ball as falling at the 'wrong feet' of a particular player he did not favour, and would often shower the most cutting abuse on certain footballers who, quite clearly, would never have been allowed on the same field as a young Len Shackleton.

Undoubtedly, Shackleton could be just as entertaining off the field as he had been on it. One of his most famous tricks was to flick a coin several feet into the air and then catch it on the top of his shoe – either foot, of course. After holding it there for a while he would lob it back up into the air and make it land effortlessly in the top pocket of his jacket. There would be an impish grin on his face and then he would wander off – mission accomplished.

Shack's arrival from Newcastle caused a sensation. He was already rated as one of the top players in the country, but it was the switch to Sunderland that eventually confirmed his rating among the game's elite. Sunderland managed to squeeze the best part of ten years out of Shack the player and, into the bargain, he made 348 appearances, scoring 101 goals. Len's scoring record remained a post-war best for the club until Gary Rowell managed to beat it by one goal 27 years later. Shack the gifted footballer was also a great talker. He once said:

I'm not big-headed. I was given a gift and you can't be big-headed about that. But I made mistakes as well. I stayed with Sunderland for 11 seasons because I liked the club and I loved the North-East. Durham and Northumberland have the best people in the world. But, back then, I wouldn't have made any more money by joining a London club, for example. Not then. Not with the maximum wage still being in place.

But would Shack have won more England caps if he had moved south? He laughed: 'You can bet I would have done. No one wanted to know you up in the frozen north.' Shack's pathetic haul of five England caps remains one of the biggest mysteries in football. But clearly, in the days before a manager was allowed to choose his own players, the selectors saw Shackleton as something of a threat, a mischievous rebel or simply a 'music-hall act' whose abilities could not be harnessed to top-class international football.

Shack always had his own ideas. He reckoned that the legendary Tom Finney was the best with whom he had ever played, although he did admit to being baffled by the fact that former England captain Billy Wright had amassed 105 caps: 'It was always down to faces. Some used to fit and some didn't!' Although at times he probably wished that he had quit the club in search of glory elsewhere, Shackleton had an excellent Sunderland career by anyone's standards. Having joined Newcastle in 1946, he made his debut at home to Newport County. Now there are debuts and there are debuts – but this was Len Shackleton. Newcastle won 13–0 and Len scored six of them. 'The ball ran well for us that day. And Newport were lucky to get nil!' he admitted much later.

Shack was born in Bradford, but was taken on as a teenage amateur by the all-conquering Arsenal. Dismissed as being too small to make the grade, he built up a reputation during the 1939–45 war before joining Newcastle. But it was the move to Sunderland two years later that landed him in the big time. The extra £50 on the £20,050 transfer fee was designed to frighten off other interested parties, of whom there were many. He recalled:

> And it worked! The bidding was meant to start at about the £17,000 mark once Newcastle had made me available for transfer. But Sunderland reckoned that everyone else would stop at £20,000 and that proved to be the case. As it happened, Arsenal were supposed to be interested in me at £20,000. That made me laugh, considering that they had kicked me out as a kid when they could have signed me for nowt!

With British football getting back on its feet again in the wake of the 1939–45 war, it would be almost three years before Shack was to make the 12-mile move from Tyneside. Until then Sunderland, as with every other club in the land, were concentrating on rebuilding and looking to the future. The war had knocked the stuffing out of the game and, although wartime football offered some much-needed cheer round the country, the sport needed to pick itself up, dust itself down and basically start all over again. Sunderland's real post-war action began on 31 August 1946, when they beat Derby County 3–2 at home in front of a crowd of almost 50,000, and Eddie Burbanks carried on where he had left off – by scoring. Facing Sunderland that day was Raich Carter, their former captain and inspiration. Carter had impressed Derby while playing for them during the conflict, and in December 1945 they had shelled out a significant fee of £8,000 for a 32-year-old genius whose best years had been lost to the war. The game was beginning to move on at pace and nothing, it seemed, was ever going to be as settled as it had been before the outbreak of hostilities. Sunderland's line-up on that historic day was Johnny Mapson, Jack Stelling, Jack Jones, Ken Willingham, Fred Hall, Arthur Housam, Len Duns, Stan Lloyd, Cliff Whitelum, Willie Watson and Burbanks.

The game marked a debut for Watson, the club's new £8,000 signing from Huddersfield Town. He was 26 and his claim to fame was that he had been capped by England at both football and cricket. The all-rounder was a gentlemanly footballer who went on to make 223 appearances for the club as either a wing-half or an inside-forward, doing much to help to re-establish Sunderland's place among the game's elite. When he arrived at Roker, Watson had already been capped by England as an outside-left, but his intention was to be in the centre of the action, and manager Billy Murray offered him the opportunity. He quickly became a wing-half of international standing and remained a Sunderland player for more than eight years. He died in South Africa in April 2004, aged 84. Just weeks after his death, it was announced that his adopted country would stage the World Cup in 2010. How he would have loved to hear that! Watson won four England caps and was selected for the 1950 World Cup. In 1968 he and his wife Barbara moved to Johannesburg, where he took up the post of sports manager at the Wanderers club. After six years with Wanderers he joined a rubber company with which he remained until his retirement at 65. In his spare time, Watson coached the Zoo Lake club and managed Northern Transvaal in the 1985/86 season. He was 66 then and loved every minute of it.

When the stylish Watson was signed by Sunderland, it had been nine years since they had won the FA Cup and ten since their last First Division championship triumph. But, with the war years intervening, it did not seem that long ago in football terms. Now it was Murray's task to restore the glory days to the town. Sunderland were still perceived to be giants of the game, and their supporters were desperate for a repeat of the success attained during the 1930s. Birkenhead-born Johnny Mapson, who would live to be the oldest-surviving member of the 1937 Cup win, was still the regular goalkeeper, while wingers Len Duns and Eddie Burbanks were the only other two players from the Wembley triumph to be wearing the red and white stripes after the war. Fresh faces were arriving on the scene, many of whom would be around for some time. There was Arthur Wright, an ever-dependable wing-half who went on to star in the club's Bank of England side before becoming their first-team trainer in the days of tin buckets and the 'magic' sponge. Wright was not actually a new face immediately after the war, because he had made his Sunderland debut at 18 and played 13 times before League football was suspended. But seven years later he returned as a mature wing-half with a cracking shot. Wright hailed from Burradon in Northumberland and loved the club throughout his life. He died back in his home village in 1985, aged 65.

And then there was Fred Hall, an uncompromising centre-half who looked as if he was capable of eating centre-forwards alive. Hall was a typical no-nonsense defender who originated from the delightfully named No Place, near Stanley in north-west Durham. He arrived at Sunderland on a roundabout route, having been a Blackburn Rovers player since 1935 and making the move to Roker 11 years later after requesting a transfer. He was 28 when he returned to the North-East and was appointed captain. The full-back berths were filled quickly by former colliery plumber Jack Stelling and Arthur Hudgell, quite an expensive buy from Crystal Palace at £10,000. Such was their total reliability that, by strange coincidence, they both went on to clock up 259 League games apiece for the club. Centre-forward Dickie Davis was still at Sunderland, while winger Tommy Reynolds had arrived from Felling Juniors. Centre-half Bill Walsh was signed from Horden Colliery and England international Jackie Robinson followed in a £5,000 move from Sheffield Wednesday. The free-scoring Robinson was born in Shiremoor in Northumberland and revelled in his return to the North-East. As with many other players, his best years had been lost to the war, but he scored 34 goals in 85 appearances for the club. A year after Robinson's arrival, Ron Turnbull was signed from Dundee. Turnbull was another Northumbrian and he could not have wished for a better debut. The centre-forward was handed the No. 9 shirt two days after signing and scored all four goals in a 4–1 mauling of Portsmouth at Roker. With the virtuoso Shackleton arriving in February 1948 – and making his debut in a 5–1 home defeat by Derby – Sunderland were beginning to feel that they were making some genuine headway with the rebuilding task. It probably did not look that way in the immediate aftermath of that battering at Derby. A certain Raich Carter had declared himself in the mood for the visit of his former club, and Sunderland's one-time golden boy practically inflicted all the damage himself, helping himself to four of the five goals.

Sunderland had to be content with ninth place in their first season after the war, while the following campaign resulted in a lowly 20th. In 1948/49 they pulled up to eighth place, but it was the next season that really stood out – unfortunately for all the wrong reasons. That was the season in which Sunderland were coasting towards the end of the campaign as favourites for the title. Sadly, it all went drastically wrong right at the finish.

One more crucial addition had been made early in 1949 when Ivor Broadis shocked football by moving from Carlisle United to mighty Sunderland. Broadis, a commissioned officer and RAF bomber pilot during the war, had been appointed Carlisle's player-manager at the tender age of 23. That was no mean feat, but it was all the more remarkable because he had never played a League game at the time of his appointment. It is true that Broadis, a Londoner, had guested for both Tottenham Hotspur and Millwall during the war, but he had yet to taste League action. Ivor – the name stuck after someone had misread his handwriting on a contract and failed to spot that his actual Christian name was Ivan – cost Sunderland £18,000, and suddenly the inside-forward from the Isle of Dogs found himself cast as one of the leading lights in Sunderland's Bank of England team. Broadis, who went on to win 14 England caps, arrived just days after Sunderland had been humiliated at tiny non-League Yeovil Town in the FA Cup.

The mighty Wearsiders had been expected to bag a hatful of goals against Somerset's part-timers. But Yeovil, led by future Fulham and Queen's Park Rangers manager Alec Stock, pulled off one of the greatest Cup upsets of modern times with a 2–1 win on their famous sloping pitch. It was reckoned that 15,000 crammed themselves into the Huish Park ground, with a further 5,000 outside, while desks from a local junior school provided extra press facilities. The notorious slope did not appear to unsettle the Sunderland party when they inspected it the day before the tie, and chairman Colonel Joseph Prior and manager Billy Murray agreed: 'If we should happen to get beaten, there will be no complaints about the pitch or the slope from us.' That defeat at Yeovil is still part of FA Cup folklore. As it turned out, it was a defeat that Sunderland needed to get out of their system – and quickly. The club picked themselves up and prepared for a genuine tilt at the First Division title. The 1949/50 season was to be their greatest League campaign since 1935/36, when they were champions. And all the early omens looked good.

With the free-scoring Davis at centre-forward and Shackleton and Broadis providing the spadework from the inside-forward slots, the

Wearsiders looked a powerful, attacking unit. Right-winger Tommy Wright – the father of Tommy junior, the former Leeds United and Middlesbrough forward, and uncle of former Newcastle winger Jackie Sinclair – had only just arrived from Partick Thistle for £8,000. And with Tommy 'Tich' Reynolds operating on the opposite flank, Sunderland looked a more than formidable outfit. Reynolds had replaced the veteran Burbanks two years earlier and settled into the role comfortably. Whether he knew it or not at the time, Murray still had plenty of spending to do to bring Sunderland up to 'Bank of England' standard. Yet to arrive were players such as Trevor Ford, Ray Daniel, Billy Elliott, George Aitken, Jack Hedley and Billy Bingham. But the 1949/50 side played with a great flair of its own, and missed out on the title by a single point behind champions Portsmouth and runners-up Wolves. Although one game alone never cost any team a championship, it was widely regarded that the shock 2–1 home defeat at the hands of relegated Manchester City did the damage. Sunderland, unbeaten at home, were expected to thrash doomed City, who had not won an away game all season. But it all went horribly wrong with German goalkeeper Bert Trautmann saving a twice-taken penalty by the normally reliable Stelling. And the record books prove that, if Sunderland had won that day, then the title would have been theirs for the first time since 1936. As it is, the people of Sunderland are still waiting for such an honour to return to the city.

Davis was the First Division's top goalscorer that season with 25 goals, and his on-the-field relationship with star schemers Shackleton and Broadis had been impressive. In fact, Shack always liked to recall that, when selected to play for England Schoolboys as an outside-right, he had managed to swap places with the No. 8 and play his more familiar game as an inside-forward. That other promising, and obviously most obliging, teenager had been one Dickie Davis! 'We had some great individuals back then. But there were always those who insisted that individuals – myself included in that naturally – did not make a football team. But I always admired Billy Murray for sticking to his guns and doing his best to bring in players who he knew would entertain the fans,' recalled Shackleton.

And, not long before his death in November 2000 at the age of 78, Shack took a moment to compare football in his heyday with the modern game: 'I find it hard to watch football these days. I'd rather be on the golf course. But in recent times there's really been only Paul Gascoigne who, at his best, managed to excite me. Apart from possibly George Best, Gazza was the nearest I ever saw to a British player being as gifted as I was!' That was typical Shack. He did not mess about: he just told it as it was.

And he did so when Sunderland paid Aston Villa a record £29,500 for centre-forward Trevor Ford in October 1950, just five months after missing out on the First Division title by a point. It made the highly rated Ford the most expensive player in the history of the game, but money was becoming something of a dirty word at Roker Park. In the end it was to catch up with Sunderland when an illegal-payments scandal broke in 1957. But in the meantime Shack, himself a record-breaking signing, had cost almost £10,000 less than the new centre-forward with whom he was expected to gel. The two of them did not get on at all, and Ivor Broadis summed it up succinctly when he said, 'Let's put it this way – Shack and Fordy didn't socialise together.' And one of the sticking-points that ostracised some players was the fact that Ford was given an extra-curricular, part-time job as a car salesman by one of the directors. In those days, it was one way for a player to make some extra money!

Broadis himself considered the timing of Ford's arrival as odd:

I remember thinking how strange it was that the club had signed Fordy. We had almost – and should have – won the title the season before he arrived, and Dickie Davis was the First Division's leading scorer. Fordy was a good player, arguably the best centre-forward in the land at the time, but Dick had done nothing wrong. Shack and he just didn't gel, and maybe sometimes Len would carry some resentment onto the field with him. Shack could play a ball through that would look a perfect pass, but then he had the ability to play it so that it was only just unreachable. I watched him do that to Fordy, leaving the lad with no chance of catching it as it ran out of play. 'That's the last pass I give you,' he would yell. Len could make you like an idiot, even with a pass that would look perfect when he delivered it. But Len was a marvellous player and thoroughly deserved many more England caps.

Broadis, a cultured inside-forward whose England career took off after leaving for Manchester City and then Newcastle, adored his time with Sunderland

They looked after their players and it was the best of everything for them. Of course, nothing could be done about the other side of it – the money side – because we were all in the same boat. There was a maximum wage of £15 a week at that time, although it would finally be abolished some years later. I was on about £12 a week at Sunderland with win bonuses of about £2. Having said that, moving there from Carlisle with their crumbling ground was like going from the Jungle Cafe to The Savoy.

Broadis never lived in Sunderland during his spell with the club. Instead he would make the car journey from Carlisle on an almost daily basis, sometimes remaining at Brunton Park where he would train with his former club. By then, an up-and-coming manager called Bill Shankly was in charge of Carlisle. Broadis recalled:

> Bill would ask me what I was planning to do on certain afternoons and I would probably reply, 'Not a great deal.' Then he would invite me to Brunton Park, put down two up-turned chimney-pots in the car park and challenge me to a one-a-side game. And there we would be, playing all afternoon in the car park. The idea was to knock down the chimney-pots to score a goal – and if I hadn't tended to let Bill win, we would have still been playing at midnight!

Broadis revealed that Sunderland had wanted him to put an end to his long-distance commuting in an Austin A40 sports car and buy a house in the town, as had the rest of their big-name stars: 'I remember the club showing me a lovely house on the seafront near where Shack and that delightfully elegant player Willie Watson lived. It was a super house, but I couldn't afford it – not on 12 quid a week! Then I picked up a newspaper and saw the headline: "£20,000 star refuses £4,000 villa!"'

The future England international almost picked up a championship medal in his first season and, if it had not been for that disastrous home defeat by relegated Manchester City, he would have done. He remembered:

> I was told to play centre-forward that day. I was never a centre-forward, but I think Dick Davis must have been injured, and I was handed the No. 9 shirt with Harry Kirtley coming in at inside-right. Anyway, Bert Trautmann had one of those days that he had obviously been waiting for. He saved everything we threw at him, including that penalty missed by poor Jackie Stelling. It was just not to be. But we had a very good side and just missed out by a whisker.

It was easy to see what Murray had envisaged by bringing together an attacking trio of Broadis, Ford and Shackleton. It was highly unlikely that any other club in the country at that time could have matched such firepower and rich individual talent. Ford's home debut was certainly a cracker – he scored a hat-trick in a 5–1 demolition of Sheffield Wednesday, and one of his sizzling shots managed to dislodge a goalpost

79

at the Fulwell End! But although there should have been fireworks on the field week in and week out, the whole expensive plan turned into one enormous damp squib. The three star players performed as a trio on just eight occasions, although Ford and Shack operated together regularly following the £18,000 departure of Broadis to Manchester City in October 1951. Yet, even back then, supporters spoke regularly of the discord between the Clown Prince and the swashbuckling Swansea-born goal-getter.

The obvious clash of personalities on the field did little to help the club's desperate longing for that elusive First Division championship. And, although Ford's individual club record of 70 goals from 117 appearances was an outstanding one, Murray's initial blueprint never really got beyond the drawing-board. Sunderland returned to mid-table mediocrity, finishing 12th, 12th and ninth in Ford's three full seasons on Wearside. Many at the time subscribed to the theory that Shack had not been too taken with the club's willingness to offer Ford a regular part-time job in the motor trade, and the would-be golden partnership was dissolved in December 1953 when Sunderland sold Ford to Cardiff City for the same £29,500 they had paid Villa. By then Ford had been fined £100 for a breach of FA rules. It was alleged that he had asked for more than the maximum £10 signing-on fee while negotiating with Sunderland, and was fined £100. The fine did little to upset Ford who boasted that he had already agreed to sell his story to a national newspaper for £100 while also collecting the same amount from an anonymous Welsh benefactor!

The whole episode clearly elicited little sympathy from Shackleton, who later commented dismissively that 'The fining incident was the only real highlight of Fordy's career at Roker Park!' But there is still no shortage of Sunderland fans who talk of Shack feigning to play a brilliant through ball to Ford, only for the pass to have so much backspin on it that it would bounce and start to roll back towards its master as if it were a table-tennis ball rather than a heavy leather football. As Broadis himself explained, Shack could make the best player look like an idiot if he felt so inclined. Indeed, it was during a friendly in Holland that Shack danced his way through an entire bemused defence before delivering the ball into the six-yard box for the unmarked, goal-hungry Ford. 'Don't say I never give you a pass!' screamed Shackleton as Ford tapped the ball into the gaping goal.

Another who witnessed the Ford–Shackleton situation first-hand was a young Stan Anderson, who went on to make 447 appearances for his home-town club: 'I don't know what it was all about. Actually, I don't think Len liked the way Trevor combed his hair. Fordy would stand in front of the mirror for ages doing it and then tell himself how good-looking he was! Also – and it's just my guess – maybe Trevor came off better with under-the-counter payments when he joined the club.'

Ford, who died in May 2003 at the age of 79, was a centre-forward from the old school. His move from Aston Villa to Sunderland had made him the most expensive player in the world, but money – or rather the players' lack of it – was still a huge problem back then. And Welsh legend Ford was never afraid to tell tales out of school, either. He spoke openly of both the financial situation and his personality clash with Shackleton. Like Shack, Fordy was never afraid to tell it as it was. He probably was not just as subtle with it! He said:

> Shack could make the ball talk. On one occasion he got the ball on the touchline and put on a one-man act that would have won him a lifetime contract with Bertram Mills' Circus. Twenty-one other players stood transfixed, but where did it get us? The result was precisely nowhere because, when he did make a move, the opposing defence was ready and in position. Time and time again, when I thought Shack was going to slip a goalscoring pass to me, he would veer off – unlike Ivor Broadis, who was like a prince to centre-forwards.

And, in one cutting comment, Ford rebuffed Shackleton's earlier put-down:

> Shack once wrote that the only thing of note I did while I was at Sunderland was to be fined £100. Well, the only thing of note he did while I was there was when he pipped me at the post by one goal as leading scorer! But I don't care what Shack believed. The record books say that I was leading scorer in two of the three seasons I was there – despite the indifferent service I often received on the field. And did Shack discount the cup-tie we played at Scunthorpe? It was 1–1 when I came out of a tackle with a broken ankle. Did he ever consider the decision I had to make at that time? Did he know that I had to decide between the pain of playing with a broken bone and the ignominy of defeat by Third Division minnows? I played on, went on the wing and scored the winning goal. Maybe that wasn't notable enough for Shack because it happened against a Third Division side. I wonder what he would have said if it had happened to him?

The Shackleton–Ford dispute was beginning to do far too much damage on the field, and their open feuding was now also an open secret. It all came to a head early in the 1953/54 season. Ford explained:

> The months of frustration in a disjointed forward line were beginning to tell and my effectiveness as leader of the attack was rapidly diminishing. I could see myself not only hammering the nails in my coffin, but digging my grave and stitching my shroud at the same time! I went to see the manager Billy Murray and, for the first time in my career, asked for a move without any thought of a slice of the lolly on the side. That just shows how anxious I was to get out. Manager Murray tried to talk me out of it, but eventually my request went before the board. The directors' reply knocked me as cold as a corpse – it was 'No!' The weeks went by and then came the first big moment of decision in my football life. The team had travelled to Birmingham for a game at Aston Villa, and for some time there had been rumours that I had not been hitting it off with Shackleton. They said that it was our avowed policy not to combine.
>
> That was not altogether true, but it had reached the stage of make or break. And the break came in that game at Villa Park. I refused to play the following week. I told Mr Murray that, if Shackleton was in the side, he could count me out. As far as I was concerned, I had never made a better move. I felt myself coming back to life and I had only one answer when Mr Murray called Shack and me together in his office and asked us to shake hands and make up. The answer from me was, 'Not on your nelly!' Was the club right in trying to get us together again? I think not. Soon after this Shack was injured and had to drop out of the side. I came in and we had a great run. I never played with Shackleton again. But Shack and I were not the only misfits at Roker Park. Any club that lays down a policy of spending to the hilt for the stars is bound to end up with a team of individualists. There's no one in the side who is prepared to do the fetching and carrying. They all want to stand aloof like poodles at a dog show, waiting for their turn to parade before the crowd.

Ford basically spoke the truth. Sunderland's obsession with buying success was not working. But while the club lavished cash on the purchase of big-name stars, the players themselves were still struggling to maintain a cost of living that was a step or two ahead of the man in the street. It explained the offers of part-time jobs, the willingness of the better players to keep moving from club to club and the appeal of the club house. Football clubs would buy respectable houses in residential districts and rent them to their players at a nominal amount. Ford, for example, paid 30 shillings (£1.50) a week for his stay on Wearside. But still the battle against the maximum wage or, as Broadis called it, football's slave trade, rankled.

Ford became the most expensive player on the planet when Sunderland paid £29,500 for him – and all he was entitled to was a meagre £10 as a signing-on fee. It was not difficult to understand why there was such resentment among the country's top players at the time or even why some, such as Jack Hedley and Neil Franklin, headed for South America in search of riches. All the same, the Welsh wizard enjoyed the majority of his time at Sunderland even though he later described it as a graveyard for centre-forwards! 'I kicked centre-halves all day,' he said. 'But I was always prepared to take stick as well as give it.' Amazingly, hard man Ford was never booked in his entire career, let alone sent off. He claimed:

I was proud of that record. But it was goals that really mattered to me. I used to consider myself a bad turn if I didn't score a goal. I enjoyed the public adoration and thrived on it. Supporters meant everything to me and I was the most miserable man in the world if I couldn't deliver the goals. In fact, I hated anyone whose job it was to stop me scoring. They were all my enemies because there's only one way to entertain the crowd and that's by scoring goals. I'd bet that everyone would prefer to see an awful match with five goals in it than an average one without any goals at all!

Left-winger John McSeveney was in and out of the first team at the time and remembers the era well:

When I signed for Sunderland, I felt the same as someone who wins the National Lottery nowadays must feel. I was only 20 and very fortunate, but, when I came down from Scotland, I had no intention of signing. But when they started talking turkey and I saw Roker Park, which was like a colosseum, I soon changed my mind. The club was known as The Bank of England team then and we would fill grounds wherever we went. We had plenty of good players – Ford, Shackleton, Mapson, Hedley, Hudgell, Hall, Wright, Bingham and so on. The manager, Bill Murray, was a dour Scot who never said anything much to anybody. He never let anyone know what he was thinking. The only exception I can

remember came after I'd been at the club for a while and he came
up to me and asked, 'How do you think you're doing?' I told him
I thought I was doing all right, but he replied, 'We don't play your
style here. We don't need you to try to beat your full-back four or
five times – we need you to pass the ball.' We'd play a lot of head
tennis in training, but I had some ideas of my own at Roker Park
and I would run up and down the steps at the Roker End. There
were little steps, so it was pitter-patter to the top and pitter-patter
down again. It was the best thing I ever did in training because it
made me lightning-quick over a short distance, it gave me quick
feet and I never pulled a muscle. Occasionally some of the other
players would try it and I can remember one time when Tommy
Wright ran up and down the terraces as he was getting fit again
after an injury.

McSeveney also recalled Ford most vividly:

I knew Fordy well because I was with him at three different clubs
– Sunderland, Cardiff City and Newport County. But I thought he
had his limitations and that Dickie Davis was a better player than
he was at Sunderland. Ford was a whirlwind at times. I can
remember when we beat Huddersfield Town 7–1 one Easter and
he rattled their goalkeeper Jack Wheeler so hard that he had to go
off, and Jimmy Glazzard had to go in goal for a while! Ford had a
thunderbolt of a shot and he was quick to see a half-chance and
score goals. Shack was a quiet person at times, but he was still the
star showman and I had a lot of respect for him. There was one
occasion when he had to play for the reserves at Blyth, but he still
turned on the magic and ran the show. Len loved the banter and
saw the funny side of everything. But above all, he was just a
wonderful player. Johnny Mapson was wonderful and in training
he would dare anybody to beat him by shooting from the arc on
the edge of the penalty area. He'd offer people money to score
against him, but he was rarely beaten. Freddie Hall, who was a
great striker of the ball and was very strong from having worked as
a pit engineer at Wearmouth, gave him the most trouble, while
Shack often tried to cause him problems by deliberately landing
the ball on the crossbar. There again, Shack would play the ball
against the corner-flags during matches!

By the time the fiery and ferocious Ford had returned to South Wales,
Sunderland were doing battle in the 1953/54 season. The Roker Park

chequebook had been out several times since Ford had first breezed into the club, and the faces in the first team were changing again. One player who had arrived shortly before Ford was full-back Jack Hedley, from Willington Quay, but it had taken him some time to force his way into the side on a regular basis. Hedley had cost Sunderland £10,000 from Everton, although he had returned to his native North-East via a controversial summer spell in Colombia with Bogota. He had been lured to Colombia with a handful of others, including England's centre-half Neil Franklin. The South American country's league clubs had broken away from their own football association and, therefore, from FIFA. Hedley was one of those who made the lengthy trip with the intention of earning far more than was possible in a country with a £20 maximum wage for footballers, although he eventually refused terms in Bogota and – after a ban on all the travelling rebels had been lifted – signed for Sunderland. Wearside was no South America, but Sunderland were seemingly unstoppable when it came to signing top talent of the day.

In one brief flurry in June 1953, in came Welsh international centre-half Ray 'Bebe' Daniel for £27,000, Burnley and England outside-left Billy Elliott for £26,000 and Scottish international goalkeeper Jimmy Cowan from Morton for £8,000. More followed during the next season, even though Sunderland were bottom of the First Division at Christmas. Money was buying the game's biggest stars, but it clearly was not buying results. In through Roker's revolving door came Scottish inside-forward Ken Chisholm from Cardiff City for £15,000. 'Chis' was a more than useful player and a genuine character. He quickly became a big pal of Shack both on and off the field, and in Chisholm Len finally found the soulmate he had failed to recognise in Ford. South African centre-forward Ted Purdon was snapped up for £15,000 from Birmingham City and full-back Joe McDonald arrived from Falkirk for a bargain £5,500. Purdon did well for Sunderland, scoring twice on his debut and hitting a hat-trick a week later in a 4–1 win at Arsenal. By the time he left for Workington in 1957, he had bagged 42 goals from 96 appearances, which was no mean feat. McDonald, meanwhile, got on with his job quietly and without fuss. As the immediate post-war pairing of Stelling and Hudgell began to find the going tough, Hedley made the right-back slot his own, while McDonald became a regular in the No. 3 shirt. One more new face that season was goalkeeper Willie Fraser, who was signed from Airdrieonians for £5,000 and won his two Scottish caps while with Sunderland.

So, armed with an array of big-name players, Sunderland's quest for the title continued. But the 1953/54 season proved to be one gigantic flop, and they finished in 18th place. Amid the mayhem of chequebook football, one key purchase had been defender George Aitken. A Scottish international, Aitken came from Third Lanark following eight seasons with East Fife. He had arrived in 1951 for £19,500 and had gradually begun to ease Arthur Wright out of the left-half slot. Big George was also used at centre-half – which in those days was a totally different position – and became a huge hit with the Roker faithful. Aitken had proved to be a reliable, tough wing-half who, although an international, never found himself in the 'glamour' class of players such as Ford, Shackleton, Broadis, Watson and Elliott. But if Sunderland had been able to rely on more players in the mould of the robust Aitken, their obsession with becoming champions again might have turned into reality as opposed to remaining a dream.

This was the mid-1950s, and Roker Park was as big and as famous a ground as you would find anywhere in Britain. Crowds of 50,000-plus were considered normal and, when arch rivals Newcastle made the short journey to Wearside, the gate would be much nearer the 70,000 mark. The record attendance for a League game had been set in March 1950 when 68,004 witnessed a 2–2 draw with the Magpies. Broadis, who scored that afternoon, looked back on what was a time of lofty ambition on Wearside: 'The Sunderland crowds were amazing. And their supporters were always such great people as well. They understood the game and their passion flooded down from the terraces and spurred you on. You couldn't fail to respond to a crowd such as that.' For those supporters familiar only with the modern-day Stadium of Light, that was what it was like when Roker Park was in its pomp!

The following season saw the bright, young talent of Stan Anderson begin to pin down a regular place among the leading lights of English football. By now, Sunderland's reasonably settled side consisted of Fraser, Hedley, McDonald, Anderson, Daniel, Aitken, Bingham, Shackleton, Purdon, Chisholm and Elliott. Shack had been switched from inside-left to inside-right to accommodate Ken Chisholm, who enjoyed his best season with the club, scoring 18 goals in 37 appearances. But Murray's men again fell short of their aim. Sunderland finished fourth, and people were beginning to wonder whether the Bank of England team was destined to flirt with success rather than to find it. But still the game's big spenders kept shelling out in the hope of getting it right. Midway through the season, Charlie 'Cannonball' Fleming was signed from East Fife for £7,000 plus the out-of-touch Tommy Wright as a makeweight in the deal.

Fleming was yet another Scot whose Sunderland career record of 71 goals from 122 games was excellent. All the same, impressive individual goal hauls were doing little to bring any silverware to Roker Park. And it was during the 1954/55 season that the Wearsiders battled their way to an FA Cup semi-final only for yet more agony to be heaped upon them on a mudbath of a pitch at Villa Park. Sunderland had been hoping for a Wembley date against Newcastle in what would have been quite a special FA Cup final appointment. But while United managed to see off lowly York City at the second attempt – at Roker Park of all places – Sunderland went down to a 1–0 defeat at the hands of eventual losing finalists Manchester City. Most agreed at the time that the semi-final against City should never have been played because of the atrocious weather conditions in the Midlands. But played it was, and by now Murray's miserable money men could have been excused for believing that they were going to win precisely nothing. How right they were! It was as if The Bank of England side had peaked and was now on its way down again.

The following season brought about yet another FA Cup semi-final defeat, Birmingham winning 3–0 at Hillsborough. Bill Holden had arrived that season as a centre-forward from Burnley, but his signing owed more to desperation than long-term planning. Newcastle had just beaten Sunderland 6–1 in a Boxing Day derby encounter at Roker Park, and morale was understandably low. The following day, less than 24 hours after Holden's arrival, the new boy did manage to score in the return at St James' Park. But it was to little avail because United won 3–1.

Still the new faces kept coming, but the really big spending was over. Don Revie was signed from Manchester City for £23,000, and left-winger Colin Grainger cost £17,000 from Sheffield United with Sam Kemp moving in the opposite direction. Goalkeeper Johnny Bollands was snapped up on the cheap from Oldham Athletic although he did keep Willie Fraser out of the side for the bulk of the 1956/57 season before breaking a leg. Both Revie – the 1955 Footballer of the Year – and Grainger were England internationals, although the ageing Revie was already past his best. Fellow Yorkshireman Grainger collected seven England caps, the final one while with Sunderland, and was regarded as one of the club's most exciting wingers of the era. Indeed, Grainger, the uncle of former Middlesbrough and England winger Eddie Holliday and the brother-in-law of former Newcastle wing-half Jim Iley, was a valuable addition to a team nearing its demise. Grainger recalled:

Billy Murray signed me, and at the time we had a team of individuals with everyone playing for themselves. It was brilliant for me to go there because they were the millionaires' club. But everyone wanted to play for themselves. It wasn't until Alan

Brown came in as manager that we were told what to do. We had all the ability in our team, but other sides put in the effort and teamwork. We had some great players and great characters too. Shack was a nice fellow and he wasn't big-headed, while Charlie Hurley was a tremendous player and a gentleman. In fact, Charlie and I used to back horses together. Our local shopkeeper had given us a system so that we couldn't lose. In fact, we were making so much money that the bookmakers banned us from putting on bets. Then there was big Ray Daniel. He was a lovely man and a footballing centre-half, not a clogger. He was a great fellow and a bit of a character. He would take off Robert Mitchum with a cigarette hanging from his mouth and walk and talk just like him. But when Alan Brown came in as manager, that was the end of that. Ray would just lie on the bench with his arms on the back of his head. Alan Brown didn't like that and let him go not long afterwards.

Grainger, himself a successful cabaret artist who was known as 'the singing winger' in his heyday, revelled in the star-studded Roker Park dressing-room: 'Billy Bingham was a good pal of mine at Sunderland, a typical Irish lad who always had a smile on his face. He was one of the nicest lads you could wish to meet and he did a good impression of Rod Steiger, too.'

But while frivolity still reigned in the Roker dressing-room, results out on the pitch were gradually getting worse. Time was clearly running out for the long-serving Billy Murray, for Sunderland and – most importantly – for their frustrated fans. Supporters had been used to the best – even if the best Murray could muster had consistently fallen short of winning trophies. Suddenly survival was becoming the name of the game. And that was a worry that was beginning to make the writers of the day reach for their history books. The once mighty Sunderland had never played in any division other than the top flight. It was indeed a proud record, and one to which no other team in the land could lay claim.

5

'WHEN WE WIN PROMOTION...'

Sunderland's Bank of England team had collapsed like a house of cards. In fact, the entire once-proud club was in total disarray and, by the summer of 1957, it looked as if there were no aces left in the pack. Manager Billy Murray had just resigned in the wake of a Football League Commission's findings that the club had made illegal payments to certain players. Former defender Murray departed on 26 June after 28 years with the club. Supporters who had been enthralled by Murray's great team of entertainers had also been frustrated by the failure of such an expensive and multi-talented side when it actually came to putting trophies on the table.

Murray's successor was Alan Brown, a former Burnley centre-half who hailed from Corbridge in Northumberland and used to pride himself on the fact that, as a young Sunderland supporter himself, he used to run from his home to Roker Park on matchdays. Brown was a disciplinarian. His tall, iron-backed figure would strike fear into players who probably wished that they were not even in the same corridor as their manager, let alone his office. He arrived directly from Burnley, where he had already made a name for himself as a manager with an astute eye for young talent. Indeed, the bulk of the great Burnley side who went on to win the First Division championship in 1960 had been groomed by Brown. He had played a major part in bringing together players such as the great Jimmy McIlroy, Jimmy Adamson – himself a future Sunderland manager – John Angus, John Connelly, Tommy Cummings, Jimmy Robson, Brian Miller and Adam Blacklaw. Turf Moor was to become the pinnacle of English football shortly after Brown's switch to Roker Park, and it was no coincidence that the nucleus of the team hailed from the North-East.

Brown had looked to his native region as a breeding-ground for teenage talent, delighting in the fact that he was snapping up future stars from under the noses of Sunderland, Newcastle United and Middlesbrough. After leaving for his dream job at Sunderland, Burnley replaced Brown with Billy Dougall. But he lasted just one season before Clarets legend Harry Potts – yet another North-Easterner – was handed the reins. Potts, who hailed from Hetton-le-Hole, went on to steer them to their 1960 title triumph. There was no doubt, however, that Brown had done much of the spadework – literally. Before becoming Burnley manager, hard man Brown had spent two years in the police force and he recalled:

> We learned to dig ditches among other things. And after doing it for days on end I became good at it. A couple of years after that, when I was at Burnley, we were building a training-ground on the edge of the town. Ditches needed digging then, so I got on with it – alongside players who were only too willing to help!

There would be many changes during Brown's first spell as Sunderland's manager, although the highlight of his two stays on Wearside was still seven years away. After relegation to the Second Division, promotion back to the First was the holy grail as far as Brown was concerned, and by the time he had actually achieved it Sunderland's side bore little resemblance to the team he inherited from Murray.

The 23-year-old Stan Anderson – later to become the first man to captain each of the North-East's big three of Sunderland, Newcastle and Middlesbrough – was Brown's first-choice right-half from the start. He recalled the wind of change that swept through Roker Park at the time:

> We were still in the First Division. But the previous season had been a struggle and we had just stayed in by the skin of our teeth. The club wanted new blood and it certainly found it in the shape of Alan Brown. Obviously his first task was to keep the club in the top flight and, in that respect, he failed. I had played alongside Len Shackleton quite a bit and he was still playing when Brown arrived. But I don't think the two of them would have got on somehow. Len was 35 by then and an old ankle injury was causing him a lot of trouble. I remember that he played in Brown's first game – the opening game of the season at home to Arsenal – but it proved to be his last in a Sunderland shirt. Len played one game for Alan Brown and then quit. Well, I mean, come on! Shack had done all the pre-season training with the rest of us and then he quit after just one game. I think that he'd thought to himself, 'I'm not playing for this fellow!'
>
> I did discuss it with Len many years later and asked him why he'd quit at that particular time. He just smiled back at me. But

one thing is for certain – Len and Alan Brown would definitely not have got on. But then not too many people did get on with Brown. He tried to rule people by fear, and it's a fact that most people were frightened of him – although I was not one of them. I would always speak my mind – not that it did me a great deal of good with Alan Brown, I might add!

Anderson was soon to become Brown's captain in a new-look team. But for the time being, Don Revie was in charge on the field – the same Don Revie whose Leeds United team was to be promoted with Sunderland in 1964 and whose star-studded side tasted bitter defeat at their hands in the magical 1973 FA Cup final. Revie was 30 during the season in which he captained his side to relegation. And, with his best days and his six England caps firmly behind him, he could do little to halt the rot setting in at Roker. Anderson said:

Don had been a good player and a thinking footballer, and Browny made him captain. But we needed fresh blood then and, after Don had left for Leeds at the end of that sad season, the boss appointed Charlie Hurley captain with me as vice-captain. However, I took over when Charlie was injured and, when he was fit again, he insisted that I remained in charge. That was typical of Charlie.

Brown, meanwhile, knew that he would forever be remembered as the manager who allowed such a proud club to slip into the Second Division for the first time in its history, and was already planning his major reconstruction job. As it happened, they were relegated on goal average – as it was then – despite Don Kichenbrand's double which gave them a 2–0 away win at Portsmouth on the final day of the season. The side at Fratton Park on that fateful day of 26 April 1958 was Willie Fraser, Jack Hedley, Billy Elliott, Anderson, Hurley, Reg Pearce, Ambrose Fogarty, Revie, Kichenbrand, Alan O'Neill and Colin Grainger. Anderson can still recall the feeling when, after winning at Pompey, the players learned that Leicester City had won 1–0 at Birmingham City. Defeat for Leicester at St Andrew's would have ensured Sunderland's safety. Just to add insult to injury, Leicester's last-ditch escape had been masterminded by Dave Halliday, Sunderland's one-time goal machine. Anderson remembered:

We were simply stunned. Walking off the field at Portsmouth, we knew that we were the players who had put an end to the club's glorious record of never having played outside the top division. We were devastated and it took some time to recover from that feeling

91

of utter dismay. I was a local lad and had joined the club from school. I took it really badly, I can tell you. But we should never have gone down in the first place. Alan Brown tried to make far too many changes that season and untried youngsters are not the ones you need when you are trying to avoid relegation. If you look at some of the players he picked that season, you would be hard-pushed to remember some of them and say where they moved afterwards. It was too hard a job for youngsters, but that was Alan Brown for you.

One player added by Brown quite late on that season was the South African centre-forward Don 'Rhino' Kichenbrand. He had picked up rave reviews at Glasgow Rangers and had only just lost his place in the side when Sunderland snapped him up for £8,000. The gamble was that his goals would keep the club in the First Division – and it nearly worked. 'Rhino' scored six times in his ten games for the club late on in that fateful season. But, despite his brace at Portsmouth on the day of reckoning, it just was not enough. Considering that the season had been such a sickener for all concerned, though, there were some silver linings amid the ever-darkening clouds that gathered over Roker Park in 1958.

Charlie Hurley had arrived from Millwall as a relative unknown. After a baptism of fire during which the young centre-half watched 13 goals fly into Sunderland's net in just two games, there were immediate doubts about his credentials. This, of course, was where Brown deserved credit. He saw both the dominance and the culture in Charlie's footballing abilities, he had camped out in Hurley's parents' Essex home until Hurley finally agreed to sign, and he nurtured the Irishman with the Cockney accent into one of the finest centre-halves in the game at the time. Whether or not even Brown could have foreseen Hurley eventually being voted as the Player of the Century by the club's supporters is another matter. But what was not in dispute was the fact that Hurley was the rock upon which the Sunderland manager built a team who finally achieved Sunderland's first-ever promotion six years later. Brown, who died in 1996, aged 81, once recalled:

It took me ten solid consecutive hours of hard talk to persuade 'King Charles', as he became known, to leave London and move north. All his family was there and at the end of ten hours Charlie turned to me and said he would sign. I jumped to my feet and actually cheered. The whole family rose with me and cheered as well. I thought we were going to lift the roof off! But I never once had the slightest cause to regret the signing and I considered it to be one of my happiest moments in football. No player commanded a higher respect from the manager and the players than Charlie Hurley. For a big man, he was the most skilful player on the ball I had ever seen and he knew better than most how to use that skill. But he was also one of the bravest players I ever knew. Charlie sustained a badly swollen ankle on his debut when we were soundly thrashed. Against my better judgement I allowed him to play in what was to be his first home game. I would not have attempted to play myself if I had been in such a condition, but Charlie performed admirably. Charlie had such great courage and skill. He was the best buy I ever made.

Hurley offered his own version of events:

I hadn't even wanted to go. But 'Bomber' Brown – as I later christened him – had met me in the morning and then taken me for lunch because I was still refusing to sign, so then he arranged to meet my parents in the evening. I briefed Mum and Dad and the whole family to tell him that I wouldn't be going, but he had them eating out of his hands in no time. He was a very clever man. Bomber told me at the time that he had spotted something in me and that, as a former centre-half himself, he could turn me into the best. But I was just 20. A 20-year-old these days is probably more like 30 now, but I was just a kid. I was one of seven children, but I was earning more than my Dad, who worked at the Ford plant at Dagenham. I was earning £15 a week and I felt as if the family needed my money. But I made the move thanks to Alan Brown's persuasive powers.

Hurley also recalled the early days:

I can remember driving up to Sunderland in my first car, a Ford Consul, and wondering just how far north I had to go. I thought I was driving to the end of the world. It was town after town and there were no motorways then. And, after my first two games for Sunderland, I thought I'd fallen off the end of the world! I couldn't have had a worse start. We lost 7–0 at Blackpool on my debut and then 6–0 at Burnley. The Sunderland fans must have been thinking, 'Who is this duffer we have signed?' They must have thought they'd signed a colander, not a centre-half! But I was determined to show them what I could do. One reporter mentioned my first two games to me, naturally enough recounting the scorelines. All I could reply was, 'Well, you've seen an improvement already!'

Then there was the usual wag who told the story that he had been to the bingo hall and the caller had shouted out, 'Seven and six, 76.' Of course, he claimed that he had shouted back, 'Seven and six, Charlie Hurley!' But seriously, I remember that I was carrying an injury after the defeat at Burnley, and there was no way I wanted to miss my first home appearance against Preston North End. I insisted on playing even though Alan Brown was not too keen on it. It was a goalless draw, which was a good result after those two defeats, and I thought that I did quite well in front of the Sunderland fans for the first time.

Hurley quickly settled in, with Anderson tending to play alongside him at right-half and either George Aitken or Reg Pearce at No. 6. Charlie's arrival had offered Sunderland fans a glimmer of hope. But the odd glimmer was all that they were going to get during the first few months of 1958. Sunderland were sinking fast. Relegation meant rebuilding, and Brown was the man for the job. He concentrated on his youth policy, introducing players such as Len Ashurst, Ian Lawther and Jimmy McNab.

Lawther was an interesting case. He explained: 'I am one of the few lads who turned down a chance to join Manchester United. As a 15-year-old, I had a six-week trial at Old Trafford, but I didn't fancy the set-up at all. Perhaps it was because I was young and rather homesick.' Lawther, who followed in the footsteps of his uncle, Fred Roberts, by representing Northern Ireland, eventually joined Sunderland instead. But he found it tough going:

I came to Roker Park and a depressing atmosphere because Sunderland had been relegated for the first time in their proud history and many famous stars, such as Len Shackleton, Ray Daniel, Billy Bingham and Charlie Fleming, had moved on. But after only six months in Sunderland's reserve team I was flung into the Second Division side at the start of the 1959/60 season. It was the beginning of a very worrying time for me. The Roker Park fans were impatient with the club's efforts to fight their way back into the First Division and, as the centre-forward, I was one of the most criticised players in the team. Nobody seemed to appreciate that I was only 20 and in my first season of League soccer in a side which was painstakingly being rebuilt from youth-team level by Alan Brown, but he always encouraged me most when things seemed blackest.

During the next few years more youngsters followed, such as Jim Montgomery, Cecil Irwin, Martin Harvey, Nick Sharkey and Brian Usher. But promotion was to remain elusive for Brown. There was, however, a stirring FA Cup run in 1961 when Sunderland and eventual Double winners Tottenham Hotspur drew 1–1 in a fifth-round tie at Roker Park. Sunderland lost the replay 5–0, but the tie at Roker was, for many, one of the most memorable and certainly the loudest that they had ever known. The official attendance was 61,326, although a great many more were believed to be packed in that day. Anderson explained: 'We were gradually putting a decent side together. And that day against Spurs showed us all what would be there for us if we could be successful on the field. The noise was deafening, and I can remember Danny Blanchflower saying that he had never heard anything quite like the Roker Roar!'

The Sunderland goalkeeper against Spurs was Peter Wakeham, at that stage established as the club's No. 1. But it would not be the case for much longer. A 17-year-old Southwick lad called Jim Montgomery was attracting rave reviews as the club's youth-team goalkeeper. And once Monty was given his chance in the first team, history was in the making. Montgomery would make a club record 623 appearances, carving his name into the very fabric of Sunderland AFC. But if the vastly experienced Wakeham had not put a sudden end to his own Wearside career with one moment of madness, Montgomery might have had to wait a while longer for his debut. Monty revealed:

I was just a young kid who had been brought up on Sunderland. In fact, I was still playing for the youth team when I suddenly found myself thrown in at the deep end. Alan Brown was the manager and Peter Wakeham was the first-team keeper. But Peter had given a V-sign to the crowd and that was it. He was dropped, it gave me my chance and I grabbed it. As a kid, I had stood behind the goal at Roker Park, marvelling at the agility of Johnny Bollands. He was my hero when I was a lad and how I hoped that one day I would be out there in the green jersey as Sunderland's goalkeeper. As it happened, the opportunity arrived a lot earlier than I had expected.

Sunderland were gradually developing into a side that, Brown felt, would be strong enough to go up. During that time there were players whose contribution tended to be forgotten simply because they were not part of the 1964 promotion-winning team. But wingers Harry Hooper, Jimmy Davison and Jackie Overfield, inside-forward Willie McPheat, the veteran Ernie Taylor and Colin Nelson all helped to drag Sunderland back to the top flight. With Wakeham edged out by Montgomery, others such as Ambrose Fogarty, Alan O'Neill – who also played as Alan Hope – John Goodchild and Norman Clarke also featured.

There was, of course, one player who would, without question, have become the scourge of practically every First Division defence in the land if injury had not wrecked his career when he was just 26 – Brian Clough, who had been one of Brown's big-money signings. Clough brought fresh flair to the club, alongside other expensive arrivals such as George Mulhall, George Herd and Johnny Crossan, and his extraordinary goalscoring feats earmarked the youngster from Middlesbrough as an all-time great.

Clough had returned from a cruise in July 1961 when, as a Middlesbrough centre-forward with an astonishing 204 goals in the bag from 222 games, he was met at Southampton Docks by Brown. The deal was done there and then with the rest, as they say, being history. Cloughie scored 63 goals in just 74 Sunderland appearances and had already found the net 28 times in half a season when an ill-fated collision with Bury goalkeeper Chris Harker on Boxing Day 1962 left him with a cruciate knee ligament injury from which he never recovered. Clough's incredible managerial achievements need no introduction. But it all began at Roker Park for the abrasive Yorkshireman with the cutting wit and sharp eye for a footballing talent. George Hardwick, Sunderland's manager at the time of Clough's failed comeback during the 1964/65 season, saw the coach behind the player. And Hardwick, like Clough a Middlesbrough legend, handed the broken-hearted goalscorer his first opportunity to work with players when he placed him in charge of the club's youth team.

Clough who died of stomach cancer in September 2004 aged 69, wrote in his autobiography:

> Browny met Barbara and I on the quayside at Southampton. He looked me straight between the eyes in a way that made lesser men freeze on the spot and asked, 'Would you sign for Sunderland?' I blurted out 'Yes' without the need to be asked again. Brown said he'd see me at Roker Park in a week and assured me I would be on top money at Sunderland. I didn't know Alan Brown personally, but I knew of him. I was aware of his reputation as a strict and honest man. I took him at his word.

Clough's switch from Boro had cost Sunderland £42,000 – no mean fee in 1961. But the centre-forward with goals in his boots was a good way down the road towards repaying it when tragedy struck that Boxing Day afternoon at Roker. He remembered:

It was a bitterly cold, snowy, sleety day on Wearside – the kind of day when seagulls fly backwards to stop their eyes watering. That day the Clough playing career effectively ended in its prime – done and dusted, dead and buried. Bury goalkeeper Chris Harker's shoulder slammed into my knee as we challenged for the ball. My head hit the ground and everything went black. I came round soon enough and knew immediately that this was no minor injury, no simple sprain. Instinct demanded that I should get up, but I could only crawl and I'll never forget the voice of Bury's centre-half Bob Stokoe, who somehow managed to win the Cup as manager of the Sunderland side which beat Leeds against all the odds in 1973. He moaned at the referee, telling him to get on with the game and accusing me of play-acting. I'll never forgive Stokoe for that. I had a torn cruciate ligament. That knackered knee put paid to my playing days.

Clough still set the record for the quickest 200 League goals in the First Division – in his 219th game in September 1961 – and winger Mulhall said of him:

He was just a goalscoring machine. He was not one of the best outfield players in terms of his link-up play, but in the penalty area he was lethal. Time after time he would score goals with shots into either the top corner or the bottom corner of the net. For a while I thought he was just a lucky bugger, but he did it so often that eventually I realised that there was something more to it.

Clough was to play three more times for Sunderland. They were three successive appearances early in the 1964/65 season, shortly after the joyous return to the First Division. He had missed the entire promotion season, by which time the young Nicky Sharkey had taken over the No. 9 shirt and was already banging in the goals. But it was a short-lived and ill-judged return. Clough scored just one goal in the First Division – the only top-flight goal of his career – in a 3–3 home draw with Leeds:

I was totally unaware that Sunderland had insured me for £40,000 or so. But I believe they were more concerned with getting the money than with my continued belief that I could keep on playing. They got it in the end and I got about £1,000. By now Alan Brown had gone to Sheffield Wednesday and the new manager, George Hardwick, gave me something far more important and useful than a few quid. Thanks to George – and it was generous of him since neither he nor I knew whether I could coach – I was given a head start on others my age.

Brown's influence on Clough the player no doubt played a major part in his later successes as a manager with both Derby County and Nottingham Forest. Cloughie explained:

> I don't scare easily and never did. But I remember times when I was frightened of Alan Brown. A bollocking from him was like ten from anybody else. I often think of Browny. He's dead now, God bless him. I can be in the garden or sipping a cup of coffee or looking for relief from the boredom of a televised match when nothing is happening. Whatever the moment, I can catch a glimpse of him standing there, his back as straight as a goalpost. I can remember it as if it is today, looking at him at Sunderland and thinking to myself, 'This is the way I'll do the job if the opportunity ever comes.'

And, for Clough, come it did – in boat-loads. But, while all his triumphs lay ahead of him, Sunderland were still striving to get their prime objective achieved as quickly as possible. It would be almost another year and a half after Clough's injury before Brown's dream was finally fulfilled. The only trouble was that, by the time he actually led his team to the promised land, he too would be heading off for pastures new.

But at least a new era was dawning after years of broken promises and shattered dreams. Sunderland's first promotion side barely changed apart from the occasional injuries, and the regular line-up in the traditional 2–3–5 system was virtually cast in stone. The names of Jim Montgomery, Cec Irwin, Len Ashurst, Martin Harvey, Charlie Hurley, Jimmy McNab, Brian Usher, George Herd, Nicky Sharkey, Johnny Crossan and George Mulhall rolled off the tongues of the ecstatic fans. But, despite the minimal amount of change, it was not the team with which Alan Brown had begun the season. Stan Anderson was still his first-choice right-half, while Sharkey, who had equalled a record jointly held by Charlie Buchan and Bobby Gurney by scoring five goals in a match in a 7–1 win over Norwich City in March 1963, had still not been able to shake off competition for the centre-forward's shirt from the versatile Scot Andy Kerr. But Anderson's form dipped, and he was dropped in favour of Martin Harvey, already a full Northern Ireland international. Harvey made the No. 4 shirt his own, while the tiny Sharkey also managed to edge out the ageing Kerr after the first nine games.

Anderson remains an all-time Sunderland great. He made 447 appearances for the club and only Ashurst made more as an outfield player. He also picked up two England caps, becoming the only Sunderland player to represent the country during the 1960s. In fact, Anderson's stay at Roker from 1949 to 1963 was so long that he is the proud possessor of an incredible statistic. He is the only Sunderland player to have played in the same sides as FA Cup winning goalkeepers Johnny Mapson and Jimmy Montgomery. Between them, Mapson and Montgomery spanned an amazing 42 years at Roker. And the two club legends with the same initials both savoured cup success on the only two occasions that Sunderland have won the trophy. Mapson was in goal in 1937, while Monty practically made the 1973 final his own. And Anderson played with both of them.

Anderson's shock transfer to arch rivals Newcastle in November 1963 cost them a mere £19,000. And it was money well-spent. He led United back into the First Division in the 1964/65 season before completing his historic switch to Middlesbrough, whom he later also managed. Anderson had been with the club since he was 15. And to see him suddenly shipped out to Sunderland's bitter rivals as a 29-year-old England international, whose two caps had been awarded just a year earlier, was almost too much for Roker supporters to bear. In 1962 Anderson had been a member of England's 22-man squad on World Cup duty in Chile: that was how good he was. As a member of a Second Division side, he found himself alongside England wing-halves, such as Ronnie Clayton, Bobby Robson, Ron Flowers and a young Bobby Moore who, at the time, had one England cap compared with Anderson's two.

Then, just as his beloved Sunderland were en route to the top flight, the Horden-born right-half was dropped and promptly sold to Newcastle. Not even Anderson himself could take it in. And, in a revealing insight into that shock transfer, he explained:

Brown had wanted me out for quite a while. He was paying some of his new signings such as George Mulhall and George Herd more than me – I remember because I went in and asked for £40 a week and he shot a figure at me that was no good. I asked him if it was the same as he was paying Charlie Hurley and he said that it was nothing to do with me, so I refused to sign. Then, a few weeks later, he came back with an extra £5 a week – not as a basic wage, but because I was captain. It still didn't come to £40 a week.

Basically Brown was not a nice man. This was the same man who once told me that I could be at Sunderland for life and that there would be a coaching job at the club for me when I stopped playing. He said that in the presence of directors.

In fact, the chairman at the time, Syd Collings, once told me that the manager would leave the club before I did. But all this counted for nothing the night Alan Brown knocked on my front door at 10pm. To be honest – and I can say this now because the poor bloke is dead – I think there was something wrong with him. I think he was probably schizophrenic. I had been dropped, I hadn't played for about five weeks and I had asked for a transfer. As it happened, that request had been turned down. But Brown definitely wanted me out, so he arrived one night. I asked him in and made him a cup of tea. He said that a club was interested in signing me, but refused to tell me who it was. I said I couldn't agree to going just anywhere. I needed to know what he was talking about. Then, after an hour and a half of this, he said the manager of the club concerned was sitting in the car outside. He had left him there all the time. I thought to myself, 'This isn't real.' But it was. I walked outside and there, sitting in the car, was the Newcastle manager Joe Harvey.

I knew Joe and I invited him in. The talking went on, but I said to Joe that I just couldn't do it. I would be a traitor and my own family wouldn't speak to me. This was Sunderland he was talking about and I had been with the club since school. How could I, the Sunderland captain, sign for the sworn enemy? In any case, it was getting late, so I agreed to go and talk to Joe at Newcastle the next day. All the time I was telling myself that I couldn't do this. And then I would think of the things Browny had been doing to me. We just did not get on. I didn't like him and it seemed as if he didn't like me. I had asked for a transfer, but after that he wouldn't even play me in the reserves. But then, he would name me as 12th man for long trips such as Portsmouth. There were no substitutes in those days and I would shout at him, 'What do you want to take me all the way down there for?'

But that was the kind of bloke he was. He ruled people by fear. So I went to Newcastle, talked with jovial Joe and signed for them. To be honest, the moment I did it I felt terrible. I lived in Park Avenue, which was within walking distance from Roker Park. Everyone around me was die-hard Sunderland and, after I had signed for the enemy, a lot of them couldn't even bring themselves to look at me in the street!

Anderson felt that he had been pushed into a nightmare situation. He recalled:

It had always been my job as captain to meet Brown and his coach George Curtis on a Monday morning. And I would say what I thought and explain how I thought we should be playing. But all you got from Brown was the fact that everything would be done his way. So I signed for Newcastle – and as it turned out, I had two great years there, including promotion to the First Division! Back in Sunderland, though, it took time for people to come round to the idea. The club had told me to vacate my club house and had given me six weeks to get out. I contacted a solicitor who told me I had to stay there as a sitting tenant and I did. But it turned into a right saga.

Anyway, I had just signed for Newcastle when I was due to go and present the awards for darts and dominoes at Southwick Social Club. A friend of mine ran it and I had gone twice a year for many years to do it and thoroughly enjoyed it. But when he asked me this time, I told him that he must be joking. I said that they would boo me off the stage. How could I walk into Southwick Club as a Newcastle United player? He told me I would be all right, so I agreed to make the presentation. It was a bloody nightmare. The place was absolutely packed and, when I got up to do my bit, you could have heard a pin drop. Absolute silence. Blokes were coming up for their trophies and shaking my hand, but they were all looking the other way. No-one spoke a word to me. Eventually I thought I couldn't stand any more of this, so I grabbed the mike and made an announcement that Sunderland were dead certainties for promotion that year. That did the trick and everyone applauded me!

Anderson had been a hero at Sunderland, and the 12-mile move to Newcastle had been difficult for fans to stomach. He insisted:

It was all down to Browny. He was a strange, strange man. I remember Brian Usher telling me that he thought the world of the bloke at Sunderland. Brian was a young winger in the promotion side and he did well for Browny. Then Brown quit Sunderland and went to Sheffield Wednesday. He signed Brian not long afterwards and the lad thought it would be a great move for him. But he told me that Browny had treated him like a dog at Wednesday. He was a very strange man.

With Anderson gone, Martin Harvey, Nicky Sharkey, Jim Montgomery, Cec Irwin, Len Ashurst, Jim McNab and Usher all made it into the first team thanks to Brown's excellent youth set-up. Skipper Charlie Hurley had cost just £17,000 from Millwall back in Brown's first season, but by now he had added Scottish internationals George Herd for £42,000 and George Mulhall for £25,000, as well as Northern Ireland inside-forward Johnny Crossan for £26,000. It was fairly hefty spending for a Second Division club in the early 1960s, but Sunderland's long-suffering fans were growing impatient and the club needed to deliver.

Ashurst, who made 458 appearances for the club, recalled:

In 1954 I was a member of the Liverpool Boys team which won the English Schools Trophy, and I wanted to become a Liverpool first-team player. And my hopes were that they would offer me professional terms when I played for England in a series of youth internationals. But they didn't, so when George Curtis, who was then manager of the England youth team before becoming our chief coach at Roker Park, invited me to meet Alan Brown in December 1957, I accepted his offer to turn professional. At first I was a part-timer, but I was promoted to Sunderland's League side in rather unusual circumstances after playing in 12 reserve games. In September 1958 Sunderland were bottom of the Second Division and there was a big shuffle for a game with Ipswich. In fact, 22 players were ordered to report to the ground before the game and Mr Brown then picked 11.

Britain was beginning to be sucked into the Swinging Sixties, and at Roker Park everything now seemed fresh and modern. Brown had already abandoned the club's traditional black shorts in favour of white. It was the first time in the club's history that anyone had dared to interfere with the colours of red and white striped shirts and black shorts, but Brown appeared to make the switch as something of a statement.

These were new times, and Sunderland were moving forward. Brown had introduced shadow play, a training method in which the first team lined up in its matchday kit and played against...nobody! It was aimed at teaching co-ordination, timing, perfect passing and sweeping movement. In years to come, it would be claimed that Brown had tinkered with the exercise by positioning 11 dustbins as the opposition. 'And after 20 minutes the bins would be 3–0 up!' would be the cry from some disillusioned fan. But in truth, his coaching methods were fresh, new and upbeat. Generally, his players approved.

Inside-forward Herd remembered his manager's methods:

Alan Brown was ten years ahead of his time as a coach. He was a
strong man, and he took a lot of criticism because he had been the
manager when the club was relegated. But his team talks were out
of this world, and I can remember the German FA sending people
over to tape our training sessions to find out how he coached
shadow play. I'm sure all the players who worked with him would
say what a good coach he was. He always talked about the team
playing together and he didn't talk about individuals because that
got up his nose! It's true that he did do some daft, stupid things.
He was an ex-policeman and he didn't like players going ahead of
him on a training run. If you did, he would tell you to stop and take
a walk. He wasn't one for giving big slaps on the back either. He
would just say, 'You played well.' But he had charisma and, as a
leader, he was one of the best I played under.

Jim Montgomery also recalled Brown's methods:

Browny was so far ahead of his time that it was untrue. He ran the
whole club from top to bottom, and I have always said that
Cloughie modelled himself on him. Brian managed in exactly the
same way – and it didn't do him too much harm. They were both
from the same school. If either of them saw a piece of litter on the
street, then he would pick it up and put it in the nearest bin. If
there was no bin around, they would put it into a pocket and take
it home. That's the sort of guys they were.
      Alan was strict. He never let us abuse ourselves with drink and
we would practise the shadow play morning, noon and night. He
was like a father to the younger lads such as me, but then he was
also like that with the senior professionals such as Martin Harvey
and Jimmy McNab, and his system seemed to work. I think I was
on about £20 a week when we were going for promotion a few
seasons on the trot, but the secret was that we were also on £60 a
point. Imagine that – 20 quid a week, but then three times that for
every point we won! Well, I mean, you would have kicked your
granny for that sort of money, wouldn't you? We had a special
bond among the players in that early 1960s team, and a lot of us
still meet up to this day. Eventually, of course, we went up – but
the money for points won seemed to dry up. Well, of course it did.
We were in the First Division and we were not doing that well. It's
funny to say, but going up was not financially beneficial to the
players – not in those days, anyway.

For now, Sunderland were on a roll. They were promoted as runners-up to Don Revie's Leeds, a club with which they had already become used to doing battle. There was, however, plenty more of that to come during the next decade. More than 50,000 were at Roker Park to celebrate promotion with a 2–1 win over Charlton Athletic. Leading marksman Crossan, fast making a name for himself as a link-man who could both create and score goals, hit the winner for his 22nd goal of the season. Charlie Hurley recalled the moment:

> We were up. There was bedlam in our dressing-room, but sitting there and savouring that long-awaited moment made up for everything. I was glad for Alan Brown because he had put up with so much. We had gone close, missing out the previous year by just 0.4 of a goal, and the manager had needed the patience of Job. We had a common bond right then – the feeling that we had both been in it from the start. It had been a long wait, but a worthwhile one. It had never seemed right that Sunderland were in the Second Division and I don't think our supporters ever accepted it. Like men who had seen their birthright filched, they backed the team passionately and impatiently during those six seasons. In the two seasons before we actually went up, I had two experiences that I would not wish on anybody because we managed to get the First Division door open only to have it slammed on our fingers right at the end. It was a wretched, numbing experience and it cut very deeply into me because I felt so much about the team and the game. But then, finally, promotion was a reality and not that mocking mirage we had stalked for a couple of years.
>
> My greatest spell with the club was those three years leading up to promotion in 1964, not in individual acclaim, but in team acclaim. When you get an international cap, only you get any reward out of it. But so many get the rewards when you win promotion – the players, the supporters and everyone connected with the club. I was with Sunderland with the sole intention of playing my part in helping them back to the First Division, where they belonged. And, as we all did a lap of honour at Roker after the Charlton game, I saw the supporters crying their eyes out – hardened men, working men, men who grafted all day in the shipyards and in the pits. I always knew that promotion would mean a great deal to them, but I don't honestly think I understood how much it mattered until I saw their faces close up that day. No amount of money could buy the memories I have of that. The din that day was terrific, and we had to go on two laps of honour. It was

a great achievement after so much struggle, sweat and strain. That final victory tasted sweeter than vintage wine.

Hurley was 27. The granite-like centre-half with the curly hair had made such an impact on English football that season that he was runner-up to Bobby Moore in the 1964 Player of the Year award. He had attained such heights and achieved such fame – and as a Second Division player. But he took it all in his comfortable stride. Having played in the top flight as a youngster in a relegated team, Hurley was determined to stamp his mark on the First Division, but he was soon to discover that it was no easy ride. 'King Charlie' played a total of 400 games for Sunderland, of which just 114 were in the First Division. In the hectic, fixture-packed modern game that would constitute a mere two seasons' worth of appearances. Hurley, however, does not view it that way: 'I spent the best part of 12 years at Sunderland. The people are the best in the world and I couldn't have been happier.'

Hurley was idolised at Sunderland. But back in his day, when watching football actually meant going to a game and standing out in all weathers on vast roofless terraces, there was not the cavernous gap between footballer and supporter that exists today. He recalled:

We used to walk to the game with the fans, never mind driving flash cars. You always got fans wanting to chat about the game or asking for an autograph. But that was it. I saw us all as equals. It was just that we were lucky enough to be paid for playing football, but they were the people who paid our wages!

In fact, Sunderland supporters had every reason for optimism in 1964. The team Brown had built looked well balanced, with the young Montgomery now firmly established in goal and full-backs Irwin and Ashurst both crowd favourites. The half-back line of Harvey, Hurley and McNab also had great balance and the trio clicked into place like rifle bolts. Harvey operated as more of a midfield man, while the wily McNab protected Hurley's left-hand side. Pairing two players as a central defensive duo had yet to become a feature of the English game, but in this respect Brown was tactically ahead of the game. Durham youngster Brian Usher, although never a total hit with the Roker faithful, offered width on the right. As McNab said of him, 'The lad might not have been the best player in the world, but he was quick. He could catch pigeons!' On the left was Mulhall, a Scottish international left-winger who was quick, brave and excellent in the air for a small man. He also had a keen eye for goal and was to become a Roker star through and through. That left the super-fit Herd – another full Scotland cap – to help Harvey with the foraging in the centre of the park, while inside-left Crossan pushed on to form what would today be described as a two-man strike force with the goal-hungry Nicky Sharkey.

In practice, the team played a 3–3–4 formation or – with McNab dropping back into defence to play alongside Hurley – 4–2–4. The system worked a treat, with each player responding to the Brown discipline while still managing to introduce an abundance of individual skill. One player who revelled in it was Londonderry-born Crossan, who had been banned for life by the Irish League after being accused of taking a payment while still an amateur. Undeterred, he went abroad and came on in leaps and bounds as a European-style footballer. At Standard Liège he tasted action in a European Cup semi-final against the great Real Madrid, a game in which he was instructed to mark the legendary Alfredo di Stefano. Crossan made the move to Sunderland a few days after his life ban was lifted in October 1962, and slotted into Brown's promotion-winning side as if he had always been meant to be there. Crossan both scored and created goals, as well as being well-known within the game for his hard-man image. It was not, however, an image in the Ron 'Chopper' Harris or Norman Hunter mould. Crossan was far more subtle than that. As Mulhall explained:

> Johnny didn't say too much, but he was a gem and as hard as nails. In fact, he used to put Mickey Spillane detective novels down his socks as shinpads. John was as hard as anyone I met, but he was a good player and played for a long time as inside-forward to me. We played very well together and became big mates. But he could handle himself. We had a good set of lads in those days – as good as you would find anywhere in the country. Johnny and I had not been there long and we were staying in the Roker Hotel. The club really looked after you in those days, and I can remember joining the other players there for afternoon tea!

The promotion season had also included FA Cup drama of the highest calibre. Sunderland had been drawn against mighty Manchester United in the sixth round and it was a tie that was to run to epic proportions. Brown's attack-minded side drew 3–3 in the initial game at Old Trafford with goals from Crossan, who scored two, and Mulhall. Then a star-studded United side, featuring Bobby Charlton, Denis Law and a teenage George Best, came to town and drew 2–2 after extra-time. The diminutive Sharkey and an own goal by Maurice Setters provided Sunderland's salvation. But then, with hopes of a place in the semi-finals riding high, Sunderland crashed 5–1 in the second replay, at Huddersfield Town's Leeds Road ground. It was a cruel finale to a tie many believed should have been won by Sunderland at the first attempt. All the same, it had allowed Brown's boys to test themselves against a team which would become the First Division champions a year later.

Brown's mixture of home-grown talent and big-money buys certainly appeared to be ready for the First Division. But, before a ball had even been kicked in anger, the whole thing began to fall apart. The man who had led Sunderland out of the Second Division resigned to take charge at Sheffield Wednesday. And, as if that was not a big-enough shock, Montgomery injured a hand during pre-season and was pronounced unfit for the opening game of the season at home to Leicester. Monty's deputy, Derek Kirby, a goalkeeper who never started a first-team game for the club, was also sidelined, leaving the managerless club with no alternative other than to pitch in 15-year-old Derek Forster. It seems unbelievable that such a drastic step was allowed to take place, but Newcastle-born Forster, who had left school just two months earlier to begin his Sunderland apprenticeship, suddenly found himself in line to face Leicester and, perhaps more poignantly at the opposite end of the field, England goalkeeper Gordon Banks!

Forster was 15 years and 185 days old and the First Division's youngest-ever player. He started the first three games of Sunderland's return to the big time. After watching ten goals fly past him from a draw and two defeats, he was allowed to step out of the limelight in favour of Scottish goalkeeper Sandy McLaughlan, signed from Kilmarnock for £12,000 by the club's directors, who were now responsible for team affairs. Forster was forced to wait almost another three and a half years – until January 1968 – for his next appearance, ironically in another home game against Leicester. Sadly for him, victory again eluded Sunderland and the youngster found himself on the wrong end of a 2–0 defeat.

Sunderland's return to the big time had not started well, so the directors turned to former Middlesbrough and England captain George Hardwick to steady the ship. His appointment was curious. Hardwick had gone to Roker Park to collect material for his weekly column in the *Middlesbrough Evening Gazette* when, all of a sudden, chairman Syd Collings asked to see him. 'Gentleman George' thought that it would provide him with a good opportunity to gather some up-to-date information about the club – and it did do because Collings offered him the manager's job there and then. Hardwick later recalled: 'It was not a bad job for a part-time journalist! I'd had enough time to recharge my batteries and just wanted to be once again totally involved in the game that I'd loved ever since receiving my first football at the age of three.'

Hardwick guided Sunderland into 15th place in his only season at the helm, which was not a bad effort considering the chaotic start to the campaign. Two members of the promotion side left under Hardwick, Brian Usher linking up with Brown at Sheffield Wednesday and crowd favourite Crossan quitting for Manchester City, the club he would later skipper back into the First Division. New arrivals were Harry Hood, a striker from Clyde who had only just turned 20, Mike Hellawell, a right-winger from Birmingham, with whom he had won two England caps, and the versatile Northern Ireland international John Parke. Hellawell arrived in a £27,500 deal as a direct replacement for Usher, who had found life tough in the top division, but despite his electric pace he was never going to set Roker alight. His main trick was to knock the ball a good ten yards beyond the full-back and then run like the clappers. Usually it worked, but there was not a great deal of end-product and he left for Huddersfield after just 43 appearances. Hellawell's claim to fame during his Sunderland career was that he was the first player in the club's history to be substituted under new League rules when he was replaced 55 minutes into a 3–1 defeat at Aston Villa in September 1965 by winger Allan Gauden.

It was 20-year-old Gauden's debut, and he recalled the background to getting his chance as Sunderland's first substitute

It was difficult for the North-East lads to make progress. It was hard to break through because you had to get through the youth team, the reserves and then try to work your way into the first team if you were good enough to get a game. But you had to learn all the time and be respectful of your elders and senior professionals in the first team more than you do now. There were a few of us from the Sunderland area and a few canny Scots, but they were great times for me, especially being a local boy from a pit village such as Langley Park. Substitutions had just started, but they couldn't be made for tactical reasons, just if someone got injured. I came on after Mike Hellawell had broken his nose, but I found it very difficult to get into the game because I'd been sitting down on the bench all the time. I always thought that it was much easier for the prolific goalscorers such as David Fairclough at Liverpool to come on and make an impact in a game.

Gauden then had to wait exactly a month for his full senior debut:

I got in because George Mulhall was injured, and it was away to

Tottenham, who had Jimmy Greaves and all the top names. We lost, but I really enjoyed the occasion. I was quite happy just to be a member of the team at such a big club as Sunderland, but the game I remember most was at Sheffield United later that season when it was 2–2 and I scored both goals.

Hood, meanwhile, did not fare a great deal better than Hellawell during his brief stay. But the irony there was that the striker, who always looked as if he were low on confidence at Roker, later became a household name with Scottish giants Glasgow Celtic. Hood was still relatively young and stayed for two years before returning to Clyde. His Roker record was quite meagre, but, as he recalled, it was a difficult time for him. For a start, he had not played football until he was 16. He explained: 'I had to pinch time off to get my first soccer. I was a late developer and went to a rugby-playing school, but I joined Clyde as a part-timer and started to score goals.'

Parke, a cultured defender, had been snapped up by Hardwick in a £33,000 move from Hibernian. He played 93 games for the club, mostly in the full-back positions, but his trademark was his versatility in a career that earned him 14 Northern Ireland caps. For a start, he played for five clubs in four different countries – Cliftonville and Linfield in Ireland, Hibernian in Scotland, Sunderland in England between 1964 and 1968, and Mechelen in Belgium – in a 13-year career. And he played in all 11 positions for Linfield: he started in nine of them, but also deputised as an emergency goalkeeper three times because of injuries and once played on the left-wing after he himself had been injured – a traditional ploy before the introduction of substitutes. He played in four Irish Cup finals in different positions – inside-right, right-half, left-half and right-back – and represented the Irish League five times in four different positions, on one occasion again deputising in goal in an injury emergency against the Scottish League.

In the first season back in the First Division, local lad Dickie Rooks almost forced his way into the side on a regular basis. But, as a traditional centre-half, he had a battle on his hands to make it into the first team. Hurley was Sunderland's No. 5, and Rooks found his football education a tough one because he made just 18 starts in four seasons. He did, however, play 16 times during 1964/65 when Hurley was injured.

But Jim Baxter was different. If he had been a singer, he would have been Frank Sinatra; if he had been an artist, he would have been Pablo Picasso. Baxter was a virtuoso performer – a talent so rich that nowadays Manchester United, Barcelona and Real Madrid would have fought it out for his signature. As a left-half with Glasgow Rangers and Scotland,

'Slim Jim' had enjoyed a spell when he was arguably the best in his position on the planet. Even FIFA had recognised it by selecting him for a Rest of the World X1 to play England at Wembley in 1963. Yet, like so many gifted performers, Baxter was vulnerable. He was both a heavy drinker and a gambler and, by the time that Sunderland moved in for him in the summer of 1965, he needed the move to boost his sagging cash flow. Baxter was 25 when his costly £72,500 move from Ibrox to Roker shocked British football. The man who persuaded him that the North-East of England was the place for his mouth-watering talent was Ian McColl, the club's recent managerial appointment after George Hardwick's departure. The dapper Hardwick had stepped into the breach the previous season following Alan Brown's resignation and a brief uncomfortable spell when the directors handled team affairs. But Sunderland were looking to the future, and McColl, who had only just been sacked as Scotland's manager, was brought in to ride along on the wind of change. McColl and Baxter were old pals. Slim Jim had arrived at Rangers as a 20-year-old part-timer with Raith Rovers. McColl, soon to manage at Ibrox Park, was in the twilight of his own playing career and actually played alongside the young Baxter.

Baxter was a huge success at Ibrox, establishing himself on the world stage with that magical left foot of his. But the high life was always too tempting for the former miner from the village of Hill O'Beath, near Fife. When McColl became national team manager, Baxter was always one of the first names on his teamsheet. It was no great surprise that, shortly after McColl's switch to Sunderland, the pair were reunited. It might, however, have turned out very differently for maverick wing-half Baxter. As his former Scotland team-mate Denis Law explained in his autobiography The King, Manchester United were in the hunt for Jim, too:

> I remember Matt Busby telling me that he was thinking of signing either Jim from Rangers or Paddy Crerand from Celtic. I said that Baxter was the more skilful player, of that there was no doubt. But he was too much of an individual at times. I felt that, if Matt was building for the future, Crerand was a stronger, more dedicated player who would give the club more value. Jim went to Sunderland, which wasn't a particularly good move for him. He should have gone to London or Manchester. Sadly, we never saw the best of Jim Baxter – just as, in my opinion, we never saw the best of George Best – and in both instances the cause was alcohol-related.

Deep down, Baxter always knew it himself. And, shortly before his death in April 2001 at the age of just 61, he revealed:

> I went downhill after I left Rangers and I went to a bad side. I can remember walking into the Sunderland dressing-room for the first time and being introduced to people. Little Nicky Sharkey was there and, when I was told he was the club's centre-forward, I burst out laughing! I don't think I would ever have left Rangers if I hadn't gambled away all my money. But I was on £35 a week then and we were all paid the same. All I wanted was a few quid more than the less-gifted.

That was typical Baxter. Never afraid to blow his own trumpet, he will always be remembered for his outstanding performance against England at Wembley in 1967. The World Cup winners were expected to beat the old enemy comfortably, but Baxter had other ideas. Scotland won 3–2, Baxter running the show to such an extent that he enjoyed his own little game of 'keepy-uppy' with the England defence incapable of handling his sheer audacity. Baxter grinned:

> That game always makes me laugh. I remember standing next to Alan Ball in the tunnel before we came onto the pitch, and he was so wound up like a coiled spring. Bally had that high-pitched voice which people used to take the mickey out of, so I turned to him and said, 'Hey, wee man, is your daddy Jimmy Clitheroe?' Bally went mad. It just wound him up even more. All the game he kept trying to get the better of me – or at least get the ball off me – but he couldn't!

Baxter was a Sunderland player at the time, but no doubt revelled in revealing his own box of magic tricks to a wider audience. Back at Roker Park, however, his displays might be awesome one week and average the next. It appeared that he would play if and when he wanted to, turning his talent on and off like a tap. But he was battling with the booze, even in those days. A Bacardi and Coke was his regular tipple back in the trendy 1960s, although Baxter himself admitted that anything went: 'I had a candle as long as your arm and I just burned it at both ends. And I burned the bit in the middle as well. In the end, long after I had stopped playing, I got sick and tired of looking at life through the bottom of a bottle. I had done it all.'

Baxter's body was somewhat tired of its lifestyle, too. Jim had two liver transplants before cancer of the pancreas finally killed him. During his spell on Wearside he played 98 times, scoring 12 goals. Supporters still talk of his stunning performance on his home debut, a 4–1 win over Sheffield United in which he scored twice, and of another display against Nottingham Forest, which, many believe, persuaded them to pay Sunderland £100,000 for his services in December 1967. But Baxter really showed what he was made of during an ill-tempered three-game FA Cup battle with Leeds in March 1967. McColl had by now managed to assemble a half-decent team by First Division standards, even if he appeared to put the emphasis on players from north of the border.

Neil Martin, a powerful centre-forward with tremendous heading ability, was another Scottish international McColl signed. McColl had already awarded Martin two international caps while still a Hibernian player, and had obviously kept close tabs on a player whose goals were attracting a great deal of interest from top English clubs. Another Scot, the rugged George Kinnell, had been snapped up from Oldham Athletic for a bargain £25,000. In fact, Kinnell, who had been with the Latics for only two months following his switch from First Division Stoke City, was Baxter's second cousin, and McColl was already favouring the hard man's no-nonsense style ahead of the legendary Charlie Hurley, who by this time was struggling to make the first team. Jim Montgomery had seen off the challenge of former Kilmarnock goalkeeper Sandy McLaughlan. McLaughlan, who had actually managed to relegate Monty to a few bouts of reserve-team football, had blotted his own copybook by allegedly overdoing the Hogmanay bit on New Year's Eve, 1966. Sunderland lost 5–1 at home to West Bromwich Albion the following afternoon, although in McLaughlan's case it was never too apparent where his evening finished and his day began! In any case, it was the last time he played a first-team game before returning to Kilmarnock seven months later for £5,000. In the mid-1980s he emigrated to Australia, where he died.

In the full-back roles, McColl was opting for Cec Irwin at right-back and, following lengthy runs in the side for the long-serving Len Ashurst, he had installed Martin Harvey in the No. 3 shirt. One player to find himself out of favour with McColl was Jimmy McNab, which puzzled many regular supporters because the Scottish wing-half was still just 26 and had rarely, if ever, let Sunderland down. As he recalled:

McColl just didn't fancy me and that was that. I did actually start in the side that summer when he arrived, and so did Jim Baxter. But I remember that Jim had to have the No. 6 shirt, so I was made to wear No. 10. In those days the shirt number that you wore indicated the position in which you were playing. It's not like now when players have squad numbers and 1 to 11 doesn't mean anything any more. But it did back then. And when I was told I was wearing No. 10 for the first game of the season away to Leeds and that I would actually be playing inside-left, I couldn't believe it. I classed myself as a defensive wing-half. I had never been asked to play that far forward in my life. Anyway I did just that and actually scored a couple of goals in those first five games. The plan, of course, was to accommodate Jim at left-half, which had always been his position. As it happened, he actually went on to wear the No. 10 shirt quite a bit himself after that!

With McNab out of favour and heading for a £15,000 move to Preston North End, McColl's half-back line consisted of Colin Todd, Kinnell and Baxter. The young Todd had broken into the first team at the age of 17 and was fast developing a reputation as a central defender with an ability far exceeding his years. The all-Scottish forward line included another new kid on the block, Bobby Kerr. Kerr featured very much as a traditional outside-right back then, with John O'Hare, Martin, George Herd and George Mulhall completing the front line. Martin, Herd and Mulhall had all represented their country – indeed all three had been capped by McColl – while O'Hare found international success only after he had moved to Brian Clough's Derby County. Why, in years to come, Kerr was never selected for Scotland remains a mystery that still baffles many fans to this day.

Mulhall, in particular, displayed incredible consistency throughout McColl's Roker reign. He recalled:

Alan Brown signed me and he was a disciplinarian who wanted to keep things right. He was a very fit man, and if you tried to get past him on a pre-season run he would always elbow you out of the way. He was a big man and had to be at the front. But then McColl came, and I think there was a bit in the background between us. He was a Protestant man and Mulhall is an Irish name, but it never bothered me. That's what the rivalry is like in Scotland, though, far worse than anywhere in England. I always felt that I had to be playing well to stay in the team.

At this time another Scot Nicky Sharkey discovered that he was clearly not rated by McColl. And, despite a superb Sunderland record of 62 goals in 117 appearances, the man who had replaced Clough made a £15,000 move to Leicester in October 1966. He was still only 23, but had started just 19 games since Brown's departure. So, with McColl seemingly settled on his new-look Sunderland side, they took the field for a fifth-round FA Cup clash with Leeds. More than 55,000 were crammed into Roker Park, and hopes were high of a place in the quarter-finals.

McColl had by now introduced a new strip of all red with white socks. The shirts bore a large letter S on the left-hand side of the chest with AFC in smaller lettering beneath it, while the shorts came with two white stripes down each side. Sunderland were beginning to wear the kit at every opportunity, although why they were doing so at home mystified some. There were reports that McColl was trying to do away with the traditional red and white stripes in an attempt to stamp his own mark on the club. But if that was the case, it certainly never materialised. All the same, the Cup run gave the new strip a decent airing. Lower League sides Brentford and Peterborough United had already been knocked out at Roker, with Sunderland – minus their familiar stripes – hitting 12 goals. Centre-forward Martin had grabbed a hat-trick against the Posh, while Kerr was also in goalscoring mood.

Kerr had made his debut earlier in the season, scoring the only goal of the game in the 1–0 win over Manchester City at Roker Park. By the time Leeds arrived on fifth-round day, the popular right-winger had netted seven goals in 11 appearances. Great things were already expected of the former youth-team favourite, but 11 March 1967 was not to be a good day for Bobby Kerr when his leg gave way under a challenge from Norman Hunter. Sunderland drew 1–1 that day with Martin cracking home a first-half goal from just inside the area, only for big Jack Charlton to volley home Johnny Giles' second-half free-kick at the Fulwell End. Allan Gauden, who substituted for Kerr, came into the side for the replay at Elland Road, where John O'Hare's goal resulted in another 1–1 draw. It was widely accepted at the time that Sunderland were the better side in both games, but now they were heading for a disastrous evening in Hull.

The second replay was staged at Hull's old Boothferry Park, where more than 40,000 crammed in to watch the titanic struggle resume. Yet again, the game was delicately poised at 1–1 with Gauden smashing home a stunning long-range drive for the team in all red. But then, in the dying seconds, Irwin was judged to have brought down Jimmy Greenhoff in the penalty area. The referee was besieged by Sunderland players. Indeed, such was their anger over the decision that both Mulhall and the usually impassive Herd were both dismissed for their venom towards the man in black. Giles duly despatched the spot-kick, and Sunderland's FA Cup dream was over.

Mulhall recalled the sheer fire and passion of the three encounters:

'There was usually bad blood when we played Leeds. We had been promoted together in 1964, but I think it went back to a couple of years earlier than that when Willie McPheat had his leg broken after a tackle by Johnny Giles at Elland Road.' As it happened, that injury put an end to McPheat's Sunderland career because he was unable to regain his place when he finally regained fitness and was transferred to Hartlepool three years later. Mulhall said:

> I can remember Alan Brown saying that he wouldn't see it if any of our players had a dig at Giles after that. As for that second replay at Hull, it was all to do with that penalty – and Giles actually stuck it away! George Herd and I were among those who surrounded the referee to dispute the decision. But I think we were sent off because we had Scottish accents. He certainly picked us out because practically all the Sunderland players were around him and nothing happened to the rest of the lads!

Strangely enough, Mulhall was sent off only twice in his career – and on both occasions it was against Leeds. He added: 'I was also sent off at Elland Road. I told the linesman what he could do with his flag after he had made a disastrous decision. He got the referee over and that was it. Whenever I was in trouble, it was all from the mouth. I was never sent off for kicking anybody!'

Two more home-grown players, Colin Suggett and Billy Hughes, made their Sunderland debuts in 1967/68. The only ever-present was Montgomery, by now rated the best uncapped goalkeeper in the country, while the in-form Martin finished as leading marksman with 26 League and Cup goals. By now, Martin had established himself as both a consistent First Division goalscorer and a firm favourite with the Roker crowd. The centre-forward, in fact, had attended Tranent Public School in Scotland, although he did point out: 'Public is just a name and does not indicate a rich young man's seminary!'

He had joined Alloa Athletic while still serving his apprenticeship as a mining engineer, and then moved to Queen of the South on a full-time basis. From there he moved to Hibernian, proving his worth as a free-scoring centre-forward, scoring 53 times in 65 games. He earned two Scottish caps under McColl in 1965 and then a third, a year later, while with Sunderland. But he admitted:

> I did not find it quite as easy as I had thought at Sunderland. Having made the switch from Scottish to English soccer, I found goals much harder to come by. I don't think it was because of any

115

particular weakness in our own team, but chiefly because I found the English defences stronger. They were much, much tighter than they were in Scotland.

All the same, Martin became one of a select band of players to have scored 100 goals on both sides of the border.

Another interesting Scot, at this stage captaining the side, was George Kinnell. The colourful Kinnell had never harboured dreams of becoming a footballer and had, in fact, appeared more interested in a career as a butcher. Indeed, by the time he had completed his National Service, he was fully qualified and poised to don the striped apron. Raised in Cowdenbeath, he represented Fife Schoolboys and played for junior sides Ballincry Rovers, Kirkford and Crossgates Primrose. In fact, the versatile Kinnell once played 13 games in a fortnight at troop, battery and regiment level while serving with the Royal Artillery at the height of the troubles in Cyprus. Offers of trials flooded in, but the young Kinnell was rejected by Cowdenbeath, East Fife and Raith Rovers, Baxter's first club.

But in 1959 he signed for Aberdeen and, during his four and a half seasons at Pittodrie, played in seven different positions. He then moved to England with Stoke, for whom he operated mainly as an inside-forward. After his brief stay at Oldham he made the £20,000 move to Roker in November 1966. Kinnell was a rough-and-ready centre-half who loved to play the tough guy with his tightly rolled-up sleeves. He performed admirably for Sunderland before making the short journey to Middlesbrough in October 1968. He started just 13 games for Boro, scoring once, and then found himself on his travels again. This time the quaintly named club, Juventus FC of Melbourne, Australia, was the destination – and that, as they say, was that. George vanished into the distance, apparently never to be heard of again.

But Baxter did once mention Kinnell during his own latter years: 'I lost track of Kinksy. But, as far as I know, he ended up working on the oil rigs.' As it happens, Baxter was correct. Kinnell had gone 'offshore' for a living, as the Scot himself confirmed. He laughed:

People seem to think that I vanished after I left for Australia. After Middlesbrough I signed for Melbourne and stayed there for 18 months. You could say I moved around a bit. But it was Alan Brown's fault that I left Sunderland in the first place. He just didn't like me, stripped me of the captaincy and then sold me!

Kinnell was 30 when he was forced out of Roker. Then there were only a handful of appearances for Boro and the move to Juventus. But there was to be no big Italian-style pay day for him. He said:

Life was good in Australia, and it was a great place to bring up your kids. After that I played for Sydney for three years and then I became player-manager of Perth. I stayed there for four years and thoroughly enjoyed it. So then, after almost nine very good years, it was back to Scotland and I took a job working offshore. I am retired now and enjoying my golf. Back in my playing days, all footballers smoked and I was no different. But I gave up that game five years ago and that has forced me to put on some extra weight – although I suppose that might be the beer. I like the McEwans too much! But, as far as Sunderland go, I look back on those days at the club as some of the happiest of my career. And it was strange that Jim and I should have ended up together at Roker Park. We'd known each other all our lives and I suppose I used to look after him a bit. When I came out of the Army, it was time for Jim to go in, and I remember picking him up from a Butlin's Holiday Camp and taking him for his medical. It seems like only yesterday, and now he's gone, bless him! By the time I'd done my National Service, I was a qualified butcher, so becoming a professional footballer with Aberdeen was something of a luxury. But playing football was always a luxury in those days. I was paid about £65 a week at Sunderland, which was good money in those days. We had a nice house in Bywell Avenue just behind Fulwell Mill, I drove a Ford Cortina and life was great. I remember nights in the La Strada nightclub with Jim and his wife Jean and Ken Chisholm and his wife Donna. They were happy days. But we were being paid to do something we loved doing. Most of us would have played for nothing.

Kinnell's second cousin Baxter – their mothers were full cousins – might have disagreed where financial matters were concerned. But Kinnell had all the time in the world for the richly talented Baxter:

Jim could make his left foot talk. His right was just for standing on. When Jim was on his game, he was on a different planet. He was world-class by anybody's standards. In fact, funnily enough, I remember another Cowdenbeath lad, 'Ian' Porterfield, coming down to Roker as a so-called replacement for Jim after he had signed for Nottingham Forest. His right foot was just for standing on, too, although he didn't make too bad a job of using it in 1973

when he slashed that one into the net against Leeds at Wembley.
I remember sitting up at midnight that day and watching the Cup
final in Australia. It made me so proud.

I knew Ian. We had played together, but I'd also played with
Monty, little Bobby Kerr and Billy Hughes. I watched Sunderland
beat Leeds that day and I remember raising a glass and saying,
'That's for 1967 and those three FA Cup games against Revie's
team when we were robbed in the second replay and little Bobby's
leg was broken in the original tie at Roker.' Winning that day was
poetic justice, believe me! We'd had a good side under Ian McColl
in the 1960s and we knew how to knock it around as well as look
after ourselves. I liked Ian. He was a football man and he
understood how the game should be played. In fact, he must have
remembered me when he signed me because I had played against
him when I was with Aberdeen and he was at Rangers. He signed
me from Oldham, as it happens a club I had only just joined from
Stoke, so it was a big step back up the ladder for me. I remember
that Charlie Hurley was injured and that Jim had been made
temporary captain. McColl brought me in, made me captain and
that's the way it stayed even when Charlie came back into the
team. I had come into Sunderland knowing the manager, cousin
Jim and also George Mulhall. George was a fine winger, and the
two of us had played in the same Aberdeen side quite a few years
beforehand. Both of us loved playing football and basketball. We'd
played as much as we could during our respective Army days.

But Kinnell's Sunderland stay ended abruptly following Alan Brown's
return in 1968. He recalled:

We were playing a friendly at Middlesbrough when he walked into
the dressing-room and told me that I was no longer captain. That's
how he said it, just like that, as I was getting changed into my kit.
He said Charlie was going to be captain again and then, not long
afterwards, he told me I was being transferred. He just didn't like
me and that was the end of it. That was me finished there. To this
day, I still don't know why McColl was sacked. But there had been
a buzz about Brown coming back to the club for quite a while
before Ian was dismissed.

Kinnell may well have been a fan of Ian McColl, but, during the
manager's two and a half-year tenure a certain Charlie Hurley had
watched his own career hit an all-time low. 'The King' found himself

playing regular reserve-team football against sides such as Ashington in the North Regional League, when for all his career, he had been used to the big stage. Hurley admitted:

> McColl arriving was the beginning of the end for me. You could say it was a case of the end being nigh! Let's say there was a bit of bias about the first team at the time, and it wasn't unusual to have seven Scots in the side. Meanwhile, there I was, this big Irishman desperate to get a game. The club just changed when McColl came. He signed Jim Baxter, but I don't really want to say too much about that. Baxter had great talent, but I just didn't like him as a person and that was no secret at the time. Yet he was McColl's idol from their Rangers days, so, if there were any siding to be done by the manager, then it normally went Baxter's way. I remember McColl arriving and telling me that he didn't really need the Sunderland job. I told him what a big job in football it was and also what a special club it was. And if he didn't really need it, then he didn't have to take it.

McColl's response was to virtually blank Hurley out of his plans. Hurley added:

> The club was preparing to go on a tour of America in 1967, and McColl asked me if I would like to go. What would you think? I thought that, if he needed to ask me, then I would stay at home. The club returned to reports of terrible behaviour. The tour had been a disaster. But I couldn't say anything about it because I hadn't been there.

McColl was in charge of Sunderland for 109 League games, and Hurley failed to appear in 61 of them. Supporters did not need anyone to tell them that the writing was on the wall for an all-time favourite who many years later was voted the club's Player of the Century! Hurley revealed: 'I actually asked for a transfer at that time, and McColl didn't really know what to do because he knew how popular I was with the fans.'

Jim Montgomery also looked back on McColl's reign with mixed emotions:

> Ian was a quiet man and an absolute gentleman, but he was also probably the worst manager I ever played for. The club changed totally after Browny left for Sheffield Wednesday and McColl came in. Ian brought in Jim Baxter and Jim's cousin George

Kinnell – and very quickly they were running the club and not the manager. I can remember being on tour to America and McColl calling a pre-match meeting at the hotel. Baxter had failed to turn up for the meeting and the manager was furious. He said he was going to go to Baxter's room to drag him down to the meeting. Anyway, he was gone for about 10 minutes and, when he came back, he announced to the group that the meeting would now be held in Jim's room. It was just ridiculous!

Monty had forced his way back into the side despite a brief spell of pressure from Sandy McLaughlan, but, as with others, he found McColl's reign a little tricky at times. He explained:

I had actually asked for a transfer just before McColl arrived. George Hardwick was the manager at the time and it was turned down flat. Not long after that, George was told that he was no longer wanted and I wondered whether I had caused any problems for him by asking for a move. I had recovered from the injury that meant me missing the start of the first season back in the First Division, but Sandy was keeping me out of the side, so I asked to go. Thankfully, nothing came of it and then McColl came in. He actually began with Sandy in the team ahead of me, then I got back in and Sandy had another spell. But it didn't last and I settled down to be first choice under McColl. He was a lovely man but, for me, not a good manager.

Bobby Kerr was another who, like Monty, experienced life under both McColl and Brown in his two spells with the club. Kerr said:

Browny was strict, so strict in fact that you had to see him in action to believe it, whereas McColl was not like that at all. As the manager, he appeared to idolise Baxter and everything revolved around Jim. In fact, Baxter would tell us what the line-up was going to be a couple of days ahead of a game. It was a bad time for Charlie Hurley then and I think the situation was that there was probably only room in the dressing-room for 'one king', and big Charlie suffered for a while.

You had young kids coming into the side such as me, Colin Todd and Colin Suggett, and we could only watch the two different cliques in the dressing-room. Eventually I got on with Baxter and, as a player, he was magnificent even though I think he was playing on autopilot by the time he came to Sunderland. It was as if he was operating by computer when it came to passing the ball. I was a right-winger back then and I would go on runs while looking over my shoulder to see if anyone was going to hit a ball into my path. Jim saw me doing this shortly after I came into the team and called me over. He said, 'Look, son, don't bother with the looking-over-the-shoulder bit. You just go on your runs and I'll make the sure the balls will arrive' – and they did!

Fellow Scot Billy Hughes added:

We did have a lot of good players at Roker Park, but I don't think there was one of us who was on the same wavelength as Jim. The problem we had was that he was too clever for the rest of us. He was always two moves ahead of the other lads who were playing alongside him. He was an exceptional player, one of those guys you come across only once in a lifetime. I never did play with anyone better than he was.

Hurley, meanwhile, might have lost a couple of years to reserve-team football, but he had the last laugh. McColl would soon be gone and, with his mentor Alan Brown returning, Hurley would enjoy his final season at Sunderland by clocking up 33 League games – his best haul since the promotion season of 1963/64. With Hurley's would-be successor Kinnell gone, another Scot had been allowed to leave. It was, however, somewhat surprising in this instance because McColl had done the selling. John O'Hare was just 20 and a promising centre-forward. The burly striker had just enjoyed his best season at Sunderland, playing alongside Neil Martin and bagging 11 goals from 35 games. But someone else with rather strong Wearside connections had his expert eye on young O'Hare. That man was Brian Clough.

Clough had coached the young O'Hare while in charge of Sunderland's youth team and clearly knew a good player when he saw one. Sunderland felt that the young Colin Suggett was now ready to partner Martin and that O'Hare was surplus to requirements. The square-shouldered O'Hare had never proved to be particularly popular with the Roker Park crowd, despite his work ethic and his obvious technical ability as a frontman of some considerable power. So in August 1967 McColl accepted a paltry £22,000 from Clough's Derby County. It seemed a strange deal at the time, especially because O'Hare was still so young and had become a First Division regular.

But Clough did not think it strange. Under the wing of the Sunderland goalscoring legend, O'Hare picked up a First Division championship medal with Derby as well as 13 Scotland caps. And he was not finished there. When Clough was handed the job of reinventing Leeds United and then struggling Nottingham Forest, he sent for O'Hare. The barrel-chested Scot remained at Forest until he ended his career in some style, coming on as a substitute in Forest's European Cup triumph over Hamburg in 1980. Clough had certainly managed to get his money's worth: 'O'Hare? He's got more skill in his little finger than I ever had in my whole body!'

The gangly Gary Moore was another centre-forward who, as a local lad, found it a struggle to break into the first team. Moore turned professional in November 1962 and had been a promising reserve-team player at the time of the club's promotion in 1964. But when he left Sunderland for Grimsby Town five years later, he had made just 13 appearances, scoring twice. He explained:

> Sunderland were wealthy in those days and would bring in established First Division players. Every game was a big game for a young lad in those days, not least my debut which was at Wolverhampton Wanderers in 1965, where I found myself up against England centre-half Ron Flowers. It was hard for youngsters at Sunderland. In fact, it might be a nightmare just walking into the dressing-room. I can remember when Allan Gauden, John O'Hare and I made the move from reserve-team dressing-room to first-team dressing-room. We just sat together in the corner, out of the way.

Moore offered his own account of the player cliques that had appeared under McColl's management:

> here was Charlie Hurley with his friends in one corner and Jim Baxter and his mates in another area. They didn't really like each other. Then, on top of that, there was Brian Clough, who was like a bear with a sore head because he was desperately trying to play again after his injury. We would watch them all and keep our heads below the parapets. Although, to be fair to people such as Baxter and Cloughie, they treated us as equals even though we were just youngsters. Jim didn't come over with the 'big-star' attitude even though he played hard off the field as well. In fact, I remember Ian McColl putting up all the players at the Five Bridges Hotel in Gateshead before home games to stop them from drinking on Friday nights!

Like many other local lads at that time, Moore was forced down into the lower divisions in search of regular first-team football – but not until he had enjoyed a run-out in Clough's testimonial game:

> Cloughie was great and he let me and John O'Hare play half a game each that night just to give us some more experience. He didn't have to do that. But, by and large, he was a good guy – even though we were wary of him. When we played together, all he would shout was: 'Give me the ball, give me the ball...' All he wanted to do was score goals. In the end it made me forget about going for goal myself!

Meanwhile, the sands of time were beginning to leak by the sack-full for Ian McColl B.Sc. Sunderland had won just six games as the end of January 1968 approached and had failed to clinch victory in any of their previous ten League games. The final straw for him came later that month when Second Division Norwich City came to Roker Park in an FA Cup third-round replay and won 1–0. Three days later, Alan Brown returned for a second spell in charge. Ironically, his first game back at the helm came against Sheffield Wednesday – the club he had only just quit in favour of Sunderland. Sunderland won 1–0 with the goal coming from Ralph Brand, another former Scottish international forward signed from Manchester City for £5,000 by McColl. Brand, who spoke at the funeral of his close friend Baxter in 2001, was in the twilight of his career.

So too was a Sunderland player making his debut that day after Brown had signed him from Burnley for £65,000 – Gordon Harris. He had been a flying left-winger during Burnley's heyday in the early 1960s. But, having been converted to a midfield player, he now looked slow and cumbersome. It seems amazing that he was still only 27 when he arrived at Roker – many supporters looked upon the Brylcreem-haired Harris as an old man, and promptly christened him Grandad. The shock arrival of both Brown and Harris, coupled with the signing of Stoke's utility man Calvin Palmer for £70,000 just two weeks later, clearly marked the start of yet another new era on Wearside. Brown had returned to a mixed reception. There were those who still had little time for him following his shock walk-out in the summer of 1964, but according to another school of thought, he probably knew the club better than anyone else and would therefore bring a measure of stability.

McColl had at least brought some degree of flair to Sunderland. But Jim Baxter had preceded him out of the door when Nottingham Forest's £100,000 bid had been accepted in December 1967. Many believed that Forest's offer – probably too good to turn down at the time – had been made on the back of Slim Jim playing them off the park at Roker just a couple of weeks earlier! Then the free-scoring Neil Martin, whose Roker record of 46 goals in 99 games was highly impressive in such a mediocre side, was sold to Coventry City for £90,000 within two weeks of Brown's return. Brown, in fact, never played Martin. He could have started with him in that first game at Sheffield Wednesday, but dropped him to substitute in favour of new boy Harris. Martin, who had already scored 12 goals in a struggling side that season, was promptly 'cashed in' by Brown, who would no doubt have argued that he used the £90,000 towards the cost of two players – Harris and Palmer.

One player plunged into the middle of this game of ever-revolving doors was full-back Geoff Butler. Unfortunately for him, McColl had paid Chelsea £65,000 to sign him just before being sacked! Naturally, he was keen to play his new signing in place of Len Ashurst, and play him he did – in one League game, which was a 2–2 home draw with Burnley in January 1968. Butler was then selected for the two FA Cup ties against Norwich – ironically the club he later joined – and never started another first-team game.

One of Brown's first actions on his return was to wind back the clock and reinstate his old full-back pairing of Cec Irwin and Ashurst. Amazingly, the tried and tested partnership of the two defenders who had made their debuts together as far back as 1958 was to last until March 1970. Meanwhile, Brown was attempting to pull out all the stops in a concerted attempt to drag the club away from the lower reaches of the First Division. He did actually manage to pick up seven wins from 17 games that season, which was one more victory than McColl had managed from eight games more. But the best was kept for the final day of the campaign.

It had been quite a season in Manchester, and both United and City were going for the title on the last day – 11 April 1968. At Old Trafford they were confident that they had the championship in the bag. Victory over visiting Sunderland would be enough to do it as long as City, ironically playing at the home of the Wearsiders' rivals Newcastle, did not win as well. Brown's Sunderland side had little to play for other than pride. But the team that performed in front of more than 62,000 at Old Trafford certainly had a tale to tell for the rest of their lives – Montgomery, Harvey, Todd, Hurley, Ashurst, Herd, Harris, Porterfield, Bruce Stuckey, Suggett and Mulhall. Amazingly, Sunderland took a 2–0 half-time lead against mighty United. The teenage Colin Suggett whipped home the first with a near-post flick, while the wily old Mulhall climbed unmarked to head home the second. But one small detail of the two goals tends to be lost in the mists of time. Right-winger Bruce

Stuckey had been one of McColl's last signings, a bargain £5,000 buy from Exeter City. McColl had made a special trip to watch Exeter only for the highly-rated 20-year-old to be sent off! Stuckey provided both right-wing crosses for Suggett and Mulhall to score that day and rob United of the First Division title. George Best did pull one back in the second half, but while Sunderland were winning against all the odds that afternoon, City were pulling off a sensational championship-clinching 4–3 victory at St James' Park!

The following season, Sunderland avoided the drop by just four points, and in the summer of 1969 'King' Charlie, Mulhall and Brand were all granted free transfers. Suggett, who had captained the club to FA Youth Cup glory in 1967, had established himself as a stylish striker with a keen eye for goal. But he found himself in a struggling side, and in July 1969 Brown sold him to West Bromwich for a not-insignificant £100,000. Suggett had scored 25 goals from 93 appearances and was the most expensive player ever to leave the North-East. With their star striker gone, Brown again turned to youth. Players such as Colin Todd, Bobby Kerr, Billy Hughes, Dennis Tueart, Mick McGiven, Richie Pitt, Bobby Park, John Lathan and Paddy Lowery were becoming familiar faces. But in 1969/70 Sunderland simply ran out of steam and were relegated on the final day of the season thanks to Chris Lawler's almost apologetic goal in a 1–0 win by Liverpool at Roker Park.

Former Arsenal and England striker Joe Baker, by now a shadow of his former self, had arrived from Nottingham Forest in a £30,000 deal and found the going tough. The quick-stepping forward made 24 appearances that season but managed just two goals. Baker, who died in October 2003, aged just 62, had been a great player in his international prime. But, like several players who arrived at Roker Park in the late 1960s, he was well past his sell-by date even though the crowd liked him because of his sheer endeavour, his ridiculously long sideburns and his white boots. He will probably best be remembered for his hat-trick against Charlton early the following season, but he had struggled to find the net since arriving on Wearside and, having scored 10 goals in 15 Second Division games, he made a sudden £12,000 return to his first club, Hibernian.

The team that was relegated for only the second time in the club's history, on 15 April 1970, consisted of Montgomery, Irwin, Harvey, Todd, Pitt, McGiven, Park, Kerr, Hughes, Harris and Tueart. The majestic Hurley, who had joined Bolton Wanderers just a year earlier, missed the wake. If he had not been granted a free transfer the summer before – it was seen as a reward for service in those days – Charlie would have still been around at the age of 33. But, having suffered relegation in 1958 and then waited another six years for the eventual return to the promised land, he would surely have found a second slip through the trapdoor just too much to stomach. Alan Brown had taken the club into the Second Division for the second time in his career. Yet that was not the end of his own personal misery. Sunderland finished in 21st place, one point adrift of Crystal Palace. The First Division's anchor club was Sheffield Wednesday, cast adrift by Brown just two and a half years earlier. But the long-suffering Sunderland supporters were disillusioned, feeling that only a miracle could turn things round. For that, they would have to wait another three years.

Alan Brown was a patient man. Known throughout the game for his strong belief in youth policies, he stuck to his guns at Sunderland. Now in his second spell with the club, the dark days of that first relegation 12 years previously were well behind him. It was true that he would go down in history as the manager who had taken Sunderland through the First Division trapdoor on not just one occasion, but two. But Brown did not panic as they prepared for life in the Second Division. He recalled:

> The previous season had been hard for us. But I still had to pay tribute to my team for the way they battled against eventual relegation. I knew that, back then, every single lad cared about the position the club found itself in. And I could say with all honesty that, despite everything, we managed to keep morale high. Team spirit was good, right up to the last game when we went down. In fact, I had never come across a team in such a position which displayed such goodwill to one another. It's never easy when you are losing, believe me. Life is always much easier when you are winning. But the boys who were in that relegated side had immense spirit, and I always knew that they would go on to produce better times for the club. In fact, I viewed it as a temporary setback. I knew the club would come bouncing back.

Brown was never one to mince his words. And on this occasion he spoke quite prophetically. As the 1970/71 season began to take shape, Brown was relying on players whose moment of FA Cup fame was still more than two years ahead of them. Montgomery, Dick Malone, Dave Watson, Pitt, Kerr, Hughes, Porterfield and Tueart all featured strongly during the first season back in the Second Division.

Watson, whom Brown signed as a centre-forward, was the club's first £100,000 buy. He came from Rotherham United and arrived in December 1970 as a virtual unknown from the lower reaches of the game. But Brown could always spot talent. Watson, the raw-boned centre-forward with an incredible leap and stunning heading ability, would earn 65 England caps, making Brown a very proud man. By then, however, he was Dave Watson the world-class centre-half. Brown had always sensed that in Watson, but, because of Sunderland's dire need at the time for an old-fashioned centre-forward, he was handed the No. 9 shirt.

'Alan Brown was a big influence on me,' said Watson. 'He was a very hard man and I learned a lot from his philosophy.' Watson was a giant of a man and perfectly built for a centre-half, but he spent the best part of two years as Sunderland's centre-forward and, in the main, they were wasted years for him. He had been a late arrival in the professional game and admitted:

> I had been playing for only four years and then I found that I had gone from electrician to £100,000 footballer. It was a lot of money for a player back then and to me it was a fairy story come true. Everything was big at Sunderland – the ground, the training grounds, the gymnasium and, of course, Alan Brown. He always treated me well.

'Signing Dave was a joy,' said Brown. 'I had never felt so elated since the day I had signed Charlie Hurley. Dave had been number one on my list for a while by the time that I had the money to buy him.'

Another new arrival that season was Dick Malone. A gangly defender who loved to attack, 'Tricky Dickie' cost Sunderland £30,000 and eventually became the regular right-back in place of Cec Irwin. Malone was often branded something of a buffoon during his early days with the club, mainly because many of his ridiculously long and loping runs down the right wing appeared to confuse himself as much as it did the opposition. But he quickly matured into a fine right-back and spent the bulk of his time at Roker Park as a huge crowd favourite.

Sunderland finished 13th in their first season back outside the top flight. It had not been the best of tilts at immediate promotion and, to make matters worse in the eyes of the fans, one of their all-time heroes was sold. Colin Todd, the England under-23 international wing-half who had matured into a fine centre-back alongside players such as Charlie Hurley, George Kinnell and Richie Pitt, cost Derby County £175,000 – then a record British fee for a half-back. But Todd's switch to the Baseball Ground was never a gamble. The wily Brian Clough, his former boss at Sunderland youth-team level, knew exactly how far Todd could go in the game and, as ever, he was proved right. Todd forged an outstanding central defensive partnership with Roy McFarland, picking up two First Division championship medals with Clough's dynamic Derby. Todd represented England 27 times and was widely regarded as one of the most cultured defenders of his era. It seemed unbelievable at the time that Brown could even contemplate parting with such a talent. But £175,000 was an enormous sum, and at the time he clearly felt that the club's immediate future would benefit greatly from such an influx of cash.

In fact, Todd had become desperate to quit Roker Park. The best young defender in the land bombarded the club with transfer requests until, in the end, he was allowed to leave. Todd said:

> I remember going to play in a youth tournament in Holland when I was 15. Alan Brown was the manager and took a great interest in me. I could see he was a tough disciplinarian and I didn't mind that. But I never realised that in five years' time I would be fighting Alan Brown to get away from Sunderland. When I was captain of the first team and we were struggling, I asked to be rid of the captaincy several times. I simply didn't feel that I had it in me to become a driving captain. That has never been my nature. But Alan Brown kept assuring me that I had hidden qualities as a leader. But then the club went into the Second Division and I kept putting in transfer requests. I decided that Sunderland in the Second Division was not good enough. I was single-minded about putting in those transfer requests. It was not something I liked doing, but it had to be done.

As soon as Todd was placed on the list, Clough pounced. With Todd gone, the veteran Martin Harvey was handed his familiar No. 4 shirt. The Northern Ireland international, given his big break by Brown back in the early 1960s, had been filling in as a left-back in place of Len Ashurst, one of just two outfield players to have clocked up more than 400 League games for Sunderland, the other having been Stan Anderson. Early in 1971, Ashurst finally left Roker to become player-manager at Hartlepool.

So, with Harvey back as Pitt's central defensive partner and players such as Bobby Park, Brian Chambers and Mick McGiven being given regular first-team football, Brown was steadily shaping yet another Sunderland side. Sadly, tragedy was to strike for Harvey the following season when he injured his back after scoring a rare goal in a 1–1 draw at Norwich in March 1972. The ever-reliable defender was just 30 and playing some of the best football of his career. But he was never to play another game following the injury at Carrow Road. Harvey had been an

Sunderland's squad for 1905/06 (left to right): back row, JJ Wilson (director), F Taylor (chairman), B Williams (trainer), Farquhar, Rhodes, Naisby, Watson, Barrie, Kyle (secretary-manager), S Wilson (vice-chairman); seated, Hogg, O'Donnell, Gemmell, McKenzie, Bridgett, Buckle, McConnell, F Foster (director).

Winger Billy Ellis, who made more than 200 appearances for Sunderland during the 1920s and was known for supplying 'many a dandy cross' for the legendary Charlie Buchan.

Soccer icon Charlie Buchan, who became Sunderland's leading marksman of all time with 209 goals to his name. He was an England international and later founded his own football magazine.

Sunderland's squad for 1928/29 (left to right): back row, AG Ferris (groundsman), Yorke, Clack, Hobson, Dempster, Scott, Ferguson, Staley, G Holley (coach); second row, E Birnie (assistant trainer), Haggan, Mitton, Parker, Gregory, Johnson, Gibson, Kasher, England, Poole, W Williams (trainer); third row, Young, Stephenson, Power, Best, Stannard, Buchan, R Marshall, Martin, Ellis, RH Kyle (secretary); front row, Marsden, Goldie, J Marshall, Black.

Sunderland's 1935/36 First Division championship-winning squad (left to right): back row, Urwin, McNab, Spuhler, Ferry, Saunders, Bell, Wilkinson; second row, Russell, Royston, Thorpe, Ainsley, Ives, McDowall, Scott, Middleton, Lockie, Burbanks; seated, J Cochrane (manager), Thomson, Johnston, Hall, Murray, Shaw, Clark, Hastings, A Reid (trainer); front row, Davis, Carter, Gurney, Goddard, Gallacher, Connor.

Raich Carter, one of Sunderland's all-time heroes who was born locally in Hendon. An England international, he skippered the club when they won the FA Cup for the first time in 1937.

The front cover of the 1937 FA Cup final programme when Sunderland beat Preston North End 3-1 at Wembley.

Sunderland's 1936/37 FA Cup winners (left to right): back row, Thomson, Johnston, Gorman, Mapson, Hall, McNab; seated, J Cochrane (manager), Carter, Gurney, Gallacher, A Reid (trainer); front, Duns, Burbanks.

Sunderland's club badge in 1936/37 when they won the FA Cup for the first time.

An Agreement made the ... day of *April* ... 19** between *George Cross* of *Sunderland* in the County of *Durham* ...

Part of Sunderland winger and Wembley goalscorer Eddie Burbanks' contract with the club for the ill-fated 1939/40 season.

Sunderland's squad for 1952/53 (left to right): back row, Hall, Watson, Kirtley, Mapson, Threadgold, McNeill, Walsh, Reynolds, Bingham; front row, Shackleton, T Wright, Hedley, Ford, Stelling, A Wright, Hudgell.

Len Shackleton, Sunderland's 'Clown Prince of Soccer' whose box of magic tricks bamboozled opponents and, unfortunately for him, the England selectors too!

Ivor Broadis, an outstanding inside-forward of his day and a future England international when he joined Sunderland. He spent many an afternoon playing one-a-side football against the legendary Bill Shankly with old chimney pots for goals.
Picture, The Sunderland Echo

Brian Clough, who had an astonishing record of scoring 63 goals in just 74 games for Sunderland before a knee injury ended his career prematurely.

Johnny Crossan, Sunderland's goalscoring Northern Ireland international inside-forward who was said to have used Mickey Spillane detective novels as shinpads.

Sunderland's stylish and immensely-popular wing-half Stan Anderson, who made 447 appearances for the club. An England international, he was stunned when manager Alan Brown transferred him to arch rivals Newcastle United during the 1963/64 promotion season. Picture, The Sunderland Echo.

Charlie Hurley leads newly-promoted Sunderland out before a 3-1 defeat at Chelsea on 29 August 1964. Behind him are Cec Irwin (left) and Len Ashurst with the heads of 15-year-old goalkeeper Derek Forster and Brian Usher also visible.

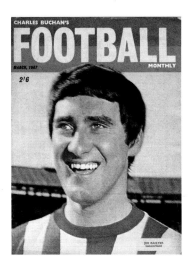

Two Sunderland favourites for the price of one – Jim Baxter poses on the front cover of Charles Buchan's football monthly.

An early shot of Ian McColl – with hair! The former Sunderland manager whose 2¹/₂ - year spell in charge of Sunderland was sandwiched between Alan Brown's two stints at the helm.

Sunderland's Player of the Century Charlie Hurley is condemned to a reserve line-up against Ashington at Roker Park in October 1966 – an all-too-familiar occurrence during Ian McColl's reign as manager.

Sunderland line up before the start of the 1967/68 season (left to right): back row, Montgomery, Ashurst, Todd, Baxter, Kerr, Forster; middle row, Heslop, Suggett, Gauden, Hughes, Shoulder, Irwin, Hurley; front row, Harvey, Kinnell, Mulhall, O'Hare, Parke, Herd, Martin.

CHARLIE

ROKER PARK   SUNDERLAND

TESTIMONIAL
MATCH

WEDNESDAY, 4th OCTOBER, 1967

SOUVENIR PROGRAMME   1/-

YOUR LUCKY PROGRAMME NO. IS

Nọ   8075

HURLEY

The front cover of the programme for Charlie Hurley's testimonial match on 4 October 1967.

Jimmy Montgomery, the legendary
Sunderland goalkeeper who made a
record-breaking 623 first-team
appearances for the club.

George Kinnell, Sunderland's tough-guy
centre-half and second cousin of Jim
Baxter who spent 25 years working
offshore after retiring from the game.

Sunderland train on the beach at 'The Cat and Dog Steps' in the late 1960s. Jimmy
Montgomery saves from George Mulhall as youngsters Colin Suggett (left) and Billy
Hughes look on.

Alan Brown, the only person to manage Sunderland twice. His players either loved him or loathed him, but few have been able to forget him. Picture, The Sunderland Echo.

The front cover of the 1973 FA Cup final programme when Sunderland beat Leeds United 1-0 at Wembley.

Sunderland's captain Bobby Kerr lifts the FA Cup aloft in 1973, watched by a grinning Jimmy Montgomery, whose amazing double save had played such a major part in their Wembley triumph.

Probably Sunderland's all-time golden goal as Ian Porterfield uses his less-favoured right foot to smash the ball into Leeds United's net and carve the club's name in FA Cup folklore with a fairy-tale 1-0 win at Wembley on 5 May 1973.

Sunderland's manager Bob Stokoe, complete with trademark trilby, cannot disguise his joy as he hugs FA Cup winners Dennis Tueart (left) and Ian Porterfield after the 1973 Wembley triumph.

Sunderland's 1972/73 FA Cup winners (left to right): A Cox (coach), Halom, Malone, Montgomery, Pitt, Watson, R Stokoe (manager); front row, Young, Guthrie, Hughes, Kerr, Tueart, Porterfield, Horswill.

Gary Rowell, the Seaham-born forward who became Sunderland's first player since Len Shackleton to score more than 100 goals for the club. Picture, The Sunderland Echo

Sunderland's dashing striker Marco Gabbiadini, who became a huge crowd favourite after manager Denis Smith had paid York City £80,000 for him. Nicknamed 'Marco Goalo,' Gabbiadini was sold to Crystal Palace six years later for £1.8m. Picture, The Sunderland Echo

Prolific marksman Kevin Phillips, who set a Sunderland record of scoring in seven successive games in 1997/98. He became an England international and his partnership with Niall Quinn played a big part in the club establishing themselves in the FA Premiership's top 10. Picture, The Sunderland Echo

Kevin Ball, the former Sunderland skipper whose never-say-die attitude and leadership qualities endeared him to the fans. He captained the 1999 First Division championship-winning side and more recently joined the club's backroom staff.
Picture, The Sunderland Echo

Alan Brown man through and through, even though McColl had also featured him strongly, albeit as a left-back. Brown had planned on the likeable Harvey providing much-needed experience for the youngsters around him, but unfortunately he was never given the opportunity to play on. If he could have avoided the injury, Harvey would surely have picked up an FA Cup winners' medal at Wembley a year later – and probably as skipper.

Serious injuries to key players were beginning to cost Brown dearly. On the subject of cruel career-ending blows to talented footballers, Sunderland had lost the services of young midfield player Bobby Park when he broke a leg in the opening game of the 1971/72 season. Less than 10,000 turned up to watch Sunderland and Birmingham draw 1–1 in a rain-soaked match that, arguably, should never have started. If it had been postponed or maybe even abandoned at an appropriate moment, the richly talented Park might never have been injured and might well have gone on to great things. As it was, the young Scot with the delightful left foot never kicked another ball in earnest. The frail-looking midfielder had played 57 games for Sunderland and was undoubtedly destined for a great career. But that August day in 1971 marked the end for him at the age of just 19.

Brown, meanwhile, continued to ring the changes. In came even more youngsters, such as full-backs Keith Coleman and Joe Bolton, yet more products of the club's highly successful youth system. And there was also a shock debut for a young flame-haired and naturally fiery defender from Annfield Plain, Micky Horswill, who burst onto the first-team scene as a confident young man sporting the then-trendy red boots. Horswill had made rapid progress through the youth system after joining the club on a weekly training basis. But Brown had spotted something combative in him that would eventually hit the jackpot a further year down the line. Micky Horswill's Sunderland career was about to take off in style.

The injury to Harvey gave Horswill his chance. The versatile Brian Chambers had filled in initially, but then Brown elevated the unknown Horswill without a second thought. Horswill said:

I would have died for Alan Brown. When he signed young lads, they always went to the club. But he actually came to my house to sign me, and I can still remember it perfectly clearly to this day. I'd heard that Sunderland were going to watch me in a cup final for Stanley Boys against Newcastle Boys. I went over to take a throw-in and saw Alan Brown standing there. He threw me the ball, but then walked around the ground and straight out. I thought that was it – I had blown my chance. But Sunderland's scout Charlie Ferguson saw me and told me that Mr Brown would be coming round to my house later that night. I rushed home and waited there for a couple of hours. But then he turned up and came to the back door. He offered me £8 a week and warned me to do as I was told from then on. In fact, he turned to my dad Eric and said, 'You've just lost a son because I'm his father from now on!' It was great at Sunderland. I was just a scruffy lad from Annfield Plain who wanted to play football. I became captain of the youth team and I remember being asked to travel with the first team to Preston in 1972. I thought I was just going for the experience and expected to be the kit boy. But then, just 45 minutes before kick-off, Alan Brown asked to see me and said that I had done well since joining the club and that I was going to play that night. I didn't know what to say. I was speechless.

Horswill played in the last seven games of the season as Sunderland finished fifth. It had not been a great season, and the crowds backed that up. Roker Park was averaging gates of about 14,000 when Horswill was busy staking his claim, but still Brown's youngsters kept coming off the production line. Many of the talented teenagers were forcing their way into the first team virtually unnoticed as supporters looked to results and league tables to see where the club was going under his leadership. But one rookie striker certainly hit the headlines when he was handed his debut during 1971/72. Jimmy 'Chico' Hamilton was just 16 years and 103 days old when he became the club's youngest outfield player. The unknown Hamilton was named as substitute for Preston's visit on 25 September 1971. And, with the game delicately poised at 3–3, Brown decided to throw the youngster in at the deep end and create a piece of club history. Hamilton did not need a second invitation. The 16-year-old Scot with the sweet left foot did not look the type of forward whose heading ability was going to worry too many defences. But Hamilton climbed high at the far post to head home a late winner and knock himself out against the woodwork at the same time!

It was a sensational strike by the kid whose nickname came from the Aston Villa star of the day, Ian 'Chico' Hamilton. But it was definitely not a day to remember for the former Sunderland favourite Jimmy McNab. McNab, by now a Preston stalwart, was the regular left-back at the time and was caught off-guard, allowing the hungry Hamilton to nip in.

But despite all Brown's determined efforts to make amends for a second relegation and lead the club back into the big time, Sunderland were beginning to tread water. Up front the partnership of Dave Watson and John Lathan looked promising, and in wingers Billy Hughes and Dennis Tueart there was more than an ample supply of flair. But by November 1972 struggling Sunderland had won just four games. The directors were beginning to come under increasing pressure from the fans. Following a goalless draw at home to Fulham on 28 October, Brown was sacked. As is so typical in football, the Sunderland boss had been given a vote of confidence by chairman Keith Collings shortly before the start of the season: 'Alan leads by example. We have the utmost faith in him making this club great again. There's a great spirit in the club and we are looking forward to the future.'

Sadly, the future for Brown was looking bleak in reality. He was relieved of his duties on 5 November, leaving the club under the caretaker management of coach and former Sunderland favourite Billy Elliott. Brown mused:

> My dismissal didn't really come as a surprise. You read the signs, and the politics of the situation were such that I knew it would be inevitable in the end. But, if I had been allowed to stay, I think I would have taken the club back into the First Division. I had to sell in order to buy and also make a profit. I sold Colin Todd and Colin Suggett for more than £250,000 and spent half that amount on two players. I had been faced with another rebuilding job, and it was finished apart from the topping-off when I was sacked.

Brown kept himself fit after being sacked. The previous year he had completed the Pennine Way in 12½ days, carrying 35lb in weight, and made a film of it. This time his schedule was 'six to ten miles a day, walking and running'. And, he insisted defiantly, 'I have been a manager-coach all my life. I suppose it would be hard convincing people that I could outrun and outwork any trainers I have ever worked with, but I still can.'

Bobby Kerr said of Brown's second stint in charge:

> Some of us knew Alan from his first spell with the club. I was only a kid, but he gave me my apprenticeship when I was 15. It was a case of 'You will' and 'You won't,' but we all abided by his rules. In fact, talk about abiding by rules, Browny would not let anyone wear jeans, and to this day I can't bring myself to wear a pair of them! He created that in me and the mentality has never left me. You couldn't have a beard or even a moustache. Look at everyone who played under Browny at Sunderland and you won't see a

moustache. Jimmy McNab never had one at Sunderland, but he soon grew one when he went to Preston. It was the same for me, too. Browny left after his second spell and I grew a moustache straight away. I couldn't have done it beforehand!

And he was tough. I was recovering from breaking my leg the second time when he was back as manager. We were training at Cleadon and the rest of the lads had all gone home. But Alan told me that I would be cutting the grass as part of my recuperation while he would do some tidying up himself. So, there I was, with this great big mower, doing as I was told, and I saw Browny wade into this enormous patch of nettles and start pulling the whole lot out with his bare hands – not a moment of pain, not a squeal, nothing. That's what the man was like. I told the lads about this the next day, and I was telling Jimmy McNab about the place where Browny waded into the trees to pick the nettles. But then Jim told me that he and some of the older professionals had been made to plant those trees in the first place!

It was about that time that the club was having a new gym built at Washington, too, and we thought we would be training up there soon, inside the smart new place which was three-quarters the size of a football pitch. We were up there all right, but Alan Brown had us laying the concrete paths after training! There we were, in sandshoes, waiting for the next batch of ready-mix to be delivered so that we could actually build the pathways. Cec Irwin and Colin Symm ended up with cement burns, but Browny didn't seem to care. I suppose at the time a lot of us probably thought of him as some sort of nutter. But then you speak to a lot of the lads who have gone on to manage or coach themselves and they will tell you how good his ideas were and what a good coach he was.

But I think he lacked man management. By that I mean he treated everyone the same. He would talk to Charlie Hurley in exactly the same way as he would talk to me or another youngster. Sometimes he would talk to Charlie as if he was a kid. I remember before one home game that Browny told George Mulhall that he wanted to see white lines on his boots at halftime. In other words, he didn't want George to leave that left-hand touchline. But after 20 minutes George realised he wasn't getting the ball and started coming inside for it. That was enough for Browny. He came running down from the directors' box and took George off – and the game was just 20 minutes old!

As Brown left Roker Park for the last time, the club began its search for a suitable successor. And it did not take them long to find their man. He was a Northumbrian, a former Newcastle United star and a virtual sworn enemy of Sunderland legend Brian Clough. But none of that was going to stop Keith Collings and his board from appointing Bob Stokoe as manager on 27 November 1972. History was now just around the corner.

6

FAIRY TALES REALLY DO COME TRUE!

Dave Watson was still a centre-forward and, as powerful No. 9s went, an impressive one. But the wily Billy Elliott had played with the best during his own heyday and knew a natural centre-half when he saw one. It was thus Sunderland's caretaker manager Elliott – not new manager Bob Stokoe – who changed the destiny of a former electrician who was soon to become one of England's finest post-war stoppers. Elliott's first of four games in charge was at home to Aston Villa a week after the sacking of Alan Brown in November 1972. Fewer than 12,000 had turned up at Roker Park to watch Brown's final match as Sunderland manager, but now almost 19,000 trooped in to see what difference a change of face would make. The supporters were greeted by two major changes. Firstly, Billy Hughes, who had been in and out of Brown's line-ups after asking for a move, was recalled. And secondly, Brian Chambers was brought in from the cold to play in the centre of midfield. John Lathan and Mick McGiven were dropped.

Hughes and Bobby Kerr both scored in an entertaining 2–2 draw, and the spirits of long-suffering supporters were lifted. Now Elliott had a week to plan for the next game, a derby encounter at Carlisle United. Sunderland lost 4–3, but it was not the scoreline that was the major talking-point, but a further tactical switch by Elliott. Watson was handed the No. 5 shirt and told that Micky Horswill would partner him in the centre of defence. Replacing Watson at centre-forward was young Jimmy Hamilton, and suddenly the entire structure of the side looked different. Elliott recalled:

> Dave Watson was always going to be an outstanding centre-half. In fact, it was not long after I moved him into that position that we went on the FA Cup run. I said at the time that Dave was a better player than John Charles. I was sure he would get a chance in the England team because there was no-one else to touch him then, not even Roy McFarland. And, of course, he did get his chance and went on to pick up 65 caps!

134

A 1–1 draw at home to Hull City followed, with Lathan recalled and scoring. Then Elliott's men went down 1–0 at Bristol City before Stokoe finally breezed in and took hold of the reins. Perhaps understandably, Stokoe kept faith with Elliott's final selection for his own first game in charge. The side which lost 1–0 at home to Burnley on 2 December 1972 included Jim Montgomery, Dick Malone, Keith Coleman, Horswill, Watson, Ian Porterfield, Bobby Kerr, Billy Hughes, Lathan, Chambers and Dennis Tueart. As it happened, eight of that line-up would find themselves defying all the odds to pick up FA Cup-winners' medals just five months later. But, for now, it was climbing up the Second Division that mattered to Stokoe.

He brought a new lease of life to the club. Although most of the players had admired Alan Brown, many of them had felt stifled on the field. Brown had always been a stickler for discipline and detail, and a clearly talented Sunderland team had often lacked the flair many thought they ought to have displayed. Stokoe brought something else with him, too. One of his first acts as manager was to ditch the club's white shorts – introduced by Brown in 1961 – and replace them with the more traditional black. Younger fans found it strange at first, but to those who could remember The Bank of England team and beyond, it represented a welcome return to old-fashioned club values. It was a small yet clever piece of PR by the new man and it sent out the important message that a new era was dawning.

Stokoe, who became a Wearside legend long before his death in 2004, at the age of 73, tended to let players off the lead. Suddenly there was a cavalier style to Sunderland's play. It was almost as if some first-teamers were finally coming out of their shells – and the free-flowing football worked! The new manager wasted no time in signing four new players – although, if one of them had not lasted a mere 45 minutes in a Sunderland shirt, the name of the hugely popular Vic Halom might never have entered Wearside folklore. The first to arrive in a bargain-priced £30,000 double deal from Stokoe's former club Newcastle United were Ron Guthrie and David Young. Stokoe had sensed that youngsters Joe Bolton and Keith Coleman needed to step aside in favour of a more experienced left-back, and that man was Guthrie.

Young, on the other hand, was a versatile defender who – as with Guthrie – had flitted in and out of Newcastle's side for several seasons. Stokoe saw him as the perfect foil for Watson although, in practice, Richie Pitt made the slot his own during Stokoe's early months at the helm. The third new arrival was something of a bolt out of the blue. He was John 'Yogi Bear' Hughes, the former Glasgow Celtic and Scotland forward, whose younger brother Billy was already a Sunderland striker.

Hughes senior had left Parkhead for Crystal Palace and was in the twilight of his career when Stokoe paid £30,000 for his services. The media lapped it up. Here was the great John Hughes set to play alongside his brother, 'Billy the Kid', for the first time. And it looked as if it might be pure theatre at Roker as almost 23,000 turned up to watch the Hughes boys make their historic bow at home to Millwall. John was still only 29 and great things were expected of him. But sadly the famous charging runs and powerful shooting were consigned to the history books. Hughes picked up a knee injury in the third minute of a 2–0 win and never played again.

Stokoe's response was immediate. Determined that his side needed a strong No. 9 following Watson's switch to defence, he raided Luton Town in another £30,000 swoop. This time the target was Vic Halom, a player Stokoe had nurtured as a youngster when they had been together at Charlton Athletic. Halom was a barrel-chested centre-forward from the old school. He played the game with a smile on his face and was never afraid to dish out stick as well as take it. He was an instant hit with the Sunderland crowd and delighted in ploughing a lone furrow down the middle, with Hughes and Tueart providing the all-important width. Halom's home debut came in the 4–0 mauling of North-East rivals Middlesbrough, and Halom began his love affair with the Fulwell End by joining Hughes, Tueart and Horswill on the scoresheet. The comprehensive win came in February 1973, but there was something a lot more significant about it other than the fact that it was a derby triumph – it was the first time that Stokoe assembled the 11 players whose lives would have changed forever by the end of the season. In Stokoe's words:

What was to come a few months later was still beyond the wildest dreams of all of us. I had jumped at the chance of returning to the North-East from Blackpool and managing a club the size of Sunderland. Like many other people, I knew of their past and of their tradition. I also knew that they had to be lifted up and carried forward. They were slumbering at the time and something was needed to awaken the place. We all know what did the awakening in the end – and that was only five months after I went there! But it was all to do with the players and how they responded to me as well as to each other. They were a great set of lads and really they made it easy for me. We had players such as Monty, who was still absolutely top-class and one of the best goalkeepers in the land, and in big

136

Dave Watson we had a centre-half who was quite obviously destined for great things. I had little Bobby Kerr in there as my captain, running non-stop and organising all the time. Bobby had been a great right-winger as a kid, but by then he was a little maestro, a little general. I called Bobby my little general because that's exactly what he was on the field. He understood what was needed and what was wanted of every player. He was a gem.

Billy and Dennis were also 'on fire' at that time. Billy had been on the transfer list, but came off it when I arrived and I was delighted about that. The two of them were still playing their football in the Second Division, and Dennis was yet to go on to bigger things, including England caps. But you could see that their directness, their speed, their flair and their goalscoring abilities were going to be enormous pluses at Sunderland. And then we had Vic at centre-forward. It turned out that Vic was the final piece in the jigsaw as far as the FA Cup win was concerned and he was such a lovely lad. We needed someone up there to hold things up and Vic had been doing that job for years. Who knows what might have happened if John Hughes had not been forced to retire? But that's football for you. One man's misfortune is so often another man's gain.

By the time that Halom arrived at Roker, Stokoe had guided his players into the fifth round of the FA Cup. It had taken replays against both Notts County and Charlie Hurley's Reading to make such progress and, because of a lack of firepower, Watson had been moved back to centre-forward for the fourth-round replay at Reading. He scored, too, with Kerr and Tueart adding the others in a 3–1 midweek win. But there had been some sticky moments against both County and Reading.

It all began on 13 January with a third-round trip to Meadow Lane. Watson, playing against his former club, grabbed a late equaliser to force a Roker replay in front of more than 30,000 – a bumper crowd for a side whose form had been attracting gates of less than half that. And Watson scored again, with Tueart grabbing the other in a comfortable 2–0 win. That led to the fourth-round visit of Reading and an incredible reception for Hurley. The only trouble was that Hurley and his players seemed to respond to the atmosphere, and Tueart's strike in a 1–1 draw paved the way for a replay at Elm Park.

Sunderland had little trouble in finishing off the job with emergency striker Watson scoring yet again, as did Tueart. Kerr added the other in a 3–1 win. By now, Cup fever was gradually beginning to grip Wearside. In truth, Sunderland had struggled to knock out two mediocre sides and both at the second attempt. Yet that seemed to count for little when Stokoe's men were drawn away to First Division giants Manchester City in the fifth round. This was the Manchester City era of Mike Summerbee, Colin Bell, Francis Lee and Rodney Marsh. Second Division Sunderland were meant to be in for a thrashing, and almost 52,000 fans crammed into Maine Road to witness what was expected to be a comfortable victory for the big-time glamour boys. But Sunderland had other ideas, although they took time to settle and Stokoe admitted: 'I thought that I would have to throw another ball on the pitch for us to get a kick.' But goals from Horswill, now a midfield terrier, and a supreme solo effort from the dashing Hughes, put the underdogs 2–1 up. Sadly, for the Wearsiders, the experienced Montgomery punched a left-wing corner into his own net while under extreme near-post pressure, and victory was snatched from their grasp.

The two previous rounds had produced replays, so what would be so difficult about this one? That at least was what the more optimistic members of Sunderland's fan-base were counting on – and how right they were! Roker Park had become used to attracting gates of less than 15,000 when City came to town on a cold February night in 1973, so an awesome atmosphere was generated by an incredible attendance of 51,872. And, as many fans would recount over the years, it would be impossible to describe the feeling of sheer electricity pumping through the famous old stadium to those who were not there. Sunderland simply took it all in their stride. It was as if a new kind of self-belief and supreme confidence had flooded their veins. City were demolished by two goals from Hughes and an unbelievable Fulwell End sizzler from new crowd favourite Halom. All of a sudden, the sixth round beckoned. Sunderland were a club on a roll. Halom recalled:

What a match! We murdered them. After all the ballyhoo that City would put four past us, it was tremendously satisfying to see my goal fly in. It was probably the best goal of my career and it went like a rocket from the moment it left my boot. It gave Joe Corrigan no chance whatsoever. Billy Hughes got another for us, and then there was a difficult stage when Francis Lee pulled one back. But then Billy got a second. What a night!

Second Division rivals Luton, Halom's old club, were next on the agenda. Having scaled the dizzy heights of the fifth round, few feared that Luton were capable of putting the lid on Sunderland's FA Cup run. And defenders Watson – with his fourth FA Cup goal – and Guthrie duly stole the glory on quarter-final day when 53,151 packed Roker to see them march into the last four. Things were beginning to get serious and Watson revealed: 'I had a dream that I was going to score against Luton, but I kept quiet about it. When the ball came across from the corner, I knew that would be it.' It was the opposite of Clem Stephenson's dream that came true in 1913 when Sunderland lost in the final against Aston Villa.

With the semi-finals beckoning for the first time since 1956, Sunderland fans were not quite sure whether they were in a state of shock or euphoria. Yet there comes a time, probably in the history of most clubs, when supporters simply sense that this is going to be their moment. The mighty Arsenal, Double winners just two years earlier, were Sunderland's opponents at Hillsborough, while Don Revie's Leeds United had been pitted against Wolverhampton Wanderers.

Stokoe knew his best team by now. And an injury-free run allowed him to stick with his first-choice 11. The fact that Halom scored early in the first half following a fumble by centre-half Jeff Blockley rocked the Gunners and handed the underdogs a surprise momentum. And after Hughes had made it two after the break with a clever looping header, Hillsborough belonged to Sunderland. Charlie George did pull a goal back with a low drive, but Sunderland, playing in all white, held on for a historic victory. It was very much a team triumph, with Watson and Pitt immense at the back and Hughes and Tueart pulling Arsenal's defence wide at every opportunity.

But at the hub of the amazing win was a young midfield man still in his first full season as a regular. Micky Horswill put in a man-of-the-match performance to snuff out the danger expected to emanate from Arsenal and England midfield man Alan Ball, and on that pivotal battle in the centre of the park Stokoe's braves built their valiant victory. The Arsenal fans gone from the stadium, Hillsborough remained a sea of red and white for what seemed like hours. The Sunderland players saluted their supporters, but not one of them was going to leave until Stokoe had reappeared from the tunnel to take his own bow. It was a very special moment for a club whose last FA Cup final appearance had been in 1937.

Many still believe that the raw emotion of winning an FA Cup semi-final as a Second Division club and knowing therefore that the final was to come was somehow more nerve-tingling than the eventual triumph itself. Stokoe recalled the win over Arsenal:

Obviously we weren't fancied against them, but they had said the same about us against Manchester City. They were the big team with the big names, but anything is possible on a given day. We outfought them, out-thought them and – in the end – outplayed them. They must have expected us to have a go. After all, semi-finals are not for sitting back. But Vic's early goal seemed to knock the stuffing out of them, and they couldn't cope with Dennis and Billy running at them all day long.

It was an amazing turnaround for Sunderland, and for their new manager in particular. Stokoe said:

I had been sacked by Charlton six years earlier and had battled my way back into the game as manager of Rochdale. That little club handed me a passport back into the game and I never forgot that. Then it was off to Carlisle and Blackpool. Every time I left those clubs, I did so of my own accord and to better myself. I had not been able to say 'no' to the Sunderland offer, but never in my wildest dreams did I expect to be talking about us going into the FA Cup final to play Leeds just five months after arriving at the club. It seemed crazy, unbelievable. But in many ways, it wasn't either of those things. I had inherited a great bunch of players, who just needed to be allowed to express themselves a bit more. I added one or two, not many, and that helped. But we enjoyed every minute of that Cup run. And, if there were any trick or magic to it, it was just that we lapped it up and always made sure the pressure was on sides such as City, Arsenal and Leeds. We didn't feel any pressure. The players were laughing all the time. Billy Hughes had a laughing-box that he would set off at the most ridiculous times and that would relieve any slight tension we were feeling. Later, after the final, someone referred to us as the team who laughed their way all the way to the FA Cup. There was an awful lot of hard graft in there, too, and some momentous displays from the players. But, yes, there was probably a lot of truth in that comment, too.

The date of 5 May 1973 is one that no Sunderland fan will ever be able to erase from the memory. It was the day that football was the winner. It was the day that the underdog triumphed over the odds-on favourite in the world's best-loved and most traditional cup final. It was the day that Wearside wept with tears of joy. Ian Porterfield's 32nd-minute strike with his so-called wrong foot – his right – sent shock waves reverberating through the football world.

The mighty Leeds, built by former Sunderland captain Don Revie and by now one of the greatest club sides, were widely expected to rattle up a record FA Cup final victory over the Second Division upstarts. But sometimes miracles really can happen in sport. Stokoe had revelled in the pre-match build-up, announcing that he would not stand for Revie 'refereeing' the final. The press loved it and, understandably, anyone anywhere who was not a Leeds supporter was always going to become an adopted Wearsider for the day. Sunderland's players gave every last ounce and more as Billy Bremner and Johnny Giles were blunted in their increasingly desperate attempts to provide the ammunition for star strikers Allan Clarke and Mick Jones.

But there was one pivotal moment in the game – one piece of blinding genius that would send out a specific signal to Sunderland's players and fans alike that now they simply could not be beaten. The magical moment belonged to long-serving goalkeeper Jim Montgomery. It had been very much backs-to-the-wall stuff for Sunderland when Leeds' full-back Trevor Cherry found himself so far forward and in so much space that he looked a certain scorer with a diving header. The header alone would have been enough to beat most goalkeepers. But Monty, not always at his best with long-range efforts, was the master of the reflex save. He somehow managed to paw away the England international's header, only to knock the rebound into the path of a grateful Peter Lorimer, who was reckoned to have the hardest shot in British football and was not prone to missing gaping nets from a few yards. Striking what he assumed to be the all-important equaliser with his famous right boot, Lorimer was already raising an arm in celebration when the unimaginable happened. Montgomery, at this stage flat out on the ground, threw himself upwards and, with a breathtaking, panther-like reaction, flicked Lorimer's goal-bound drive onto the underside of the bar. Sunderland supporters looked away as Lorimer unleashed his shot. Even BBC commentator David Coleman announced to millions at the time: 'And Lorimer makes it 1–1…no!'

Everyone saw Lorimer hit it, and thousands of those sporting the red and white of Sunderland could not bear to look. They did not need their faces rubbing in it as Leeds finally made the breakthrough that was expected of them. What an irony it was, then, that those who turned away missed *the* FA Cup final save of all time! Monty's magnificent double denial had, in effect, won the Cup for the Wearsiders. If Leeds could not score via Cherry and Lorimer in the space of a single second, then surely they would never score at all.

With one final piece of inspiration drawn from their goalkeeper,

Stokoe's heroes found added heart and extra legs. The FA Cup was theirs, and Wembley went wild with delight. The pictures of a jubilant Stokoe sprinting onto the pitch in his trademark raincoat and trilby, and racing across to hug Montgomery, whose grin was by now as wide as the River Wear, will never be removed from the annals of Wembley's FA Cup history. Sunderland had done it: they had become the first Second Divison club to lift the trophy since West Bromwich Albion in 1935. Stokoe insisted that he would never experience anything like it ever again: 'It was just a one-off – a day when the underdog won and so did the game. I think Sunderland warmed millions of hearts that day.' He had worked with coaches Arthur Cox and Billy Elliott alongside him that season and Elliott recalled:

> We had been dismissed as mere 'scrubbers' before the final because we were playing the mighty Leeds. But sometimes you can rise to the occasion and that's what happened that day. We spoke to the players before the game about the little teams which had overcome the giants and we told them that there was no reason why they could not repeat that. If a team can put in that little extra on a day when its opponents are not quite up for it, you can beat anyone. And, as a Bradford lad, beating Leeds that day was one of the highlights of my career – a day I shall never forget.

And Dave Watson, whose own Cup-final performance was absolutely outstanding, remembered: 'Winning the Cup that day was one of the greatest moments in my career. It was a fairy tale for everyone concerned because we were simply not expected to win. But we threw ourselves in front of every ball, played good football and worked for each other.' Micky Horswill, again an immense force as a ball-winning midfield man, was the youngest member of the side at 20, and explained:

> Bob Stokoe had moved me from a defender to a midfield player. I had been brought up as a defender and had never thought of myself as a midfield player, but it did me the world of good. I would run all day and cover for people such as Bobby Kerr, Ian Porterfield and Dennis Tueart. That day in 1973 had to be the highlight of my career – in fact, I'm still living on it all these years later. I don't suppose I appreciated it at the time, but it's probably given me half of what I have now because it was so special. When I played football with a tennis ball in the shed at home, getting to the FA Cup final had always been my dream. I had always wondered what it would be like to go up those stairs for the Cup,

142

but I can't even remember it! It was such a big day that I can hardly remember any of it. But afterwards Dave Watson and I took a bottle of champagne each and went back into an empty stadium to drink it out of red and white plastic bowler hats that the fans had bought for the day. There wasn't another soul inside the ground and we never spoke a word. We just looked round and took it all in. I had passion for my local club and a sparkle and enthusiasm for the FA Cup. It was an incredible experience.

And match-winner Porterfield, a player who at the time had tasted both the ups and downs of the game during his six years with the club, insisted:

The special thing for me was the collective impact it had on the people of Sunderland. They have a great passion for football, and that was such a great day. The highlight was the camaraderie between the supporters and the atmosphere in the stadium. I think we had great self-belief, from Bob Stokoe down to us all. It was epitomised by Jim Montgomery's great double save, probably as good a save as you'll ever see in a cup final.

Monty has always remained typically immodest about *that* save:

It was a mixture of everything I knew – all thrown into one moment. Yes, I was on the ground when Peter Lorimer struck it, but I just thought to myself that I had to have a go for it. It worked, but the funny thing was that I never realised at the time what I had done. Dick Malone was out on the right by now and the ball was going out for a throw-in. You had to adjust yourself accordingly for the next piece of action. Leeds were coming at us all the time at that stage, and you didn't have any time to think about any saves you might have just made. It wasn't until Bob came running across the pitch to hug me after the final whistle that I realised something was going on. And then I can remember celebrating in the dressing-room with the obligatory bottle of milk when the press wanted me to go out and talk about the save. Then I watched it on the monitors for the first time and talked them through it. All I could say was that I had done my best to throw myself at the line of the ball. Obviously everyone still wants to talk to me about it to this day. But I am happy to do that. Why shouldn't I be? It was a special day for Sunderland Football Club.

Bob had come in and let the players express themselves.

Remember that nine of the 11 on that day had played under Alan Brown, so you could argue that it was Browny's team who won the FA Cup. But of course, in reality, it wasn't. Bob came in and put his own mark on things. It was just a one-off occasion, and we even caught the BBC off-guard. They clearly hadn't expected to be visiting the Sunderland team's hotel that night for the celebrations, so they had to adjust their plans.

And Monty revealed: 'After the banquet, the players were not quite sure what to do with themselves, so we found ourselves sitting in a Wimpy Bar somewhere in London in the small hours of the morning eating burgers. You couldn't imagine that happening to players in this day and age!'

Watching the match had been Raich Carter, Bobby Gurney and Eddie Burbanks, the goalscorers in Sunderland's first FA Cup final triumph in 1937. Members of that great team had also been invited to join the next great team in the after-match celebrations. Burbanks' wife Joyce recalled:

We got an invitation to the 1973 FA Cup final, and it was a great day. The whole occasion was wonderful from start to finish, especially because so many people recognised Eddie. There was a reception in London at the Park Lane Hotel, which was a sumptuous place, and the Alan Price Set supplied the entertainment. Everybody had a lot to drink, but nobody was drunk and it finished at four in the morning. I can remember Bobby Kerr going round the ballroom. He just kept pouring drinks and even asked the directors what they wanted!

Captain Kerr, in fact, had found some poetic justice in the fairy-tale Wembley win. Six years earlier, as a young right-winger, his leg had been broken in a challenge with Norman Hunter. Now, against all the odds, the tiny Scot was holding the FA Cup aloft while Hunter and the rest of Revie's shell-shocked players trooped dejectedly from the pitch. He recalled:

The day and the lifting of the Cup were all something of a haze at the time. But it's all pretty clear now because everyone still wants to talk about it more than 30 years later. I don't mind that at all, though, because, even if Sunderland were to win the Cup again some day, it would just never be the same. We had a great team and we did it from the Second Division against the mighty Leeds. We were in the right place at the right time, but we could play.

And, on top of that, we stopped Leeds from playing. No-one can ever take those memories away from me.

Naturally enough, there was a homecoming to end all homecomings and, for some of Stokoe's heroes, life would never be the same again. But football had to go on and, after all, the FA Cup winners were still a Second Division side. Promotion had to be the aim from now on. When the 1973/74 season began, the Wembley fairy tale needed to be edged ever so gently into the background.

The new season was always going to be difficult in the wake of the wondrous win at Wembley. And in truth, players and fans alike began the campaign knowing that changes would be inevitable. Stokoe kicked off the season with one change from his FA Cup Final line-up. Horswill was suspended after being sent off during the final game of the season, a surprise 3–0 home defeat by Queen's Park Rangers after the final. That handed the versatile Mick McGiven a brief chance to reclaim a regular place, although he failed to make the most of it and joined West Ham United soon afterwards. The season did not turn out as planned. Sunderland finished in sixth place for the second year in succession, and some of the expected changes had been a little more drastic than most people had imagined. The major shock was the double departure of FA Cup final heroes Tueart and Horswill. The popular Tueart had grabbed a hat-trick in a 4–1 home win over Swindon Town on 10 November. Yet a week later he found himself on the wrong end of a Bob Stokoe rollicking as Sunderland lost 2–0 at Bristol City. Tueart said:

> I had scored what I thought was a perfect hat-trick, but in one national newspaper I did not even get the man-of-the-match rating. I started to think I was not appreciated and I realised that day that I had to go. It was acrimonious from the club's point of view when I left. Bob had a go at me after the match at Bristol City, a week after the Swindon game. I admit I had a bad day. Even though I tried 100 per cent physically, I had a complete mental block in that game. Bob had been a breath of fresh air when he first came in. We were not that bad, but Alan Brown had kept us on a short leash whereas Bob wanted us to play. He was a smashing bloke, but missed the chance to capitalise on our Wembley win. The club did not seem as ambitious as the players.

Tueart was gone four months after his run-in with Stokoe. He joined glamour club Manchester City in a joint deal that involved Horswill going with him and midfield man Tony Towers moving in the opposite direction. Tueart was valued at £275,000 in the agreement, with the two midfield terriers – valued at £100,000 apiece – moving in a straight swap. As it happened, only Horswill failed to make the grade on the back of the deal. Tueart went on to fame and fortune with City, picking up six England caps on the way, while Towers played the best football of his career while at Roker and also won three international caps. Horswill recalled:

> I didn't want to go to City in the first place, and when the deal was done I sat at home and cried. I think the FA Cup changed my life. City wanted to buy Dennis and they took me at the same time, working a swap with Tony Towers. But I was young and impressionable and also about to become one of the biggest tearaways in Manchester. Rodney Marsh took a shine to me and put me up at his place. He introduced me to George Best, and suddenly I found myself trying to live the life of a superstar. I remember Besty taking me for a night out on my 21st birthday and bang went another two weeks' wages on a club fine. The high life and the booze got the better of me. I had never been a big drinker at Sunderland, but the move changed me. I was missing training and being fined all the time. I went from £25 a week to £100 a week and I thought I'd made it.

In the end, Horswill's first manager saved him. He explained: 'Alan Brown helped to get me to Plymouth Argyle after just a handful of games for City. If he hadn't, then I would have been on the scrapheap at 21.' Meanwhile, Stokoe was looking to progress without two of his Wembley wonders. In came former Leeds striker Rod Belfitt from Everton for £65,000 and midfield man Dennis Longhorn, a £22,000 buy from Mansfield Town. It has to be said that the highly-rated Belfitt was a flop as a Sunderland striker, although he did perform surprisingly well that season as a stand-in for Dave Watson's defensive partner Richie Pitt, who had picked up a knee injury after playing just four games that season. The injury would force the powerful young defender to retire from the professional ranks just two years later. The long-legged Longhorn, on the other hand, often flattered to deceive and found himself being cast as a bit-part player during his four seasons with the club.

The 1973/74 season also resulted in European competition coming to Roker Park for the first time, in the European Cup-Winners' Cup. But, having disposed of Hungary's Vasas Budapest in some style, Sunderland crashed out to Sporting Lisbon in the next round. Promotion was again the main talking-point when they began the following season, but it was to elude them once more as Stokoe's side finished fourth. Former Newcastle skipper Bobby Moncur had been snapped up in the summer for £30,000 and swiftly forged a sound defensive partnership with Watson, who by now was an England international and attracting the attention of several major clubs. And into the attack, breathing a new lease of life into Stokoe's side, came another ex-Newcastle star. Bryan 'Pop' Robson had been scoring goals for the Geordies, and more recently West Ham, all his career. Stokoe was a long-time fan of the free-scoring Robson and forked out a not-inconsiderable £145,000 for the Sunderland-born striker just in time for the start of the new season. And Pop did not disappoint the fans. He was an ever-present, forming an impressive and potent link with Halom. The ever-popular Robson hit the net 21 times during his first campaign in a red-and-white shirt, and in his three different spells with the club scored 67 goals in 164 games. Still, despite Robson's goals, Sunderland had to plough their way through yet another season before promotion was finally theirs, but this time they did it as champions.

There were more new faces, too. Sunderland were finding it increasingly difficult to hold on to the talents of Watson, and in June 1975 he was sold to Manchester City for £175,000, with centre-half Jeff Clarke finding himself almost thrown into the deal as an added incentive. Centre-forward Mel Holden – who died from a tragic illness in 1981 – arrived from Preston North End for £120,000 and gradually edged Halom out of the reckoning, while Roy Greenwood, Hull's flame-haired left-winger who had been a thorn in Sunderland's side practically every time the clubs had met, was signed for £140,000. Stokoe was beginning to assemble a team he knew was capable of making the big push, and in March 1976 he forked out another £80,000 for Carlisle's popular little midfield man Ray Train. As a result, the club stormed to the Second Division title with a first-choice side of Montgomery, Malone, Bolton, Towers, Clarke, Moncur, Kerr, Train, Holden, Robson and Greenwood. Sunderland were back in the First Division thanks to only the second-ever promotion in their history. But a horrendous start awaited them. Stokoe had been happy enough to stick with the players who had taken the club back into the big time. But after struggling through the first nine games without a win, he insisted that he was too ill to continue and quit without winning a First Division match.

Perhaps it was more by chance than design, but Stokoe's Wembley hero Jim Montgomery bowed out at practically the same time. Monty played in his final game for Sunderland, a 1–0 home defeat by Everton, in October 1976, before being replaced by Barry Siddall, an £80,000 buy from Bolton Wanderers. Stokoe handed Siddall his debut in the 1–0 home defeat by Aston Villa in the next game – and then announced his resignation immediately after the match. Monty was just a few days short of his 33rd birthday – not particularly old for a goalkeeper – when he pulled on Sunderland's green jersey for the last time. It was almost 15 years to the day since he had made his first-team debut, and his total of 537 appearances for the Wearsiders remains a club record. All of a sudden Sunderland were managerless again, and Montgomery was not there between the posts. There were shades of 1964 when they had gained promotion only for Brown to quit and Monty to be sidelined through injury.

But Sunderland's greatest goalkeeper was far from finished once he realised that his days at Roker were over. He joined Birmingham City on a free transfer after a brief spell on loan to Southampton and made 73 appearances for them. And still he was not ready to hang up his gloves for good. His old mate and former Sunderland colleague Brian Clough was winning everything in sight with Nottingham Forest and snapped him up as back-up for Peter Shilton. Jim never started a game for Forest, but did collect a 1980 European Cup-Winners' Cup medal as compensation.

It was a little more than three years since that glorious FA triumph, and the team which Stokoe had led to victory at Wembley were almost no more. Only Kerr and Hughes were still regular first-teamers, and even their days were fast becoming numbered. The free-scoring Robson had gone too, in an £80,000 return to West Ham just five days before Stokoe resigned. It was all beginning to fall apart.

The club needed a new man at the helm, and on 30 November they announced him. Local man Jimmy Adamson, who as a player had done much to transform Burnley into a major force 25 years earlier, quit his post as manager at Turf Moor and headed for Roker Park. Struggling Sunderland were again facing a game of 'all change'. They had made a disastrous start to their first season back in the First Division. For reasons of his own, big-money buy Roy Greenwood had good cause to remember the build-up to what was being heralded as an exciting return to the big time. Greenwood had found himself caught up in a bizarre battle with Stokoe that was to become known as 'the battle of the beard'. Greenwood explained:

> I remember some of the lads asking me when I was going to shave off my beard. I'd had it for quite a while and I thought they were taking the mickey. But just before the start of the new season a notice went up in the dressing-room announcing that everyone had to be clean-shaven for the annual photo-call. I went to see Bob

Stokoe and told him I would be staying as I was – and he told me that I wouldn't be in the picture. I asked him whether it would affect my playing in the first team, and he said it wouldn't. I was in the dressing-room reading a paper while the photo-call took place, but then quite a few photographers came in wanting pictures of me with the beard. The *Sunderland Echo* then ran a poll as to whether footballers should have beards, although I'm not sure how it went. I did ask Stokoe if there was any particular reason why he thought I shouldn't have one, and he said that it made the referees notice you more. I said that it wouldn't make much difference in my case because they would probably notice me with my ginger hair. Besides, we had players in the team with moustaches, and the captain, Bobby Kerr, was one of them!

Perhaps, in retrospect, Stokoe's ridiculous run-in with Greenwood was a sign that the Sunderland manager was beginning to lose his grip. But just two months later the club had bigger things to worry about than beards. It was only October, Stokoe had quit and even that early in the season it looked as if it was going to be a close shave between survival and relegation.

7

HOW ARE THE
MIGHTY FALLEN!

As with Bob Stokoe, Jimmy Adamson was a Northumbrian. Born in Ashington, he had been a one-club man, captaining Burnley to the First Division title in 1960. Adamson had been named Footballer of the Year three years later, before becoming coach and finally manager of his beloved Burnley. He was widely regarded as one of the top thinkers in the game, and his appointment as Stokoe's replacement looked highly promising. But while the new broom did sweep clean, he failed to stop the rot. Sunderland were relegated after just one season back in the First Division.

Like all managers, Adamson wanted his own players in. He did persevere with Stokoe's final two signings, record £200,000 buy Bob Lee and former Manchester United and Scotland centre-half Jim Holton. Striker Lee, signed from Leicester City, had played just two games and Holton just three. Lee was perfectly built but appeared to lack the passion and power that Sunderland fans wanted of their centre-forwards, and he never really hit it off with the Roker faithful despite scoring 33 goals in 122 appearances. Holton, on the other hand, proved popular in the short-term, playing in 15 successive games – which proved to be the sum total of his Sunderland career. Tragically, big Jim died from a suspected heart attack in 1993, aged just 42.

Sunderland's form under Adamson failed to improve, and by the turn of the year they had won just two League games. Now he raided his old club Burnley, snapping up Mick Docherty, Colin Waldron and Doug Collins. Centre-back Waldron and left-sided midfield man Collins were past their best although, in all fairness, the same could never be levelled at young Doc. The son of Tommy Docherty came into the side in his favoured position of right-back, but was later used as a midfield ball-winner and became much respected as team captain before injury ended his career at the age of 28. Despite making a valiant recovery in the New Year thanks to a bizarre upturn in form which saw successive wins – 4–0 against Middlesbrough, 6–1 against West Bromwich Albion and 6–0 against West Ham United – Sunderland slipped through the relegation trapdoor.

But at least there was some light at the end of the tunnel. Adamson had introduced three youngsters, Gary Rowell, Shaun Elliott and Kevin Arnott, and the former youth-team trio excelled in a struggling side. The three home-grown lads clearly understood neither fear nor pressure and stood out in a side that always looked doomed. Elliott, who would later become a cultured centre-back as well as captain, was dropped into midfield as a ball-winner, while the elegant Arnott revelled in the space he found against some of the best teams in the land. Young striker Rowell, who had already made a handful of first-team appearances, scored just five times that season. But the best of Gary Rowell, the legendary Sunderland goalscorer, was yet to come.

As it happened, Adamson's side almost pulled off a great escape. A draw at Everton on the final day of the season would have kept them in the First Division at the expense of both Coventry City and Bristol City. But a 2–0 defeat at Goodison Park sent them spiralling back into the Second Division. Much was made of the fact that Coventry and Bristol City kicked off seven minutes late on the same night – allegedly because of traffic congestion – and so knew what they had to do to stay up. The two sides went through the motions in the final stages, playing out a goalless draw safe in the knowledge that Sunderland's defeat had sent them down. Be that as it may, Sunderland could still have saved themselves by drawing at Everton.

And so it was back to the Second Division yet again. Swashbuckling striker Billy Hughes had never hit it off with Adamson and was sold to Derby County in September 1977 for £30,000. That meant that Bobby Kerr was the only member of the 1973 FA Cup-winning team still on the books at Roker – and even he was no longer guaranteed a regular place. With a couple of additions – namely centre-forward Wayne Entwistle from Bury for £30,000 and Sunderland-born winger Wilf Rostron from Arsenal for £40,000 – Adamson went for the immediate return ticket. But crowds slumped to about the 15,000 mark towards the end of a disappointing campaign in which Sunderland finished sixth.

The following season, 1978/79, was slightly better to the extent that Sunderland missed promotion by a point. But Adamson had left for Leeds United just two months into the season, and his assistant Dave Merrington linked up with him again in December following a brief spell in charge on a caretaker basis. That left club stalwart Billy Elliott to take the reins temporarily, and from December to the end of the season he made a pretty good fist of it. Indeed, if Crystal Palace had not won their game in hand right at the death, Sunderland would have been promoted.

It was during the back end of yet another disappointing season that Bob Stokoe's 'little general', Bobby Kerr, finally severed his ties with Sunderland. Kerr had turned professional in 1964 and, apart from having the distinction of captaining his side to a legendary FA Cup win, had made 413 appearances, scoring 67 goals. It marked the end of an era. Kerr had finally lost his place to an Adamson buy, Mick Buckley, a £60,000 purchase from Everton during the summer of 1978. And although the immensely popular Kerr went on to play for Blackpool and Hartlepool United, nothing would ever rival the rapport he had with the fans and the respect he drew from everyone who had ever worked with him at Roker.

Despite the clamour from local media and supporters for Elliott to be handed the manager's job on a long-term basis, Sunderland turned to coach Ken Knighton. He brought in ex-Newcastle United left-back Frank Clark as his assistant. Knighton could not have wished for a better introduction to management, steering the club to second place and automatic promotion in his first season. Knighton naturally wanted to put his own stamp on the club, so Roker's revolving door was soon back in action. One of his first moves was certainly astute. He persuaded West Ham to sell Pop Robson back to his home-town club for a bargain £40,000 – exactly half the amount they had paid for him three years earlier. Robson was 33, but still as sharp as ever in front of goal. And he proved it by netting 20 goals in 40 League appearances as Knighton's new-look team marched to promotion. Knighton was certainly not afraid to dabble in the transfer market despite being new to management and, with the season just two months old he bought target man John Hawley from Leeds for a club record £200,000, with Wayne Entwistle moving in the opposite direction.

Hawley and Knighton were former Hull City team-mates and the new Sunderland boss clearly saw the barrel-chested centre-forward as the ideal partner for the ever-nimble Robson. Unfortunately, an injury early in his Roker career restricted Hawley to just nine League appearances that season. He never really picked up the momentum again, finishing his Sunderland career with 11 goals from 31 games two years later. Hawley recalled:

Jimmy Adamson and Dave Merrington didn't like me at Leeds, so the deal was done involving a Sunderland player whose name sounded as if it was a Welsh veterinary disease! But I was happy to sign for Ken Knighton, whom I knew. And I remember my first training session when coach George Herd took me for some sprints and exercises to test my 'legendary' fitness. I had to do some knees-to-chest exercises and after five minutes George complained to Ken, 'This one can't get his chest to his knees!' But at least I scored a hat-trick on my League debut for the club. It was against Charlton Athletic, and I can't remember the first two goals. But the third one came from a cross by Barry Dunn. I went to head it into one corner of the net, but it hit my shoulder and went into the opposite side!

Knighton, meanwhile, was not content with the firepower he had in Hawley, Robson and Gary Rowell. And in November 1979 he forked out a further £300,000 for the services of Middlesbrough's richly talented forward Stan Cummins. Sedgefield-born Cummins was a mighty atom of a striker who, former Boro manager Jack Charlton had once predicted, would become the game's first £1m player. That never materialised for the mercurial Stan, but he certainly entertained the Sunderland fans along the way. Cummins racked up 159 appearances for the club, scoring 32 goals, but undoubtedly created far more than that with his intricate, tantalising, twisting style of play.

Strange to say, Knighton clearly did not fancy the striking talents of Rowell during that promotion season, restricting him to just eight starts in which he failed to score a single goal. Instead, Easington-born striker Alan Brown was preferred and played a major part in Hawley's absence by rattling in 13 goals. Sunderland looked impressive at the heart of their defence thanks to the partnership of Jeff Clarke and Shaun Elliott. Steve Whitworth, the former England international snapped up from Leicester for £120,000 the previous season, was an ever-present at right-back, while Joe Bolton made the No. 3 shirt his own. Tough guy Bolton picked up an injury early in the new year, forcing Knighton's hand somewhat. His solution was to bring in Joe Hinnigan from Wigan Athletic in a £135,000 deal, and the tall full-back finished the season in a promoted team. Knighton said:

> It was a hard season and we were nearly always in the top three, but we lost 2–1 at Preston in February 1980 and it was devastating, so I got everybody into the dressing-room on the Monday after the game and told them where we should be and what we needed to be. I went out and bought in Joe, who did brilliantly and made a big difference because of his sheer enthusiasm. He was a full-back who had just played for Wigan Athletic in the old Fourth Division, but he looked at the set-up at Sunderland, took it by storm and we went 13 League games unbeaten.

Chris Turner, signed by Knighton for £100,000 from Sheffield Wednesday, finally edged out Barry Siddall in goal, while the midfield duties were shared between Wilf Rostron, Mick Buckley, Kevin Arnott and Gordon Chisholm – with one notable exception.

Knighton was learning fast when it came to spending money, and he kept the big one up his sleeve until midway through the season, when he paid a club record £320,000 to Argentine club San Lorenzo for the relatively unknown Claudio Marangoni – and the deal caused a sensation on Wearside. Unlike so many of today's big-money deals when top-notch foreigners come to England and set the game alight with their silky skills, he breezed into Roker in a blaze of publicity – and promptly flopped, despite playing 16 games in a promotion side. Knighton, in fact, was never afraid to spend big: 'I tried to sign centre-half Willie Miller from Aberdeen – but it didn't work out. I had to negotiate with Alex Ferguson, who was in charge there at the time, and Willie wanted a king's ransom. He wanted the same money Kenny Dalglish was on at Liverpool!'

Sunderland crowned their promotion with a 2–0 home win over West Ham on a Monday night. The Hammers had won the FA Cup just two days beforehand and were obviously still on a high. Knighton continued:

West Ham came to us just days after winning the Cup. I remember that by 5pm the ground was full. I spoke to Stuart Pearson, who had been a team-mate of mine at Hull, and he told me not to worry about the game because the West Ham lads had been drinking all weekend after the Cup win. He said that they wouldn't be able to cope, but for the first 20 minutes we couldn't get the ball off them. Eventually it was all over for them because they were so shattered. Kevin Arnott and Stan Cummins scored the goals – they were typical of the young players who had done so well for the club that season. It had been a hard season, but we were nearly always up there in the top three. One of the first things I did as a manager was to bring Pop Robson back from West Ham. Bryan was nearly 34, but he scored a lot of goals for us that season and was a wise old head in a really good team which had plenty of home-grown players.

We had gone 13 games unbeaten by the time the West Ham game came around, but the most important thing for me was that my family was not able to be at the match because we'd arranged an end-of-season trip for them and a group of supporters to Miami. I was supposed to go with them, but the game with West Ham was rearranged because of their involvement in the Cup. It was an absolutely fantastic game, but my family and about 250 supporters had missed it because they'd had to leave from Heathrow Airport for America earlier in the day! I'd had to drop the family off at Roker Park to go London in the morning and I'd been in my office from 8am. By two o'clock in the afternoon the fans started to walk in and by 5pm the ground was full.

More than 47,000 watched Sunderland march back into the First Division that night. The roller-coaster ride was up and running again. It probably came as no great surprise to anyone – least of all the club's long-suffering fans – that life back in the top flight proved difficult to say the least. Knighton began the season with basically the same set of players. But a serious knee injury to key centre-back Jeff Clarke left a huge gap, and Knighton opted to plug it with the £150,000 signing of Bolton Wanderers' tough guy Sam Allardyce. Big Sam, who would prove to be a huge success as Bolton's manager years later, was appointed captain and played 26 games that season. But that, in a nutshell, was his Sunderland career.

Much later in the season Knighton signed striker Tom Ritchie from Bristol City for £180,000 and Ian Bowyer from Nottingham Forest for £250,000. It was not money well spent. Midfielder Bowyer, such an immense influence with Forest, played just 16 times for the club, while the ungainly Ritchie managed just 11 goals from his 37 Sunderland starts. The season was beginning to look bleak when Knighton and Clark were sacked in April 1981. There were only four games remaining and relegation was looking much too likely. Knighton recalled his stormy relationship with chairman Tom Cowie. The Sunderland-based motor magnate, later Sir Tom Cowie, had taken the helm in the summer of 1980 when Keith Collings stepped down. Knighton recalled:

I remember the press conference that was called to introduce Tom Cowie as chairman. At it he said that, contrary to speculation, Ken Knighton would still be manager next season. But there hadn't been any speculation in the first place. It was just something he wanted to make up. It's fair to say that we had a stormy relationship, and I left the club the following April. Remember, we were in the First Division then. And by the time he left as chairman, the club was on its way into the Third! The trouble was that he was autocratic in his car business and he wanted to run the football club the same way. But it was my remit to run the football side of things, so there was bound to be a clash of personalities.

One typical rift between manager and chairman came during the

Christmas period. It was all something and nothing really, but Cowie was not happy about the incident and Knighton appeared to be on a one-way ticket to the sack from then on. Knighton added:

> We were playing West Bromwich at home on Boxing Day and it was thought that we might get as many as 35,000 there. I asked if I could take the players away to a hotel to help them to prepare for the game. The plan was that they could have their Christmas lunches at home, spend as much time as possible with their families and we could all meet up at four o'clock. But Tom Cowie said we couldn't afford it, so I did a deal with the hotel in question and it cost me peanuts because I knew the guy there. It was all very silly, but the chairman wasn't happy.

Indeed he was not. Knighton and Clark hung on for another three months after the hotel row, but the damage was done and eventually Cowie had his way. With just four games left to achieve survival, Sunderland found an unlikely saviour in their coach and former captain Mick Docherty. Young Doc took the reins for the crucial run-in and, in his first game in charge, a hat-trick from Ritchie sunk Birmingham City in a 3–0 home win. Sunderland then lost their next two away games, at West Bromwich and Brighton, and were left needing to pull off an unlikely win at mighty Liverpool on the final day in order to stay up. No-one gave them a hope. But a goal by Cummins was good enough to do the trick, and that 1–0 win at Anfield saw Sunderland survive by the skin of their teeth.

Roker's managerial merry-go-round was cranked up yet again in the summer of 1981. After much speculation about his move, former Welsh international midfield man Alan Durban left his job at Stoke City to take over at Roker. Durban was bright, articulate and a good student of the game, having been schooled by former Sunderland favourite Brian Clough at Derby County. And, by the time the 1981/82 season kicked off, he had already brought in two new faces. One was a Scottish international defender, Iain Munro, for whom Durban paid his former club Stoke £150,000, while the other was an unknown Scottish teenager whose international career was then no more than a pipedream. But Ally McCoist, a £250,000 signing from St Johnstone, always had talent in his boots. It was just that he had neither the time nor sufficient opportunity to allow it to shine through at Roker. McCoist, who went on to pick up 58 Scotland caps while establishing himself as an all-time great at Glasgow Rangers, found himself in and out of the side as Sunderland tried desperately to re-establish themselves as a First Division outfit. He started just 46 games in a Sunderland shirt, coming on as a substitute on another 19 occasions, and scored nine goals before Rangers saw something in his raw talent and paid £180,000 to take him back north of the border.

With Jeff Clarke having recovered from his knee injury, full-back Jimmy Nicholl arrived from Manchester United, initially on loan and eventually signing for £250,000, while home-grown youngsters Barry Venison, Nick Pickering and Colin West also established themselves on the Roker scene. Big defender Rob Hindmarch and midfielder Gordon Chisholm were also products of Sunderland's youth scheme and featured heavily under Durban's guidance. Tragically, Hindmarch, who made 125 appearances for the club before joining Derby and Wolverhampton Wanderers, died in November 2002, aged just 41.

Durban's side finished 19th that season and, with the ever-dependable Ian Atkins arriving from Shrewsbury Town for £30,000 plus striker Alan Brown in time for the following campaign, Sunderland were expected to build from that position. Durban opted for some extra flair and panache with ageing forwards Leighton James and Frank Worthington. Although Worthington showed some delightful touches on the ball, his two goals from 18 games hardly marked him down as a worthwhile contributor to the cause. Former Burnley and Wales hero James, on the other hand, stayed a little longer and clocked up 57 appearances.

There was a slight improvement, Sunderland edging up to 16th in 1982/83, but Durban had hardly set the place alight. And towards the end of his third and final season in charge – with new boy Paul Bracewell, a £250,000 signing from Stoke, pulling the strings in midfield – he was sacked and replaced almost immediately by former club favourite Len Ashurst. The change came in early March 1984, leaving Ashurst, who had just quit as Cardiff City boss, to oversee the final 13 games. Back in the side were old favourites Pop Robson, now in his third spell with Sunderland and a player-coach, and Mark Proctor, who had been brought back from Nottingham Forest by Durban. But it still took a final-day win – at Leicester – to secure First Division survival. Durban had signed Lee Chapman from Arsenal for £200,000 and, although his Sunderland career was nothing special, he did grab one of the goals in that crucial 2–0 victory at Filbert Street. The ageing Robson grabbed the other.

There had been a fair amount of dissent among the players, many of whom had resented Durban's dismissal. Players such as Bracewell, Atkins and Gary Rowell had strongly supported him, and it always looked unlikely that Ashurst would keep them. And so it proved, with Bracewell and Atkins joining Everton that summer and all-time favourite Rowell moving to Norwich City. The evergreen Robson was another departure and headed for Carlisle United. Ashurst was determined to make a success of managing the club for whom he had made a record 458 appearance as an outfield player – and set about ringing the changes during his first pre-season build-up. Actually, it turned out to be his only pre-season because he led the side to an eminently forgettable Milk Cup final defeat at the hands of Norwich and relegation in the space of a month.

New arrivals during Ashurst's brief reign included Gary Bennett for £85,000 from Cardiff City, Howard Gayle for £65,000 from Birmingham City, David Hodgson for £125,000 from Liverpool, Ian Wallace on a free transfer from French club Brest, Peter Daniel for £18,000 from Minnesota Kicks, Reuben Agboola for £150,000 from Southampton, Steve Berry for £30,000 from Portsmouth, Clive Walker for £80,000 from Chelsea and Roger Wylde on a free transfer from Sporting Lisbon, while Stan Cummins arrived for a second spell via a free transfer from Crystal Palace. It looked promising for a while, but disgruntled supporters had been fed on a diet of 'promising' and 'potential' for far too long. They did not want to hear any more talk of 'sleeping giants.' All they wanted was someone to make them big and strong enough in order to hold down a respectable position in the top flight.

It came as no surprise, therefore, when Ashurst was sacked just 10 days after the final game of 1984/85 with a bitterly disappointing League record of just 15 wins from 55 games. Another 25 of those matches had ended in defeat, and chairman Tom Cowie, who had appointed Ashurst only 14 months earlier, was left with no alternative other than to instigate yet another change of manager. Ashurst had given the fans something to cheer about, however, with a stirring march towards a Wembley cup final. The final failed to live up to its billing, an own goal by Gordon Chisholm handing the Canaries victory, while Walker shaved the outside of a post with a second-half penalty from which Sunderland never seemed to recover.

There were still 12 League games to go when sad Sunderland slipped away from Wembley. But Ashurst's demoralised men lost eight of them and went down with their Wembley conquerors, Norwich. The main talking-point at the time of the final had been the shock omission of in-form target man Colin West. He had scored three times during the two-leg semi-final win over Chelsea, but was left out on the eve of the game. As it happened, a move to Watford beckoned for West and he completed it just four days after the Wembley woe. Ian Wallace was recalled for the final, and the inexperienced David Corner was asked to replace the suspended Shaun Elliott. The unfortunate Corner made a serious error of judgement which allowed Asa Hartford's shot to fly past Chris Turner via a vicious deflection off Chisholm. The big day out had turned into a nightmare. Ashurst admitted:

> I had never seen so many grown men in tears. We suffered a lot of wounds in that game and they were very deep wounds. It was a hard decision to leave out Colin West, but I wanted us to get the ball forward to Wallace on the ground. We just didn't play on the day and we didn't provide any service to the frontmen.

And defender Peter Daniel recalled:

> That League Cup final was one of the worst on record and was decided by an own goal. It was a disastrous season and, from what I can remember, the final was a nonentity. Losing it had a detrimental effect on the players and the club as a whole. I don't think we had accepted the fact that we were in a relegation battle at the time. But we were, and we hardly won another game after that. We had probably concentrated too much on the Cup run and subconsciously you tend to look after yourself a bit because you want to play in a Cup final. But there was a lot of turmoil at the club then, and the League position didn't lie in the end. I can remember some of the players talking everything over during the close season, and we felt that Len Ashurst had picked the wrong side for the final. We had always played 4–4–2, but he changed to a sweeper system for that game and brought in young David Corner, who had hardly played, while leaving out Colin West, who had scored a lot of important goals for us. He had even scored three in the two-leg semi-final against Chelsea. I think he suffered a broken toe in the second leg and was left out in the final. But it affected the rest of the players and we didn't really play. There was plenty of effort, but it just wasn't to be. It was a horrible game to watch and a horrible game to play in. We didn't perform, but neither did Norwich. It was one of the worst seasons in Sunderland's history, but we had some really good players, such as Barry Venison, Ian Wallace and David Hodgson. Chris Turner got a move to Manchester United later, but the most underrated of all was Gary Bennett, who was one of the real characters.

With Sunderland's lack of firepower so evident, a cruel post-match irony hit the club's supporters right between the eyes. Gary Rowell, a goalscoring legend on Wearside, had been shipped out to Norwich by Ashurst and had just missed out on being handed the Canaries' No. 12 shirt at Wembley. But, when the Seaham-born striker raised the trophy aloft in front of Sunderland's tearful fans, everyone appreciated exactly how he must have been feeling. There he stood, dressed in his Norwich cup-final suit. Somehow it might be sensed that the Sunderland scarf draped around his neck represented a much more poignant piece of attire.

With Ashurst gone, the search for a manager began all over again. It was becoming a painful and regular occurrence for Sunderland's dumbfounded fans, many of whom were beginning to lose patience. So, only too aware that they needed some drastic repair work in the PR department, chairman Tom Cowie went for the man he felt certain would bring both success and charisma to the ailing club. He appointed Lawrie McMenemy, the Geordie-born manager who had worked his way up the League ladder from humble beginnings before guiding Second Division Southampton to a shock FA Cup triumph over Manchester United in 1976. McMenemy had gone on to guide the Saints back into the First Division, but it was felt that he needed a fresh challenge. Sunderland certainly offered him one.

The appointment of such a well-known football figure, a television pundit and a straight-talking North-Easterner who had always seemed able to charm the birds off the trees, set Wearside alight. The fans went crazy. Here, at long last, was their saviour. Big Lawrie was the man to right all the wrongs. Surely it could not get any worse. But it did. In fact, it got so bad that McMenemy, who had promised to lead Sunderland out of the Second Division, actually kept his word. Unfortunately he led the club into the Third Division for the first time in their history. Sunderland were becoming a laughing-stock in the game, and McMenemy's appointment turned out to be nothing short of a disaster.

Players were sold, including such money-making assets as Chris Turner to Manchester United, Barry Venison to Liverpool, Nick Pickering to Coventry and Shaun Elliott to Norwich. The £800,000 that it generated helped to pave the way for McMenemy to go down the road he had known so well as Southampton manager. He bought experience – only this time the plan was a gigantic flop. George Burley, who cost £80,000 from Ipswich Town, former Newcastle favourite and Penshaw-born left-back Alan Kennedy, a £100,000 buy from Liverpool, centre-half Steve Hetzke, bought from Blackpool for £30,000, Dave Swindlehurst, signed for £150,000 from West Ham, £100,000 capture Frank Gray from Leeds, and goalkeepers Seamus McDonagh and Bob Bolder were all clearly past their best. And while another – Eric Gates, a £150,000 buy from Ipswich – suffered a miserable time under McMenemy's management, at least he came good at a later date and played a major part in steering the club straight out of the Third Division.

McMenemy's introduction could not have been more dramatic, but it was for all the wrong reasons as Sunderland produced their worst-ever start to a season. And it did not really get much better. By the time the miserable 1985/86 season was drawing to a close, the situation was drastic. Two wins were required from the last two games in order to avoid the drop into the Third Division for the first time in the club's history. They were achieved over Shrewsbury and Stoke and Sunderland finished 18th, but the damage was already done. Lawrie McMenemy and Sunderland supporters were on a collision course.

McMenemy – still one of the biggest names in the game – had signed a three-year contract. But his second season at the helm was just as miserable as his first, and by Easter 1987 new chairman Bob Murray had no alternative but to terminate the deal. Sunderland were sinking so fast that this time relegation was beginning to look a certainty. Murray did pull one trick out of the hat by bringing back fans' favourite Bob Stokoe for a second spell at the club, albeit as caretaker-manager. Sickened supporters responded, Stokoe's trademark raincoat and trilby were donned for the media scramble and some hope was rekindled. It was all too late. Try as he might, even Stokoe was unable to wave a magic wand over such a moribund set of disheartened players. The play-off system was still relatively new at the time, and Sunderland were forced to battle it out with top Third Division side Gillingham for the one remaining place in the Second Division. Sunderland went down 3–2 in the first leg at the Priestfield Stadium before winning the return 4–3. But Tony Cascarino's late strike at Roker saw the Gills swap divisions thanks to away goals.

Newcastle-born midfielder Gordon Armstrong was well placed to reflect on the slide, having served under nine managers even though he did not make a senior appearance during Alan Durban's spell in charge:

> I didn't make it into the first team under Alan Durban, but I did under Len Ashurst and it wasn't the best of introductions. He played me right at the end of the 1984/85 season when we were already relegated. Ashurst did not get on very well with a lot of the players and there was a load of dissent in the camp. A lot of the senior professionals were taking the mickey out of him because of his strange phrases and so on. He was a sound enough fellow, but he just couldn't communicate. I remember the Friday of the last

match of the season, which was at home to Ipswich Town. The fans had already had enough and so had many of the players – so much so, in fact, that quite a few were not willing to play and there was all kinds of trouble. I think that Len had managed to muster nine who said they would play, but then the club threatened to cancel an end-of-season trip – and amazingly quite a few injuries miraculously disappeared there and then! It was not a good time for the club, but then Ashurst went and Lawrie McMenemy came in. Lawrie did what he had done at Southampton and bought older, experienced players, but it failed miserably. He wasn't the best of coaches – he would probably admit that himself – but it was yet another sad time for Sunderland. After one miserable season in the Second Division, we had another – only this time Lawrie had gone by Easter and Bob Stokoe was brought back to try to keep us out of the Third Division. He did his best, but it was all too late.

It was almost too much for the once-mighty club to stomach, and in future years McMenemy's name would always be associated with a tumultous tumble from grace. Sir Tom Cowie admitted:

It was I who appointed Lawrie McMenemy, and at the time he seemed the right man for the job. The day that he arrived at the ground I could barely manage to push through the crowds to reach my office. But then he did what he had done so successfully at Southampton and bought experience. This time a lot of the players were past their sell-by dates and it didn't work. Things became so bad that, shortly before I sold all my shares to Bob Murray for not one penny profit, I was getting abusive telephone calls at home at three o'clock in the morning. You couldn't go on that way.

8

SEESAW SEASONS

Sunderland were in a mess. It would have been unfair to lay any blame at the door of stand-in manager Bob Stokoe, but with the Third Division now beckoning, lowly Sunderland had to look forward. And chairman Bob Murray did not need to search too far afield for Lawrie McMenemy's replacement, raiding York City for their highly-rated managerial pairing of Denis Smith and his assistant Viv Busby. The pair brought a breath of fresh air to Roker Park, waltzing to the Third Division championship in their first season.

And Smith introduced a striker who became a genuine star in the eyes of the Wearside faithful. Marco Gabbiadini cost Smith a mere £80,000 from York, and, as Sunderland marched towards the title, he hit 21 goals. In all, Gabbiadini scored 87 goals in just 183 appearances before leaving for Crystal Palace in October 1991 for a huge £1.8m. Denis Smith would never again make such a monumental profit on one player.

Gabbiadini forged an excellent understanding with the veteran forward Eric Gates, who used all his vast experience to drop deep, take defenders with him and then play perfectly weighted balls to his partner, whose electric pace was simply too hot to handle for the majority of opponents. And Gates recalled:

> My first two seasons at the club had been a nightmare. I was playing in the Second Division for the first time in my career, but dropping down a grade didn't worry me at all. All that concerned me was helping Sunderland to make a quick return to First Division football. The club belonged in the top flight, but I believe that those two terrible seasons that saw us slide into the Third Division were the result of the players' confidence and attitude being affected by all the bickering that was going on. My own form suffered and I became a target for the boo-boys. I was accused of earning easy money on my past reputation at Ipswich, and that hurt. I'd always prided myself on being a hard trainer and conscientious footballer, and it sickened me to think that I was regarded by some people as an over-the-hill player returning

home to the North-East to use struggling Sunderland as a gravy train.

To his great credit, Gates turned a nightmare scenario into a thoroughly impressive spell as an intelligent and unselfish player revelling in the twilight of his career. Having been savaged by many critics, he would end his time at Sunderland as a genuine crowd favourite whose determination to stay on board a sinking ship was much appreciated.

Smith understandably had to clear out the bulk of the old guard as well as bringing in fresh faces. Among the new arrivals who served him and Busby admirably at various stages were skipper Kevin Ball, a £150,000 bargain buy from Portsmouth, and the returning Paul Bracewell, who cost £150,000, this time from Everton. Ball, of course, became an all-time Sunderland favourite, experiencing both the almost inevitable highs and lows, while Bracewell left yet again and then returned for a third spell later in his career. Then there were strikers Don Goodman, a club-record £900,000 capture from West Bromwich Albion, and Peter Davenport, who cost £250,000 from Middlesbrough. The new defenders were John Kay from Wimbledon for £25,000, Paul Hardyman for £150,000 from Portsmouth, and John MacPhail, who had also played for Smith at York, from Bristol City for £25,000. Midfield man Colin Pascoe cost £70,000 from Swansea City, while Smith again spent a club-record fee on goalkeeper Tony Norman, who was valued at £450,000 in a player-exchange deal with Hull City which saw Iain Hesford and striker Billy Whitehurst move in the opposite direction. Home-grown youngsters Gordon Armstrong, Gary Owers, Paul 'Jack' Lemon and Brian Atkinson also excelled under Smith's guidance, although the unpredictable talent of winger Kieron Brady was never fulfilled.

Back in the Second Division, Sunderland took two just two seasons to return to the top flight, finishing 11th in 1988/89 and sixth the following season to reach the end-of-season play-offs. In the final analysis, though, they were promoted by default. Having lost 1–0 to Swindon Town in the 1990 Wembley play-off final, they found themselves back in the big time only when financial irregularities prevented Town from having their promotion ratified. Typically, it had been drama all the way for Sunderland. Drawn against arch rivals Newcastle United in the play-off semi-finals, they had found themselves involved in two titanic derby struggles before heading for Wembley and a miserable, lone-goal defeat by Swindon.

The first leg of the much-vaunted clash with Newcastle was at Roker Park and, although it finished goalless, there was no shortage of controversy. Left-back Hardyman, normally accurate with his penalties, saw his spot-kick saved by the veteran John Burridge. Desperate to race forward and knock home any subsequent rebound, Hardyman was sent off for a crude challenge on Burridge and the mood for the return at St James' Park was set. As it happened, it turned out to be a surprisingly comfortable win for a Sunderland side with Smith's G-men – strikers Gates and Gabbiadini – each scoring in a 2–0 win. Newcastle fans invaded the pitch, doubtless in the hope of getting the match abandoned, but the vastly experienced County Durham referee George Courtney was having none of it. He took the teams back to their dressing-rooms for a cooling-down period, and said later: 'I had decided that the game would be finished that night even if we had to wait until midnight!' The play-off final itself was a gloomy affair for Sunderland, whose side consisted of Norman, Kay, Gary Bennett, MacPhail, Agboola, Gary Owers, Bracewell, Atkinson, Pascoe, Gates and Gabbiadini. But there were some belated celebrations blowing in the wake of the Wembley wind that day and, with the major disappointment of being pipped at the post still rankling on Wearside, Sunderland were told that promotion was theirs.

Goalkeeper Tony Norman recalled the whole play-off saga:

We drew 0–0 against Newcastle at Roker Park and had Paul Hardyman sent off. He was the nicest bloke you might wish to meet and didn't do anything out of malice. Denis Smith didn't know what to say, but we said, 'We'll beat them at their place' because we thought that Newcastle were ripe for the picking. We went 2–0 ahead at Newcastle and some of their fans then tried to stop the match. With five minutes to go there were about a thousand people on the pitch, but the referee George Courtney said, 'I'll wait all night to finish it.' Then we met Swindon at Wembley in the final and we were torn to shreds. We couldn't get the ball from them, and it was one of the busiest games I've ever had. We lost 1–0, but then we heard that Swindon were in trouble because of allegations about some underhand stuff with signing-on fees. Swindon were demoted, and then Newcastle said that they should go up because they'd finished third, but we were promoted because we'd beaten them in the play-offs.

Back in the old First Division in 1990/91, Smith managed to keep a fairly settled team, although stability couldn't prevent them from tumbling straight back down again. His tightly knit first-team squad revolved around Norman, Kay, Hardyman, Bennett, Ball, Owers, Bracewell,

Armstrong, Davenport, Gabbiadini, Pascoe, Richard Ord, David Rush and Thomas Hauser. But these players found the step up too difficult, and Sunderland were relegated. Gabbiadini finished as the leading goalscorer with a mere nine League goals.

Sunderland were naturally enough expected to be among the forerunners for promotion in the 1991/92 season. But it did not happen. Instead there was to be yet more managerial movement coupled with a shock FA Cup run that resulted in the club marching all the way to Wembley as a Second Division team for the second time in their history. Sadly, on this occasion, there was to be no repeat of their 1973 fairy-tale triumph over Leeds United.

Smith, by now under pressure, began to show signs of a man heading for his own exit when he and his long-term ally Viv Busby parted company. Busby was a shock departure, and Smith opted to promote the highly rated Malcolm Crosby from within. But, as often happens in football, Smith was sacked himself soon afterwards, leaving the untried Crosby to take over on a caretaker basis. With Smith finding himself out of a job towards the end of December 1991, his old friend Crosby no doubt imagined that he would be asked to hold the fort while chairman Bob Murray found a new manager. What actually happened was a fairy tale in its own right. Under the leadership of the popular Crosby, Sunderland embarked on an amazing FA Cup run that swept them past Port Vale 3–0, Oxford United 3–2, West Ham United 3–2 (after a 1–1 draw), Chelsea 2–1 (after another 1–1 draw), Norwich City 1–0 in the semi-finals and all the way to a Wembley date with Liverpool.

Crosby, finding himself something of a reluctant hero under the glare of the spotlight, was a huge hit with fans and media alike. And so, with the pressure mounting on Murray, Crosby – a lifelong Sunderland fan – was finally handed a one-year contract as manager. He recalled: 'Everyone was rooting for me. And the pressure really built up once we knew we were going to be in the final. I didn't really want to lead out the team at Wembley as a caretaker manager, and the chairman handed me a one-year deal.'

Striker John Byrne hit seven goals on Sunderland's exciting road to Wembley. And, having scored in every round, there was immense pressure on the former York and Queen's Park Rangers forward to repeat the feat against Liverpool. Smith had paid Brighton and Hove Albion £225,000 for Byrne just two months before his sacking, but it was during Crosby's Cup run that he suddenly became a household name. In truth, Byrne had found himself in the right place at the right time. Smith had signed another striker towards the end of his four and a half year reign, but the free-scoring Don Goodman, who scored 47 goals in 128 appearances for Sunderland, was cup-tied when he moved to Roker, and that paved the way for Byrne. Goodman did play his part on the League front, as Crosby's side also had to overcome a relegation battle, but when it came to FA Cup duty he could only watch from the stands.

The 1992 final turned out to be something of a damp squib, with odds-on favourites Liverpool winning 2–0 thanks to goals from Michael Thomas and Ian Rush. Sunderland never really performed on a day when much was made of the omission of full-back Paul Hardyman, who had played in every round along the way. Hardyman, who was furious about being named among the substitutes, was replaced by another Smith purchase, Anton Rogan, a Northern Ireland international who had been signed from Glasgow Celtic for £350,000 earlier in the season: he was handed the role at left-back instead. Sunderland's line-up consisted of Norman, Owers, Ball, Bennett, Rogan, Rush, Bracewell, Atkinson, Armstrong, Byrne and Davenport, with Warren Hawke joining the action as the substitute. It was a depressing enough afternoon for all concerned with Sunderland, but it was a day for key midfield player Paul Bracewell to forget. He had already been a losing FA Cup finalist on three occasions while with Everton, and now it was four. It was a new – and unwanted – record, because Bracewell became the only player in FA Cup history to be a four-time loser without ever being on the winning side!

Goalkeeper Tony Norman recalled the Cup run:

In a nutshell, we were caught up in the romance of the FA Cup from the beginning – and more so because the final was at Wembley, so it was everybody's dream come true to play there in one, but also because we were in the old Second Division. We had a big mixture of experienced and young lads who would roll up their sleeves and just do it. There was a great atmosphere in the dressing-room. The week ahead of the final was a bit miserable because there were cameras pointing at you everywhere you went – even on the training pitch. And you think it's always sunny for the FA Cup final, but I remember having a training session with our goalkeeping coach Roger Jones on the morning of the game, and it was pouring with rain. The final itself was the weirdest experience. I'd watched every one since I was about ten, and I love 'Abide with Me'. As I heard it while I stood in the tunnel waiting to go out, the hair on the back of my neck started tingling. It wasn't just noise when we walked out: it was a great big cauldron and you couldn't hear yourself breathe. I just kept my head down because I knew I had a job to do. We had two half-chances early on, but we hardly had a kick and it was comfortable for Liverpool. Their experience wore us down and we couldn't get the ball. I don't think we could have won it.

But Sunderland's players did manage a brief collective smile soon after the game. Norman added:

> I kept telling myself that I wasn't going to trip on the stairs coming down after we'd gone up for the presentations, and then I would look at my medal. I realised that I'd got a winner's medal even though we'd lost 2–0, so I told the other lads to check their medals. We'd all got winners' medals, so I went over to Dean Saunders, who'd been playing for Liverpool and had been a team-mate of mine with Wales, and told him to look at his medal. It was a runners-up medal, so it ended up with the two teams swapping our medals over!'

Crosby, meanwhile, began the 1992/93 season as manager, making two major additions to his squad. He signed former England warhorse Terry Butcher as a player following a disastrous 13-month spell as Coventry City's player-manager, and Shaun Cunnington, who cost £650,000 from Grimsby Town but never really hit it off with the Roker faithful. But after the excitement of the FA Cup run Crosby found it increasingly difficult to come to terms with life in the newly named First Division, and he too was sacked – in February 1993, after just 10 months in the hot seat. His replacement was Butcher, one of his own signings, who was immediately appointed player-manager and brought in former Sunderland skipper Ian Atkins as his assistant. And, in a determined attempt to avoid the drop, Butcher later signed life-long Sunderland fan and ex-England international Mick Harford from Chelsea for £250,000. Sunderland did avoid relegation – albeit by just a point – and Harford played his part in the struggle.

Butcher forked out the best part of £2m in the close season of 1993 to bring in goalkeeper Alec Chamberlain and striker Phil Gray from Luton Town, defender Andy Melville from Oxford and midfield man Derek Ferguson from Glasgow Rangers. Youngsters Michael Gray, Craig Russell and Martin Smith were also beginning to edge their way into the first team, and the signs looked reasonably promising.

But an ever-widening gap was beginning to appear between Butcher and chairman Bob Murray in November 1993 and, as with Crosby before him, the manager was sacked after 10 months in charge. His replacement on Sunderland's managerial merry-go-round was coach

Mick Buxton. Just as Crosby had brought in Butcher, so Butcher had brought in Buxton. Now recent history was repeating itself with sacked managers being replaced from within. It was all so messy. Since Bob Stokoe's resignation 17 years earlier in 1976, Sunderland had appointed nine different managers. They were still struggling with life outside the top flight, and no-one appeared to have the ability to take the club by the scruff of the neck and drag it back into the big time.

Buxton, likeable enough and well respected in the game as a coach, was Sunderland-born and certainly felt an affinity for the club. But he was never going to pull up any trees as their manager and, after guiding his team into 12th place at the end of the 1993/94 season, he too was sacked by Murray before the following season had concluded. Strapped for cash in the wake of Butcher's spending, he still managed to sign left-back Martin Scott from Bristol City for £450,000 (with Gary Owers, valued at £300,000, going in the opposite direction), right-back Darius Kubicki from Aston Villa for £100,000 and midfield man Steve Agnew from Leicester City for £250,000. But Buxton felt the axe hovering above his neck, and he was dismissed in March 1995 after 15 months at the helm. His sacking came in the wake of two more captures when he, in effect, signed his own death warrant. A transfer-deadline-day swoop for Everton striker Brett Angell cost Sunderland a staggering £650,000, while a bizarre story surrounded the loan signing of Liverpool defender Dominic Matteo. Buxton believed that club officials had completed the necessary paperwork in time for Matteo to make his debut, but it had not been done. Sunderland were in disciplinary trouble, and Buxton was sacked.

Yet again the threat of relegation into what by then was called the Second Division was clouding everything at a crumbling Roker Park. And the under-pressure Murray turned to Peter Reid as his next manager. There were only seven games to go when he was appointed, and his brief was perfectly simple – to keep the club in the First Division. Reid made it with six points to spare. Now the club's long-suffering supporters, who had had little to shout about in living memory, were sensing the dawn of a new era. For once they were to be proved right.

Reid brought a fresh work ethic to the club and led Sunderland to the First Division championship in his first full season, 1995/96. They finished four points clear of Derby County, who were ironically spearheaded by Marco Gabbiadini, but it was efficient rather than spectacular because they scored just 59 goals in the League, Craig Russell finishing as the leading marksman on 13. From mid-February Sunderland were unbeaten in 18 League games, including nine consecutive wins at one stage, until the final day of the season, by which everything was cut and dried anyway. During the decisive run they first went five games without conceding a goal, which they bettered by keeping another six successive clean sheets a month later.

Long-serving midfield player Gordon Armstrong had seen all the comings and goings:

I was hardly playing by the time we went up as champions in 1996, although I was a substitute quite a bit. But Denis Smith and Viv Busby are the best duo I ever worked with in my entire career. When they came in it was like a breath of fresh air after the Ashurst and McMenemy eras, and we marched straight back out of the Third Division as champions. They built a decent team with Marco Gabbiadini and Eric Gates scoring plenty of goals. Denis eventually took us into the old First Division, but we weren't quite good enough and came straight back down. Things really turned sour after that, though, and Denis got rid of Viv, which shocked us all, and was a huge mistake. They were best mates, but that's what he did. I think they are friends again now, however, and I really hope that they are. But it was a massive mistake by the manager and, because of it, it killed the dressing-room for him.

Probably predictably, Denis was next to go, and Malcolm Crosby came in. Crozzer's a great guy, and we responded by going all the way to Wembley in the 1992 FA Cup final. The day itself was not great, though, and we just didn't play – I know I didn't – and we were quite comfortably beaten by Liverpool. But even that little spell proved to be an awkward time, and that's just Sunderland all over, I guess. Malcolm didn't really want to lead the team out at Wembley as a caretaker manager, so chairman Bob Murray handed him a one-year contract. The whole place was like a time bomb, and the next thing we knew was that Crozzer had gone and Terry Butcher was in charge.

Butch had come in as a player and in that respect he did a superb job. His knees were shot, he couldn't train at all and he just played on match days, but he was great out on the pitch as well as in the dressing-room. But then he was appointed manager and changed totally. He became completely introverted whenever anything went wrong – which, of course, it always did at Sunderland – and he did a lot of strange things that didn't seem to add up.

It was no surprise when Butcher went and then it was Mick Buxton's turn. For me, it was like working in a place with revolving doors for managers, but I was just an employee and I had to get on with it. Everyone called Mick the 'pigeon fancier'. He wore his flat cap, walked the dog and was a nice enough bloke, but making him manager of Sunderland was a very strange decision. I had probably been around for too long at that stage and perhaps I should have moved on. But agents were not around then and you just felt as if you were on your own.

Gary Bennett and Armstrong were part of the Roker furniture as the yo-yo years set in, staying put as managers came and went around them and showing the loyalty that had been the trademark of many of their predecessors. Bennett accumulated 444 appearances, experiencing two promotions, three relegations, a Football League Cup final and an FA Cup final. Armstrong clocked up 414 games, taking part in three promotions, three relegations and an FA Cup final. Both are in the top ten of all-time appearances for the club. Armstrong, in fact, was at Roker Park during the stewardship of *nine* managers, but is philosophical about whether he should have ventured through the players' own revolving door at some stage:

> I know that Norwich offered £1m for me and Southampton offered £750,000, but both bids were turned down. Funnily enough, I also remember something going around about Manchester United wanting me when I was still a young lad. I know Eric Gates said that Bryan Robson had been asking him about me, and big Dave Swindlehurst told me that United were genuinely interested. But nothing came of it, and these things happen in football. I seemed to spend my entire Sunderland career fighting for either promotion or against relegation. But by the time I left, I was one of the highest appearance-makers in the history of Sunderland, and that's something of which I shall always be immensely proud.

Peter Reid, too, found that the yo-yo factor seemed to be inherent at Roker Park. After just one season in the FA Premiership in 1996/97, Sunderland were relegated yet again. They had been 11th at the end of January, but finished a point behind Coventry and Southampton and went down with Middlesbrough, who had had three points deducted, and Nottingham Forest. More pointedly, they had scored just 35 goals in 38 games. Frustrated fans were beginning to lose track of the ups and downs, and it all seemed to be merging into one seemingly endless mass of misery. Relegation in 1997 meant that Sunderland could not begin life at the stunning new Stadium of Light as a Premiership club, and indeed it would be another two years before they were able to fit the two together. But Sunderland would not be Sunderland without the obligatory heartache. At the end of the 1997/98 season, there was almost too much of it around for anyone to bear.

Reid had changed things. Older stagers such as Gary Bennett and Tony Norman had moved on during his early days at the club, and by now a totally different-looking squad was at his disposal. Kevin Phillips, Niall Quinn, Lee Clark, Allan Johnston, Nicky Summerbee, Danny Dichio, Lionel Perez, Alex Rae, Darren Holloway, Jody Craddock and Chris Makin were forming the new guard, with Michael Gray, Michael Bridges and Richard Ord proving their worth as crucial home-grown talent. Quinn, the towering target man who had played for Manchester City under Reid, had been an instant hit, as had wingers Summerbee and Johnston plus Clark, who had been signed from rivals Newcastle United. But the relatively unknown Phillips, a £650,000 snip from Watford, eventually carved his name in the club's history, scoring 130 goals in just 235 appearances to become their greatest post-war goalscorer.

Sunderland had finished third behind Nottingham Forest and Southampton with Phillips scoring 29 League goals, so they were back in the play-offs as all eyes were on winning yet another passport back into the Premiership. They saw off Sheffield United in the semi-finals and then had to dispose of Charlton Athletic in the final at Wembley. A dramatic, nerve-tingling encounter ended 4–4 after extra-time with Quinn (twice), Phillips and Summerbee scoring for the Wearsiders and Sunderland-born striker Clive Mendonca grabbing a hat-trick for Charlton to go with a goal from Richard Rufus. The game, therefore, would be decided by a penalty shoot-out, and the unfortunate Michael Gray was the man to miss. His spot-kick was saved by Sasa Ilic, allowing Charlton to be promoted courtesy of a 7–6 win in the shoot-out.

Reid's answer was instant. He and his players regrouped and promptly soared to the First Division title in 1998/99. They returned to the promised land in 1999 as champions with a mammoth total of 105 points – 18 more than second-placed Bradford City. Phillips and Quinn rattled in 51 of their 91 League goals between them, Phillips finishing with 23 and Quinn with 18, and an exciting, fast-raiding Black Cats side returned to the Premiership in some style. Sunderland did not lose any of their first 18 League games or any of their final 17: in fact, they lost only three times in their 46 outings.

Captained back into the Premiership by their inspirational leader Kevin Ball, Sunderland still had it all to prove. But they surprised many observers by finishing seventh for two successive seasons. In fact, they were third for much of the first half of the 1999/2000 season, when

Phillips finished up by scoring 30 of their 57 League goals. In 2000/01 they were one of a number of mid-table teams which struggled for goals as defences held sway, but these were Sunderland's best years since the Bank of England team's era 50 years earlier. Critically, though, improvements were not made at the necessary times and the whole bubble burst before anyone could settle down and enjoy such dizzy heights.

In December 1999 the ever-popular Ball left for Fulham, who were managed by his former Sunderland team-mate Paul Bracewell, in a £200,000 deal. He had made 376 appearances for the club and later returned to the Stadium of Light to join the coaching staff in a PR master-stroke. And although right-winger Nicky Summerbee was still a first-team regular, the damage had been done with the right-footed Scottish international Allan Johnston, who had fallen out with Reid. He found himself isolated after a dispute with the Sunderland boss, and the team suffered as a result of the personality clash. Summerbee was next to find himself on the wrong end of a dust-up with Reid, and that marked the end of his Sunderland road too. The supporters were not impressed because the two wingers had been huge favourites and their supply lines for the free-scoring Phillips and Quinn had been a major feature of the club's resurgence.

Summerbee soon found himself being shown the door when Reid decided he was no longer a part of his plans, and recalled:

> I think I played the best football of my career at Sunderland, but I also think people know what happened. There was a fall-out with the manager and I don't think he did me any favours. After that, I found myself going on trial at clubs, but it's just not the same. You don't feel part of it and it's almost as if people are not taking you seriously. It got to the stage where I was having to train on my own, and it was tough having to go along and watch games on Saturday afternoons.

Reid, meanwhile, was wheeling and dealing at pace. Players were coming and going at the Stadium of Light, although the fans were willing to turn a blind eye towards some of the stranger-looking signings as long as Sunderland were holding their own with the best in the country. But then there was a sudden downturn in events on the field during 2001/02 as Sunderland slumped to a final Premiership placing of 17th, and the out-of-touch Phillips finished as the leading marksman with just 11 League goals.

Phillips, who had picked up eight England caps while on Wearside, still had one more season at Sunderland to come, but he struggled to recapture his goal touch in a side which always looked likely to crash headlong through the Premiership trapdoor. Indeed, they did not so much crash through it in 2002/03 as fly through it without trace. The under-pressure Reid was sacked in October 2002, and the dour Howard Wilkinson, who had been in the England set-up in different guises, was rushed in as his shock replacement. However, things went from bad to worse. Wilkinson and his assistant Steve Cotterill lasted just five months before Mick McCarthy, who had his own managerial pedigree with the Republic of Ireland, followed him into the hot seat in March 2003, but the damage was done and Sunderland were relegated on an all-time low. They spiralled back into the First Division with the lowest-ever points haul of any Premiership club – a meagre 19 – and ended a dismal season with a staggering 15 successive League defeats. They won just four League games, the last of them in December 2002, and scored just 21 goals in total.

It was a bitterly disappointing end to an era – one in which Peter Reid had almost banished the demons who appeared to have conspired to prevent such an enormous club from ever maintaining a position among English football's modern elite. And with the end of an era came the inevitable breaking-up of a squad. Among those to depart were former skipper Michael Gray, Danish international goalkeeper Thomas Sorensen and England international midfield man Gavin McCann as McCarthy tried valiantly to deal with the financial crisis he had inherited. As part of it, Phillips made a £3.25m switch to Southampton, who had initially rejected him as a teenage full-back, but no-one could ever take away his memories of life in Sunderland's red and white stripes:

My first four years with the club were fantastic, but the last two were not so memorable although they were still enjoyable. What opened my eyes a bit was the pre-season following the second season of finishing seventh. We never really went out and spent the money and bought the big names who had been promised to me as well as to the supporters. I thought to myself then, 'Maybe this is the time to get out.' I could just sense it. That was the time for Sunderland to go and get the big-hitters because I'm sure they would have come to the Stadium of Light. But, for me, that's history now.

Phillips left Sunderland with an incredible goalscoring record. He netted 130 times in 235 appearances, winning Europe's Golden Boot in 2000. In his first season at the Stadium of Light he scored 35 times to beat the legendary Brian Clough's record of 34 in a season in 1961/62 – although, strictly speaking, the Football League do not include goals in the play-offs in their official records. And a glorious run in which he hit ten in seven successive matches beat another record previously held by Trevor Ford. It was, of course, more than a touch ironic that he should return to Southampton, who had freed him as a youngster. He recalled:

> I was a right-back in those days, but was released because of my physique – my body hadn't grown fully. It was heart-breaking because all I ever wanted was to be a professional footballer. But I always remember my last words to the manager at the time, Chris Nicholl, when I walked out of his office. I told him that I would prove him wrong, so to go back there as a centre-forward all those years later was really quite amazing.

He is, though, in good company because Raich Carter had been allowed to leave Leicester City for being too small more than 60 years earlier and had proved them wrong by becoming a Roker hero.

Sadly, picking up the pieces and starting all over again is nothing new to Sunderland fans. Yet another journey began in the summer of 2003 when the honest and straight-talking McCarthy set about his own rebuilding task. There was a run to the FA Cup semi-finals that left Hartlepool United, Ipswich Town, Premiership side Birmingham City and Sheffield United in their wake. It led to an action replay from 1937, when Sunderland first won the trophy, as they met Millwall in the semi-finals, but this time they lost 1–0. Manager Mick McCarthy said:

> There are no heroic failures for me. I'm not into that one. We were very disappointed that we lost. It was nice to get to the semi-finals, but we wanted to get to the final. That's the achievement. It's time to be men about it. We had a disappointment, but we couldn't let it linger into our League form. It's when you've had disappointment and have to pick yourself up, then you discover if you're a decent team. It's easy when you're doing well, you get to a semi-final and people pat you on the back and say how good you are.

But as Norwich and West Bromwich eventually pulled away from First Division's chasing pack, it was always going to be a place in the agonising end-of-season play-offs for Sunderland – and so it proved, another penalty shoot-out putting an end to one more promotion dream. Defeat by Crystal Palace at the semi-final stage of the play-offs left both the club

175

and their fans frustrated, emotionally drained and wondering just what the future might hold. McCarthy observed: 'It was unbelievably tough. I asked for some luck from the play-offs, but we didn't get it.' But he sympathised with Jeff Whitley, who missed the vital penalty in the shoot-out: 'He was magnificent for someone who came on a free transfer. He's been a terrific competitor and I felt very sorry for him.'

It was exactly 40 years since the great Charlie Hurley had led an exciting and attack-minded team back into the top flight for the first time in Sunderland's history but, perhaps more significantly, 68 long years since the famous old club had finished a season as the best team in the land. Promotions and relegations had never existed for Sunderland then. The post-war seesaw seasons confirmed that they had become all too familiar.

9

MONEY, MONEY, MONEY

Relegation from the FA Premiership at the end of the 2002/03 season was catastrophic for Sunderland. It was not just the manner of it, in the wake of 15 consecutive League defeats, it also left them with a fearsome financial fiasco to face. Manager Mick McCarthy was forced to trim the wage bill drastically as the severity of the situation slowly surfaced, and it heralded a transitional stage in the club's fortunes. The brutal reality of the fiscal facts gradually became clearer, and in February 2004 Sunderland secured a re-financing package to repay a £36m debt over a seven-year period, agreed with bankers Barclay's and financiers Lombard. Vice-chairman John Fickling explained:

> The club hasn't received any new funds to invest in the team or any other issues for that matter. What it means is that we have dealt with the traumatic and immediate impact of relegation and we have survived. The club has arrested what might have been a serious decline. The position has levelled out and we can move forward.

Two months later, Sunderland were reported to have had debts of £33.2m for the six months ending 31 January. Turnover had fallen by 46 per cent to £14.4m, reflecting a 33 per cent fall in attendances. McCarthy's clear-out of players after relegation at the end of 2002/03 had reduced operating costs by 48 per cent to allow for a £3.7m profit, and the club's plc chairman Bryan Sanderson insisted: 'There is renewed spirit and determination and we are committed to getting back to the Premiership.' Reaching the end-of-season play-offs was a notable achievement in view of the transition, but going out of them without attaining promotion was not one of the money men's muses.

The future had been bleak for a while, but the money problems should hardly have come as a shock. After all, there had been all sorts of them in the past. Financial trouble and strife had haunted Sunderland even before they became a League club. In 1881, for example, one of their members offset a financial disaster by raising £1 to rescue the club with the sale of his prize canary and its cage!

And payments to players had cost Sunderland some embarrassment as far back as 1887/88, when they led to the club being thrown out of the FA Cup. They had already had to replay a tie with Morpeth Harriers for fielding an ineligible player when they reached the third round for the first time after beating Newcastle West End 3–1. They then drew 2–2 at Middlesbrough before winning the replay 4–2 at Newcastle Road. But then the all-amateur Boro complained that they had been victims of professionalism – in breach of FA Cup rules – and Sunderland's cash book was found to include a sum of £1 10s (£1.50) that had been paid to three Scottish players – Monaghan, Hastings and Richardson – for their train fares from Dumfries. Boro also alleged that Sunderland had paid the hotel expenses of several Scottish players and employed a professional trainer. Two special commissions sat in judgement on the issue, and Middlesbrough progressed at the expense of Sunderland, who were found guilty of 'technical professionalism'. The players, all of whom had been drafted in for the replay, were suspended for three months, and Middlesbrough went on their controversial way to the quarter-finals – controversial because they found themselves in trouble at the fifth-round stage when they beat Old Foresters 4–0. Old Foresters protested about the state of the Linthorpe Road pitch, and the FA ordered the tie to be replayed. But then Old Foresters scratched from the competition and a second game was not needed. The outcome for Sunderland, meanwhile, was that they recorded a loss of £370 at the end of the season.

Another payment to a player caused a stir in May 1889, when Sunderland signed Scottish centre-half John Auld from Queen's Park. He was a shoemaker by trade, and that played a part in his remarkable transfer deal. Auld, who went on to skipper Sunderland, was given a £150 signing-on fee, £20 for turning professional, help with the establishment of his own boot-and-shoe business and a hefty £300 wage for the first two years.

Not long afterwards there was another costly episode involving a Scottish player. Goalkeeper Ned Doig's registration when he was transferred from Arbroath to Sunderland in September 1890 was regarded as having been improper. He was therefore an ineligible player for Sunderland when he made his League debut for them and, not only did the club lose the first two League points it had gained, but was also fined £25. Sunderland might have been hit in the pocket, but the points deduction also meant that they finished seventh instead of fifth in the 12-team, one-division Football League in their first season.

But a cash controversy surrounding another Scottish international,

Inverness-born right-back Andy McCombie, had a more far-reaching effect on Sunderland's early history. In 1903 McCombie received £100 from the club's new chairman Sinclair Todd, who had taken over from James Henderson, the man who had masterminded the move from Newcastle Road to Roker Park. McCombie had a benefit match soon afterwards and then Todd asked for the £100 back. McCombie refused to return it, insisting that the money had nothing to do with his benefit and that it had been a gift from the club. Todd, though, maintained that it had been a loan. The dispute rumbled on until early 1904, when it became clear that McCombie was on his way out of Roker Park. He did not want to go far because he had used the £100 to start up his own business, so he made the short journey to Newcastle United for a record £700 fee. McCombie was able to link up with wing-half Peter McWilliam, a future Scottish international who also came from Inverness, and they helped the Magpies to great success. Their neighbours Sunderland slipped out of the limelight, but the matter had not ended there.

Sunderland's board took McCombie to court to try to reclaim the £100, and the ruling went in the club's favour. McCombie was ordered to repay the money, but the FA's attention had been drawn even more emphatically to the dispute and it decided to hold an inquiry into it. In October 1904 they ruled that McCombie should be absolved of blame, but it found that Sunderland's accounts books did not show a proper record of the transaction. The club was again found guilty of making illegal payments, and fined £250. In addition, Todd and five other directors were banned from football for two and a half years, manager Alex Mackie for three months, and secretary Alec Watson for 18 months.

The repercussions of the affair were considerable. Fred Taylor returned to the board to take over as the new chairman after Todd had departed with a gift of his own – a silver cigar-box – for his year's service! Taylor, a staunch Methodist who owned one of the first cars in England, rebuilt the club's foundations and served Sunderland a lot longer than Todd had. But McCombie's move was also symptomatic of the kind of big-money deals with which Sunderland were to be regularly associated, and Mackie made sure that was the case when he returned at the end of his ban.

When it came to record transfer deals, England international inside-forward Alf Common was in the vanguard because he was the first player to move for both a fee of more than £500 and for a four-figure amount. And both deals involving Common, who was capped three times while with Sheffield United and Middlesbrough, went through in less than a year with Sunderland involved on each occasion. Common had played for Jarrow and South Hylton Juniors as a teenager and first joined his home-town club Sunderland in the summer of 1900, but then moved to Sheffield United in a £325 deal in November of the following year, and was an FA Cup winner with them in 1902. It was when he returned to Roker Park in the summer of 1904 that the transfer fun really started, because he cost a record £520. But Common was on the move again by February 1905, becoming the first player to be transferred for £1,000 when he joined Middlesbrough. He later moved on twice for £250 when he joined Woolwich Arsenal and Preston North End, but it was that first four-figure fee for which he is remembered in football history. Four-figure fees gradually became common, so to speak, after that: almost a century later, eight-figure fees have become common.

But one irony is that Common, who was said to be bulky but quick, played in only 43 games for Sunderland despite the transfer ballyhoo and two spells with them. A greater irony, though, was that Alex Mackie soon followed Common to Middlesbrough as manager – after selling him to them. But after he had signed England hero Steve Bloomer from Derby County a year later, Boro were also found guilty of making illegal payments to players. Mackie was suspended again, and left the game to become a publican.

Major transfer fees, though, were becoming a regular thing at Sunderland. When Scottish international centre-half Charlie B. Thomson joined them from Heart of Midlothian just short of his 30th birthday in May 1908, there was a regulation in force stating that the maximum transfer fee should be £350. But it seemed, in effect, that Sunderland got round it, and he was signed for a £700 fee because there was a makeweight in the deal, believed to be goalkeeper Tom Allan, who also left Hearts for Sunderland at roughly the same time. Allan made only 26 appearances in three seasons at Roker Park before rejoining Hearts, but Thomson, who was capped by Scotland 21 times, was far more valuable to Sunderland and was an integral part of the side which won the First Division title and reached the FA Cup final in 1912/13, serving them until he retired just short of his 41st birthday.

A month later it was a different story when Sunderland entered the crazy world of Arthur Brown. They paid Sheffield United a world record fee of £1,600 for Brown, a centre-forward who had become England's youngest international when he made his debut for them as an 18-year-old in 1904. But Brown, who had scored four times for the Blades when they beat Sunderland 5–3 in October 1907, did not last long at the top despite his early promise. He scored 23 times in 55 games for Sunderland, but moved on to Fulham in 1910 and then left the game at the age of 28.

Then there was the case of centre-forward James 'Joe' Lane, whose family owned a printing company. At one time they had had a commission for work in Hungary, which is why he moved to Sunderland from Ferencváros Torna. But he played just two League games as a centre-forward for them in 1913 before moving to Blackpool in a £400 deal. He was, though, destined to play a significant role in football history. When he left the Seasiders in May 1920, he cost Birmingham City a record £3,300 figure and brought about an FA rule change that enabled a player to receive part of his transfer fee. He is said to have received a third of the fee when he joined Birmingham.

Less than a year later, centre-forward Bernard 'Barney' Travers, who had scored a respectable 27 goals in 63 appearances for them, left his home-town club Sunderland for Fulham for £3,000, but the following season he was banned for life for his part in a bribery scandal. He then had brief spells in Austrian and Spanish football, but eventually returned to the North-East to run a fruit-and-vegetable stall. Sunderland, it seemed, were either directly or indirectly involved in many memorable money matters, and some of their transfer deals during the 1920s confirmed it.

Warneford Cresswell was one of two footballing brothers from South Shields who played for Sunderland. Warney, a right-back who was capped seven times by England and said to be able to 'kid a forward to hand the ball over to him', made more of an impact than his younger brother Frank, especially when he left South Shields to join Sunderland in March 1922. South Shields, then a League club who were on the verge of their highest-ever finish of sixth in the old Second Division, had rebuffed bids from Aston Villa and Tottenham Hotspur before they yielded to Sunderland, who paid a record transfer fee of £5,500 for his services. The existing record of £5,000 had been set only the previous month when inside-forward Syd Puddefoot, later an England international, moved from West Ham United to Falkirk.

Centre-half Michael 'Rubberneck' Gilhooley was twice involved in record transfer deals. He cost Hull City a club record £2,500 during the summer of 1920 from Clydebank, whom he had joined during the 1914–18 war. Known for his powerful heading ability, he became a Scottish international, winning his one cap in a 2–0 defeat against Wales at Wrexham on 4 February 1922. That prompted Sunderland to sign him for record fee of £5,250 the following month. But the record was broken only a few days later, and Gilhooley played in just 20 games in three years after suffering a serious knee injury shortly after his move to Roker Park. He finished his English League career at Bradford City and Queen's Park Rangers before returning to Scotland, when he joined Troon

Athletic in the early part of 1929.

When Charlie Buchan, one of Sunderland's all-time greats, was allowed to return to Arsenal in the summer of 1925 at the age of 33, there were some complex negotiations. Arsenal's famous manager Herbert Chapman would not pay Sunderland's asking fee of £4,000 – a substantial figure in those days – so a compromise was reached. Sunderland's manager Bob Kyle accepted a down payment of £2,000 with the rider that they would receive £100 for every goal that Buchan scored in his first season with the Gunners. Buchan was a regular 20-goals-a-season man, but the deal could have gone badly wrong if, say, he had suffered an injury lay-off. As it was, Buchan promptly produced 21 League and Cup goals for Arsenal in 1925/26, so Sunderland ended up getting £4,100 for him!

Buchan was eventually replaced by England inside-forward Bob Kelly, who joined Sunderland from Burnley for what was then a record fee of £6,650 in December 1925. Kelly, originally a miner from Lancashire, was capped 14 times by England and was 32 when he moved to Roker Park. But he lasted only 14 months and 55 games with Sunderland and, when he moved on to Huddersfield Town, the fee was just £3,500.

It was not unknown for Sunderland to make losses in the transfer market in those early days. They might have had every reason to feel fated about money matters, and their experience with half-back Bill Hopkins, a local lad from Esh Winning, underlined the point. He joined the club in 1912 and played in only 10 games, nine of which were won, before the 1914–18 war intervened. Hopkins was then sold to Leeds City for £50 during the summer of 1919, but his market value suddenly rocketed three months later. Leeds were expelled from the Football League in October 1919 for financial irregularities, and Port Vale took over their Second Division fixtures. The Leeds players were then auctioned off, and amazingly Hopkins fetched a somewhat irregular fee of £600 when he joined South Shields, who were also in the Second Division in those days. Sunderland also spent £550 on Indian-born centre-forward Tom Wagstaffe in March 1923 when he was signed from non-League Fleetwood. Wagstaffe had scored 28 goals in 11 games for Fleetwood, but his career in League football was short-lived. He made just two appearances and was then transfer-listed a little more than a year later at £100.

But it was not all bad news at that time, because Sunderland made some useful profits in the transfer market to offset any losses. Full-back Ernie England cost £100 from Shirebrook as an 18-year-old in 1919 but, when he moved to West Ham 351 games later at the age of 29, his value had shot up to £500. Another full-back, Warney Cresswell, cost £5,500 from South Shields as a 24-year-old in 1922. When, also at the age of 29, he left for Everton, with whom he won two First Division titles, the FA Cup and one more England cap, Sunderland made a profit by selling him for £7,000. Goal machine David Halliday had drifted round the Scottish scene until Sunderland paid Dundee £3,500 for him in April 1925. His response was to set the record for the quickest century of League goals by a First Division player, reaching the target in his 101st game for the club in March 1928. And it was a testimony to his goalscoring craft that Sunderland sold him to Arsenal for £6,500 in late 1929 when he was just short of his 32nd birthday.

Sunderland remained at the forefront of football spending in post-war years. It was typified by arrival of inside-forward Ivor Broadis in January 1949. He had been appointed as Carlisle United's player-manager at the age of 23 in August 1946, but had never played an authentic League game despite having had wartime spells with Spurs and Millwall. Broadis may have been the youngest League manager ever, but it led to a incredible situation when he joined Sunderland in an £18,000 deal. This was the record amount to be received by a Third Division North club, and Broadis had become the first manager to transfer himself! He did not always do things the normal way, though: he may have been a manager at 23, but he was just short of his 29th birthday when he won the first of his 14 England caps soon after leaving Sunderland.

The blueprint for Sunderland's post-war spending had been set 11 months earlier when inside-forward Len Shackleton was prised from Newcastle United in a £20,050 deal, beating the British record of £20,000 set four months earlier when England centre-forward Tommy Lawton moved from Chelsea to Notts County. Shackleton joined Arsenal's ground staff in 1938 after playing for Kippax United in his native West Yorkshire. Two years earlier he had been an England schoolboy international, even though he was tiny and weighed only 6st 2lb. Arsenal, who paid him £2 10s (£2.50) a week, soon had their doubts about him, and after only two games with the Gunners he was told by manager George Allison that he was not good enough, and was released. It was later said that he always reserved some of his best performances for the London crowds – to show them what they had missed. Shackleton took a job at a paper mill in Kent, but returned north soon after the outbreak of the 1939–45 war. He had a stint as a Bevin Boy (youngsters conscripted to work in the coal mines), then signed for Bradford Park Avenue, moving on to Newcastle in a £13,000 deal in the autumn of 1946. On 5 October he made his debut for the Magpies and scored six times in what remains their biggest League win, 13–0 at home to Newport County. But there seems to have been a problem with Newcastle meeting some of his expenses, and he moved down the road to Roker Park.

Sunderland's spending also stretched to Welsh international centre-forward Trevor Ford, who cost a club record £29,500 from Aston Villa in October 1950. Originally from Swansea, Ford had plenty in common with Shack – they had both failed to make the grade at Arsenal as youngsters and were strong, opinionated characters. Both, in fact, were known as 'the stormy petrels of soccer' in those days! Ford was an immediate hit with the public after scoring a hat-trick on his home debut in a 5–1 win over Sheffield Wednesday, damaging a goalpost with one of his shots. Within a month of joining Sunderland, he played for Wales against England at Roker Park, scoring both their goals in a 4–2 defeat. Capped 38 times by Wales, Ford eventually left to go back to South Wales, signing for Cardiff City in another £29,500 deal in December 1953. He was the Bluebirds' record signing at the time, and again it was a British record fee for a centre-forward.

The animosity between Shackleton and Ford may well have originated from money matters in the first place. It was common in the 1950s for some leading players to be paid for jobs 'outside football.' In other words, a player would be signed on the understanding that he would be able to earn an extra £10 a week or more from a job to which he could trundle along in the afternoon when the day's training was over. With certain top players, some of these jobs were fictitious. But this was an era of back-handers and illegal payments. And, as it happened, Sunderland were to find out to their enormous cost just where the little tricks of the trade might lead a few years later.

When Ford moved to Roker Park, he admitted that he had chosen Sunderland ahead of other interested parties because of their offer of a house and a well-paid job outside football. The job was as a car salesman for Grimshaw Leather, thanks to their connection with Wearside-based motor agent and Sunderland director Billy Martin. Ivor Broadis said:

Fordy had been given this part-time job as a car salesman. Billy Martin employed him on a part-time basis and Trevor would drive along to training in a nice car – in fact, often three different cars a week. It wasn't his fault. What was he supposed to say to the people at the garage who were letting him use these cars? But it didn't go down too well with some of the players and I don't suppose Shack thought too much of it. The trouble was that the only way you could make a few quid in those days was to move clubs. Everyone knew that even though it was a case of back-handers – and look at the trouble Sunderland ended up in because of that! But even then you had to find someone who wanted to sign you. Players were tied to their clubs – every one of us a slave. You either got a new one-year contract every summer or else you were not retained and the club stopped paying you on 30 June.

Five months before Ford's departure, Sunderland splashed out on another son of Swansea when they signed Ray Daniel from Arsenal for £27,500. It was a record fee for a centre-half although Daniel, who became the club's captain, also turned out at full-back and centre-forward on occasions. Daniel had also played at Roker Park alongside Ford for Wales in November 1950, and was capped 21 times by his country. As with Ford, he returned to South Wales to join Cardiff, but cost just £7,500 in October 1957. Daniel then finished his League career back with Swansea Town, with whom he had started out as an amateur.

Sunderland were by now known as The Bank of England team and, in addition to signings such as Shackleton, Ford and Daniel, there were others who clambered onto the Roker bandwagon. Most of them were forwards: England international Billy Elliott moved in a £26,000 deal from Burnley during the summer of 1953, Ken Chisholm arrived from Cardiff in a £15,000 deal in December 1953 and Ted Purdon, a South African, cost £15,000 from Birmingham in January 1954. Goalkeeper Willie Fraser, an Australian by birth who won two caps for Scotland because of his parentage, arrived in a £5,000 deal from Airdrieonians two months later. Charlie 'Cannonball' Fleming was signed during the summer of 1955 in a player-exchange deal with East Fife involving his fellow Scottish international right-winger Tommy Wright, who had cost £8,000 himself from Partick Thistle almost six years earlier. East Fife received £7,000 plus Wright in the deal.

There was a price to pay, though. In 1958 came the club's first-ever relegation, but more than a year earlier there was an action replay from the early years of the club's history: Sunderland were in trouble again for making illegal payments to their players. It started in late 1956 when the football authorities became aware of an anonymous letter, mysteriously sent by 'someone called Smith', which detailed various claims of undeclared payments made to players and on the commercial side. By March 1957 a six-man joint FA and Football League Commission met representatives from Sunderland, including chairman Bill Ditchburn, manager Bill Murray and secretary George Crow in Sheffield. Three weeks later they reconvened in York with further representatives from the club. Soon afterwards the Commission announced that Sunderland had been found guilty of making illegal payments totalling £5,427 14s 2d to players via commercial agents over a period of five years.

Ditchburn and fellow director Billy Martin were banned from football permanently; while other directors, Stanley Ritson and Laurie Evans, were suspended sine die, although Ritson re-emerged to become the club's chairman for two years from 1958; and the rest of the board was heavily censured. Sunderland were fined a record £5,000 and told to pay the costs of the Commission. A few days later, though, there was an even bigger sensation when the names of the players involved were disclosed – Ray Daniel, Billy Elliott, Johnny Hannigan, Willie Fraser, Trevor Ford and Ken Chisholm. By this time Ford had come out of a brief retirement to play for PSV Eindhoven in Holland, and Chisholm had been transferred to Workington, but it did not lessen the impact. The six were summoned to appear before the FA, but Ford stayed in Holland and the other five refused to give evidence when asked – so they, too, were banned from football indefinitely. The suspensions were soon lifted, though, after a hearing in Sheffield at which the five admitted taking underhand payments. They had to forfeit benefit qualifications instead, and in June 1957 Bill Murray, who had been fined £200 after the fact that he had been acting under instructions had been taken into consideration, resigned as manager. Sunderland's trainer Bert Johnston, one of the heroes of the 1935/36 title-winning season and the first FA Cup-winning campaign the following season, also left the club, and Ditchburn's successor, Colonel John Turnbull, was left to pick up the pieces. The management team of Alan Brown and trainer George Curtis, who had been England's youth coach, was then installed.

There was no doubt that Sunderland were made scapegoats, because English football was rife with the kind of payments they had been making. Len Shackleton summed it all up in typically robust fashion after the Football League's new president Joe Richards had called for changes in the game's thinking about the maximum wage during the summer of 1957. Shackleton had previously advocated players reaching their own agreements with clubs about wages, length of contracts and benefit payments. He had this to say:

> If Stan Matthews was worth £50 a week and someone else in the Blackpool team was worth £10 a week in the eyes of the management, then that should have been allowed to happen. I think back then that the men in suits at the FA were terrified of creating disharmony in a football team. Everyone had to be equal and all that rubbish. Of course, it came about eventually, but that was after my day. But I believe that I can modestly

claim to have started this particular ball rolling in August 1955 when my book *Clown Prince of Soccer* was published. At that time I was 'murdered' by football legislators and the press. I was branded as a troublemaker, and there was even an attempt to victimise me. Yet the press decided it was a very sensible argument when an eminent gentleman such as Matt Busby expressed similar views 18 months later. Shack was a fool to say, 'Scrap the maximum wage.' But Busby was talking sense when he said, 'Scrap the maximum wage.' In my book I warned that football was being so badly run that trouble was inevitable sooner or later. Having refused to heed the warning, the FA and the League were exposed and embarrassed about the case of the 'Sunderland Scandals'. With directors, manager and players suspended or fined, Sunderland had some most unsavoury publicity, all of which could have been avoided. That evil and archaic maximum wage was the direct cause of illegal payments to players at Roker Park. When I wrote my book, I claimed that my rather outspoken views were put forward in the best interests of the game we all love. Few people believed me, but it is gratifying to realise now that other folk are beginning to see the light. If the trend continues, we may one day have football being run by football experts instead of by grocers, coal merchants and solicitors.'

Memorably, it was a point on which Shack and Ford agreed. Ford said for his part:

I would not have been prepared to let my sons go through what I went through. The star player was not paid his worth, and I feel ashamed that I had to secure my future and make my family comfortable by under-the-counter methods. Yet it was not my fault. It was the fault of the system, and something had to be done about it. The maximum wage then was £15 a week. I had a wife, two children and a house to run. And, when you are constantly in the public eye as I was, you had to dress in a way that did not let yourself or the club down. When I had taken care of all my outgoings, I didn't have enough left to keep me in smokes!

The existence of a maximum wage for footballers was always going to make it more likely that underhand payments would be made to players to enable some clubs to steal a march on their rivals. This happened in some unlikely circumstances, as the delayed signing of inside-forward Johnny Crossan showed. In effect, centre-forward Ian Lawther initially ended up being signed in his place in March 1958 because Crossan's brother Derek was a centre-half with Coleraine, for whom Crossan had been playing. Ian Lawther explained:

> I was approached by Sunderland's Northern Ireland scout Tom Coulter and manager Alan Brown, who had made an unsuccessful trip to Belfast in an attempt to sign John Crossan. I agreed to go to Roker Park for a trial, and after five weeks Alan Brown said that he wanted me to sign professional forms for Sunderland. But I had to go through the formality of signing professional forms for Belfast Crusaders, and then I was transferred to Sunderland.

The problem was that in the interim the 19-year-old Crossan, who was 11 months older than Lawther, had been accused of taking payments while an amateur with Coleraine, and the Football League refused to sanction his registration with Bristol City. He was banned for life by the Irish League and opted to pursue his career with Sparta Rotterdam in Holland and then Standard Liège in Belgium. It was only when his ban was lifted that Sunderland paid Liège £27,000 for him in October 1962.

It was all a far cry from the 1930s when Raich Carter signed for Sunderland for a basic £3 a week, Bobby Gurney earned £6 a week and Eddie Burbanks settled for £8 a week during the season with £2 less during the summer months. In fact, it was a far cry from a special provision in the contract signed by Burbanks with the club in April 1939, overseen by secretary George Crow. It read:

> If at any time during the period of this agreement the wages herein agreed to be paid shall be in excess of the wages permitted to be paid by the club to the player in accordance with the rules of the Football League, the wages to be paid to the player shall be the amount the club are entitled to pay by League rules.

It was also a far cry from Sunderland's attitude towards the up-and-coming local players taking their chances alongside the big-money signings who had earned the club their tag as The Bank of England Team. Wing-half Stan Anderson, for example, turned professional with Sunderland in 1951 after having joined the club as an amateur. He recalled:

When I was 17, I was invited to go to the secretary's office at Roker Park to sign professional forms. The youth-team trainer Tommy Urwin had told me that the club would offer me £3 a week, but said that I ought to hold out for £5. My dad came along for the meeting with George Crow. Although my father was a shy man, I remember him saying to George, 'I think Stan is worth £5 a week. He's the best player you've got in his age group.' Well, I thought George was going to have a heart attack on the spot. He replied that the most the club would be prepared to offer would be £3. We stayed in there for an hour and a half, and we must have ground him down. In the end he looked tired and agreed to £5 a week in the season and £4 in the summer. 'We've never given that to a newly signed professional before,' he moaned. We just smiled, and I signed on the spot.

Yet the big-money signings – as opposed to the local lads starting their careers by making their way through the club's ranks – continued to pick Sunderland as a priority to join after the maximum wage had been abolished in 1961. The next batch of Scots proved it. Centre-forward Harry Hood had become a hot property after becoming a prolific goalscorer with Clyde, whom he had preferred to a move to Barnsley, and Glasgow Celtic had renewed their interest in him in the autumn of 1964. But he recalled:

Celtic showed considerable interest in me, but I turned them down. Celtic had discussed a fee of about £20,000 for my services, but they were prepared to pay me only £26 a week, whereas I could pull in £30 with Clyde as a part-time professional and do a job as well. As it happened, Sunderland were said to have topped Celtic's bid by £6,000 three days later, and I decided to go to Roker because there were better wages in it for me. They weren't doing so well, but I struck up a fine understanding with little Nicky Sharkey.

Hood returned to Clyde and finally got his move to Celtic in March 1969, but at one stage he ended up with a bizarre job. He would advertise cheese on a walkabout tour of Glasgow stores and sign autographs while leaflets were distributed!

When Ian McColl became Sunderland's manager in the summer of 1965, he snapped up Scottish international 'Slim' Jim Baxter from Glasgow Rangers for a reported £72,000 fee, then a record for a Scot joining an English League club, a week after taking over. Baxter had played alongside McColl for Rangers and then under him when he became Scotland's team manager. But there was one other good reason for the move – Sunderland were paying better wages than Rangers. Baxter was paid £80 a week at Roker Park, £35 more than he earned at Rangers. In addition, the players were on a bonus of £40 a point at Sunderland, so every win meant that they effectively doubled their weekly wages!

The basic economics of supply and demand were gradually being eroded at Roker Park. The figures showed that Sunderland spent a total of £1.25m on 53 players between the end of the 1939–45 war and the signing of David Watson, their first-ever £100,000 buy, from Rotherham United in December 1970. But their gates plummeted from an average of 40,885 in 1962 to 15,095 10 years later. Sunderland were in danger of remaining a big club in name only, but those running the club were desperate to buck the trend.

In fact, Sunderland's determination to pay players above-average wages continued in the 1970s, and forward Roy Greenwood's situation confirmed it. There were hints of shock and controversy when he rejected a move to Arsenal while he was at Roker Park, but it was a decision based on financial common sense. Greenwood explained:

Terry Neill wanted to sign me when he was manager at Arsenal, so I went down on a Saturday with Martin Harvey, our coach at Sunderland, because there was a testimonial match at Highbury. Neilly, who had been my manager at Hull, showed me the marble halls and all that, and we spoke terms, but they were £20 a week less than what I was earning at Sunderland. But it was agreed that on the Monday I'd go back to chat to them again and probably complete the signing. I had to get a train to London at 7.30 in the morning, but I rang Neilly on the Sunday to confirm everything about the arrangements and mentioned that it was a bit early for me. It was said as a joke and it was taken as a joke by Neilly. I also said that I wanted to negotiate on the wages, but he said that it was the final offer on the table. I then said, 'I'm wasting your and my time' and called it off. But then Terry Neill told the newspapers that it was off because I couldn't be bothered to catch a train to London so early in the morning. I got a lot of criticism for the comment, and one journalist, Linda Lee-Potter, wrote an article about footballers being mollycoddled. She's still on my hit list! The real reason was that expecting me to move from the North-East to live in London for less money wasn't quite right.

Sunderland's financial competitiveness had also meant that, when they were involved, other clubs often set transfer records. It happened when inside-right Dennis O'Donnell returned to his native North-East to become Lincoln City's record sale when he joined Sunderland in a £350 deal in May 1905. And it was still happening in June 1979 when defender Alan Weir left Sunderland after making just one appearance for them 15 months earlier to become Rochdale's then club record buy at £12,000. But maybe a classic example involved Colin Suggett, now Ipswich Town's chief scout. He was a product of Chester-le-Street Boys at the same time as Howard Kendall and Colin Todd and made his name as a striker, scoring 25 goals in 93 appearances for Sunderland. But he became West Bromwich Albion's record buy when he joined them for £100,000 during the summer of 1969. And then he was Norwich City's record buy when they spent £75,000 to sign him from the Baggies in February 1973. A funny thing happened to him in transit because Albion's manager Don Howe converted him into a midfield player – and his record price went down, of course!

Sunderland, though, remained more of a buying club than a selling one as transfer fees spiralled out of control. It took them a long while, for example, to break their record for a sale when it stood at £275,000. That was the value of forward Dennis Tueart when he joined Manchester City in a player-exchange deal in March 1974. It was the same amount that Manchester United paid Sunderland for goalkeeper Chris Turner in August 1985. And it was the same figure that midfield player Mark Proctor cost Sheffield Wednesday when he left Roker Park in September 1987. But four years later Sunderland finally broke the seven-figure barrier for a sale when a £1.8m deal took striker Marco Gabbiadini to Crystal Palace. That record stood until July 1999, when midfield player Lee Clark hurriedly left Sunderland for Fulham in a £3m switch. Ten days later, though, the club's present record sale was established when striker Michael Bridges moved to Leeds United, who knew a thing or two about a potentially disastrous 'Spend, Spend, Spend!' mentality at the time, for a £5.6m fee.

Sunderland's record buys did not always match their sales as the latter part of the 20th century unfolded, but gradually there were more of them. Striker John Hawley, a football agent nowadays, cost a club-record £200,000 from Leeds in October 1979, but that figure was overtaken just two months later when Sunderland expanded their horizons to foreign fields by signing forward Claudio Marangoni for £320,000 from Argentinian club San Lorenzo. The record stood until December 1988, when Welsh international Tony Norman was valued at £450,000 on leaving Hull soon after returning from a mid-season club trip to millionaires' paradise Bermuda to join Sunderland in a player-exchange deal which saw fellow goalkeeper Iain Hesford and striker Billy Whitehurst move in the opposite direction. Three years later striker Don Goodman became Sunderland's record signing when he cost £900,000 from West Bromwich, but there was a spell in the mid-1990s when big-money tranfers dried up. As former chief scout David Coates explained: 'We didn't have any money and we couldn't sign players.'

It took until June 1996 for them to spend a club-record £1m on Scottish midfield player Alex Rae from Millwall, as Sunderland seemingly started to change tack. They were not quite assembling another Bank of England team, but chairman Bob Murray's previous penchant for prudence was set aside as they repeatedly set club records in the buying stakes. In June 1997 they spent £2.5m on Newcastle's midfield player Lee Clark, and two summers later former Arsenal midfield man Stefan Schwarz, a 30-year-old Swedish international, was signed for a £3.75m fee. In fact, Schwarz, who had previously played in Germany, England, Portugal, Italy and Spain, was signed from Valencia for £2m more than Arsenal had paid for him five years earlier. Then, in September 2000, Sunderland again broke the bank when they signed central defender Emerson Thome for £4.5m from Chelsea, and 15 months later they equalled that figure when they snapped up American international midfield player Claudio Reyna from Glasgow Rangers. In August 2002 their benevolence to Rangers was further extended when they spent their current record amount of £8m on striker Tore-Andre Flo. It should not, therefore, have been too much of a surprise that Mick McCarthy had to work within a much-restricted budget as he prepared for life after relegation in 2003 and that the club had to put its finances on a rigorous footing.

But Sunderland's financial excursions into the post-war inflationary world of football have led to all kinds of odd escapades. For example, during the 1969/70 season, at the end of which Sunderland were relegated from the First Division for the second time in their history, a consortium of North-East businessmen offered to put £300,000 into the club provided that the board resigned. They also wanted to appoint former Roker hero Brian Clough as manager in place of Alan Brown. But one prominent director is said to have insisted that, given the choice of £300,000 and Clough, he would keep Brown and do without the money! Sunderland then paid twice over to assemble the management team which led them to FA Cup glory in 1972/73. They had to pay compensation to Blackpool to lure manager Bob Stokoe to Roker Park, but they also had to fork out £1,000 to Preston for the services of assistant manager Arthur Cox (who announced his retirement from the game during the summer of 2004 at the age of 64) because he was under contract as coach at Deepdale.

Then there was the throwback to the good old days of Sunderland falling foul of the football authorities in March 1995. Manager Mick Buxton signed central defender Dominic Matteo, a Scot who had played for England under-21s, on loan from Liverpool – or at least he thought he had. As English football braced itself for the aftermath of Eric Cantona's sortie into the Selhurst Park crowd and dealt with the transfer deadline, nobody took the trouble to register Matteo's move. As a result, he duly appeared in a 2–0 defeat at Barnsley even though he was ineligible. Matteo never played for Sunderland again, Buxton lost his job as manager almost immediately, and the club was fined £2,500 for its administrative misdemeanour. Common sense finally prevailed in 2002, when Sunderland's Republic of Ireland international striker Niall Quinn made the momentous decision that the proceeds of his testimonial match with Sunderland should go to charity. It put footballers' finances finally and firmly into perspective, and some other high-profile players followed suit. Quinn himself explained: 'I was nearly a soccer brat, but the more I earned, the harder my conscience became.'

Money, it seems, has nearly always been at the forefront of many of Sunderland's actions. After all, it was in September 1890 when Hugh Wilson was given an impressive £70 signing-on fee – on condition that he followed treasurer Samuel Tyzack's instruction to play to the best of his ability at all times – when he left Newmilns to become captain of the blossoming Team of All Talents. And so it was again when Gerry Steinberg, the Labour MP for the City of Durham and a Sunderland fan, claimed that 'a blatant wrong decision' – an alleged foul on Estonian international goalkeeper Mart Poom against Crystal Palace – had cost the club £20m because they did not reach the play-off final and lost their chance of promotion. Money, it appears, always talks.

10

HERE TODAY, GONE TOMORROW

As with all leading clubs, Sunderland can boast their fair share of all-time heroes, the majority of whom served the club loyally for long periods. But there have been plenty of other players who have flitted in and out of the first-team picture for one reason or another. As befits an area of the North-East, where a conveyor belt of football talent has constantly been in operation, there have been those who had tenuous links with Sunderland and probably wanted stronger ones as local lads, but were allowed to get away. Then there were those who were big names in the game – often internationals – and briefly played for Sunderland. Normally they were coming towards the end of their illustrious careers and are not usually thought of as being associated with the club. Some might have been seeking one last big pay day by moving – which of course happens everywhere. Still others popped into Sunderland on loan and soon popped out again. And there are those whose short stays with the club have been coloured by a variety of odd circumstances that might often appear to be stranger than fiction. They have all had one thing in common – they have been here today and gone tomorrow.

A classic example is that of winger Chris Waddle. He was from the North-East, he had trials with Sunderland, he made his name elsewhere instead, he played for England and he ultimately ended up at Roker Park. His spell with the Black Cats was short, and most fans would struggle to identify him as a Sunderland player if they were asked to name his clubs. But Waddle had been on trial at Roker Park in 1974 and 1980 before he joined their rivals Newcastle United from Tow Law Town as a 19-year-old. He then became remarkably cosmopolitan with Tottenham Hotspur, Olympique Marseille, Sheffield Wednesday, Falkirk and Bradford City before finally joining Sunderland in March 1997 at the age of 36. He had 62 international caps to his name, but he could not prevent Sunderland from being relegated from the FA Premiership. He played in the last seven games, including a visit to his first League club Newcastle for a Tyne–Wear derby, scored once, and then became

Burnley's player-manager.

Almost 40 years earlier the experience of inside-forward 'Wee' Ernie Taylor had reflected that of Waddle. Taylor, said to have had the smallest feet in football, was born in Sunderland, but did not play for his home-town club until he was 33. He had been snapped up by Newcastle as a 17-year-old in 1942 and was an FA Cup final winner with them when they beat Blackpool 2–0 in 1950/51. Soon afterwards Taylor joined the Seasiders for £25,000 and partnered Stanley Matthews when they beat Bolton Wanderers 4–3 in the 1952/53 FA Cup final. He played in a third FA Cup final in 1957/58 after being recruited by Manchester United following the Munich air disaster, but they lost 2–0 to Bolton. At the end of 1958, Taylor, who had also made one England appearance in the infamous 6–3 defeat by Hungary at Wembley in November 1953, finally joined Sunderland in a £6,000 deal and was a first-team regular for almost two years, scoring 11 goals in 71 appearances.

Striker Mick Harford, who was twice capped by England, supported his home-town club Sunderland as a youngster, but was 34 before he signed for them in a £250,000 deal from Chelsea in March 1993, a month after Terry Butcher had become player-manager. He played for ten different League clubs, including two spells with Newcastle and Luton Town, and Sunderland were eighth on the list. Harford's homecoming was hardly successful – he scored twice in 11 games, only one of which was won, but at least Sunderland avoided relegation from the First Division by a point.

Winger Harry Hooper was not an international, but his experience was typical of the dilemma that often faced local lads, because Sunderland were his last League club and should have been his first. He was born in Pittington in County Durham, and his father, Harry senior, had played for Sheffield United when they lost 1–0 to Arsenal in the 1936 FA Cup final and had managed Halifax Town for five years. Harry junior initially represented Durham Schoolboys and played locally for Hylton Colliery. He was on Sunderland's books as an amateur, but incredibly Sunderland decided that they did not want to rob Hylton's juniors of his services because they were doing so well. As a result, he was snapped up as an amateur by West Ham United and then progressed to Wolverhampton Wanderers and Birmingham City, from whom he finally cost Sunderland £17,000 when they signed him in September 1960 at the age of 27. Hooper, who scored 19 times in 80 appearances for the club, said:

Playing for Sunderland meant a lot to me because I came from the North-East. I was asked to sign as an amateur for them by Bill

Murray, but my father wouldn't let me. He believed that Sunderland were trying to buy the title and weren't giving youngsters a chance, so I went to West Ham, who gave me my chance in the first team when I was 17. But to come back to Sunderland to play for them was fabulous because the atmosphere at Roker Park was so electric, and I jumped at the chance at the time. It did something for me and it was absolutely incredible.

Hooper left in 1963 and said of his departure:

In the end Alan Brown wanted Jimmy Davison in the team because he'd made a statement that he would play for England, so he kept leaving me out. Twice I got back in and had two blinders, but it made no difference, so, like an idiot, I asked to go on the transfer list. I should have come off the list because it meant that Sunderland didn't have to pay me and that I could only go into non-League, which is where I went!

But there were a number of other players who were good enough to be full internationals and yet drifted in and out of the Sunderland scene. Not surprisingly, some of them were Scots from the early years. Centre-forward James Logan had been capped once by Scotland by the time he arrived at Sunderland from Ayr during the summer of 1891, but rejoined them after only three months. In 1896/97 centre-half William 'Plum' Longair, who had played once for Scotland during the first of his three spells with his home-city club Dundee, was with Sunderland, but left to join Burnley in a £50 deal after only nine months. Both played just two League games for Sunderland. Inside-left George Livingston cost Sunderland £175 from Heart of Midlothian and stayed for the 1900/01 season, in which he scored 12 goals in 31 games, before moving on, eventually winning two Scottish caps while with Glasgow Rangers and Manchester City. Inside-forward Bill Maxwell had won one Scottish cap with Stoke before joining Sunderland as champions from Third Lanark for the 1902/03 season. He played in the first six games and even scored his third goal for the club in his last, isolated appearance for them against Wolves before joining Millwall Athletic.

Newcastle-born inside-left Billy Moore joined Sunderland as an 18-year-old amateur in 1912, had his career disrupted by the 1914–18 war and stayed on until 1922, but he was always in and out of the side despite scoring 11 goals in 46 appearances. Moore, who scored twice on his England amateur debut against Belgium, then served West Ham as a player and coach for 38 years. But at the end of the 1922/23 season he scored on his debut for England against Sweden a month after playing for the Hammers in the FA Cup final. He was still at West Ham as their coach when another Moore – Bobby – joined the club on his way to his own FA Cup final appearances and England glory.

Bill Marsden, who was from Silksworth, joined Sunderland in 1920 and made his League debut in March 1921 as a deputy for Moore. He did not play for the first team again until 1923/24, when he scored in both of his two further appearances, but moved to The Wednesday at the end of the season. He switched from inside-forward to wing-half and helped them to two successive First Division titles, between which they changed their name to Sheffield Wednesday. This earned Marsden three England caps during the 1929/30 campaign, but he suffered a serious spinal injury against Germany that ended his playing career.

In 1931/32 inside-forward Harry Bedford played seven games for Sunderland after joining them in a £3,000 deal from Newcastle at the age of 32. He scored twice, but stayed at Roker Park for just four months. But his prolific goalscoring had earned him two England caps during his time with Blackpool, his debut coming alongside Billy Moore and Tommy Urwin, who had also joined Sunderland from Newcastle two years earlier.

In the post-war seasons the trickle of players with international honours who played briefly for Sunderland became a stream. There were, for example, four in the early 1960s as the club sought to regain what it regarded as its First Division birthright. Forward Danny Hegan, a Scot from Coatbridge, initially joined Sunderland from Albion Rovers for £6,000 in September 1961, but left in the summer of 1963 without having broken into the first team. By November 1973, when he returned to Roker Park from Wolves, with whom he had had a disagreement, he had been capped seven times by Northern Ireland, but he played in just eight games in a little less than two months and left the following summer. Centre-forward Jimmy O'Neill, who was from Lurgan in Northern Ireland, deputised for Brian Clough in the early part of 1962 and promptly emulated Clough's goalscoring exploits. He scored twice in a 6–1 home win over Bristol Rovers and finished with six goals in seven appearances, but never played for Sunderland again and had joined Walsall in a £9,000 deal by the end of the year. In between, though, he won his only Northern Ireland cap. Another centre-forward, Andy Kerr, a Scot from Ayrshire, had played for Partick Thistle and briefly Manchester City before joining Sunderland from Kilmarnock, where he had been a productive goalscorer, in a £22,250 deal in April 1963 at the age of 31. Capped twice by Scotland during his Partick days, he made 19 appearances, scoring five times, for Sunderland before returning to

Scotland with Aberdeen after a year with them. Belfast-born right-winger Billy Campbell cost Sunderland £8,000 from Distillery in September 1964, but he made only five appearances for the club, failing to displace Mike Hellawell on a regular basis. He cost Dundee just £3,000 after a 20-month stay at Roker Park, but then went on to play six times for Northern Ireland.

Another Scottish centre-forward, Ralph Brand, who was from Edinburgh, was 30 when he joined Sunderland from Manchester City for £5,000 at the start of the 1967/68 season. He had originally made his name with Rangers and was capped eight times by Scotland while with them, but stayed at Roker Park for only two seasons. He scored three times in his first four games, but made just 32 appearances for Sunderland, finishing with seven goals. Brand was effectively replaced by Joe Baker, who also had his Edinburgh links, having had two spells with Hibernian. Baker was a Liverpudlian by birth and was capped eight times by England between 1959 and 1966, scoring four goals including one on his debut, against Northern Ireland. He had also played for Torino and Arsenal by the time Sunderland signed him for £30,000 from Nottingham Forest during the summer of 1969, but they were relegated in the first of his two seasons at Roker Park, and he did not score until his 20th League game for the club in a 1–1 draw with Manchester United. He did better in his second season, with a hat-trick in a 3–0 home win over Charlton Athletic, but finished with a total of 12 goals from 44 appearances before returning to Scotland.

Then there was the one-match career of forward John 'Yogi Bear' Hughes with Sunderland in early 1973. Hughes, whose younger brother Billy was already at Roker Park, joined the club from Crystal Palace and made his debut at home to Millwall in January 1973, but he was injured after just three minutes and never played League football again. But there was a curious reason why Hughes, from Coatbridge, had been tempted to leave Glasgow Celtic, with whom he had won eight Scottish caps, to join Palace in the first place in October 1971. He explained: 'In England they tend to accept that players can play on after they reach 30, whereas they tend to think you're a bit past it when you reach 30 in Scotland.' That one appearance for Sunderland and that final one of his League career came three months before his 30th birthday! Belfast-born winger Tom Finney made 21 appearances for Sunderland, scoring twice, after joining them from Luton during the summer of 1974. He moved on to Cambridge United after two seasons, but also played 15 times for Northern Ireland during his career. Centre-half Jim Holton made most of his 19 appearances for Sunderland during the disastrous start to the 1976/77 relegation season, when they won only twice in the opening 25

League games, but he had played 15 times for Scotland while with Manchester United. The burly Holton, from Lesmahagow, near Lanark, was signed initially on loan from the Reds just before manager Bob Stokoe's departure, but lasted just six months.

Internationals continued to come and go fairly quickly in the 1980s. Alan Durban spent £350,000 on signing 19-year-old striker Ally McCoist from St Johnstone soon after taking over as manager during the summer of 1981. McCoist scored just twice in his 28 League appearances in his first season and, although he then scored in four consecutive games, he returned to Scotland after two years. In all, he had scored nine times in 65 games for Sunderland, but when he joined Rangers for £180,000, the goals flowed. He won a host of medals with them, played 61 times for Scotland, finished off his career at Kilmarnock and became a well-known television personality. Full-back Jimmy Nicholl was also with Sunderland between 1981 and 1983, and made 40 appearances for them. Three of them came while he was on loan from Manchester United during a severe winter, so it was fitting that he spent the following summer with Toronto Blizzard. He then played 29 times for Sunderland during the 1982/83 season before returning to Toronto for the second of his three spells with them. It was again fitting because he was a Canadian by birth, but he played his international football for Northern Ireland, for whom he was capped 73 times. Another experienced international arrived during the 1982/83 season – 34-year-old striker Frank Worthington from Leeds United. Worthington, capped eight times by England during his Leicester City days, played for nine Football League clubs and Sunderland were his sixth, but he scored just twice in 19 games in a six-month stay and moved on.

Halfway through the following season, striker Ian Wallace arrived at Sunderland from French club Brest in an £80,000 deal, but found goals hard to come by as relegation from the First Division ensued. It was the same in 1985/86 after Lawrie McMenemy had replaced Len Ashurst as manager, and Wallace, a Glaswegian who has been capped three times by Scotland, scored six goals in 40 games for Sunderland before moving to Portugal. In contrast, midfield player John Cornforth made his League debut at right-back in the final game of the 1984/85 season and did not play another first-team game until October 1987. He had scored twice in 37 appearances for Sunderland before moving to Swansea City in 1991 and ended up winning two international caps for Wales four years later, even though he had been born in the North-East.

Another of the shortest stays at Roker Park by an international player occurred in February 1989 with the arrival of winger Peter Barnes at the age of 31. Sunderland were his 10th and final League club and he played just once for them. Barnes, who had won 22 England caps in the early part of his nomadic career, played in a 4–1 defeat at Swindon Town and was substituted. He was dropped the following week against Hull City, who had been his ninth League club, and two months later went to play in America.

Another England stalwart, Terry Butcher, had a brief but interesting spell at Sunderland after arriving during the summer of 1992 at the age of 33. Signed on a free transfer by manager Malcolm Crosby, Butcher had 77 caps to his name – despite having been born in Singapore – and was a natural leader who used to encourage cheers from the fans at the end of matches. But when Crosby was sacked at the start of February 1993 he found himself appointed as Sunderland's player-manager after playing just 18 League games for the club. Butcher made 42 appearances in 1992/93, but concentrated purely on management in his second season at Roker Park. Yet 17 games into the season he himself was dismissed after a run of five successive defeats.

Winger John Colquhoun, who had won one Scottish cap, arrived just before Butcher during the summer of 1992 after Crosby had signed him in a £220,000 deal from Millwall, but he lasted just a year and 23 appearances before rejoining Hearts. Midfield player Derek Ferguson, who had been capped twice by Scotland, moved in the opposite direction in exchange for £460,000 and Colquhoun. He stayed at Sunderland for a little more than two years, playing in 41 League games in his first season with the club. But Ferguson suffered some serious injuries during his career and returned to Scotland in September 1995, when Falkirk signed him for £150,000. He had played 75 games for Sunderland.

Three other internationals joined Sunderland in the first half of 1995/96, Peter Reid's first full season in charge. Striker Paul Stewart, who had won three England caps, initially arrived on loan from Liverpool in August 1995, but was then signed on a free transfer at the age of 31 the following March. He scored five times in 39 appearances for Sunderland and then joined Stoke City during the summer of 1997. Birmingham-born striker David Kelly, who was capped 26 times by the Republic of Ireland, joined Sunderland a month after Stewart and cost £900,000 from Wolves. He scored twice in 40 games for the club in two seasons before moving to Tranmere Rovers in a £350,000 deal in August 1997 after having been transfer-listed. Both strikers had been at Roker Park for a promotion season – when local lad Craig Russell had been the top goalscorer – and a relegation season. The same applied to defender Gareth Hall, who joined Sunderland initially on loan from Chelsea in December 1995 and then completed a £300,000 move the following month. He had played for Wales nine times and stayed until the end of the 1997/98 season, when he moved to Swindon after making 54 appearances for Sunderland.

In 1999/2000 Sunderland achieved their best FA Premiership finish – seventh with 58 points – after winning promotion, and signed centre-half Steve Bould at the age of 36 to help them to stabilise. Bould had been one of the backbones of Arsenal's famed defence and had twice been capped by England. He succeeded Kevin Ball as Sunderland's club captain and proved to be a valuable short-term acquisition.

Sunderland have had only minimal success when importing overseas international players. The first important foreign signing was Argentinian international forward Claudio Marangoni, who was snapped up from Lorenzo in December 1979. He played in 22 games in his year at Roker Park, scored three goals and helped the club to promotion from the Second Division. The public were not always convinced that the £320,000 outlay was worthwhile, but Ken Knighton, the manager who signed him, said:

> I'd been over to Argentina to watch him because Keith Burkinshaw had recommended him to me. Keith was in charge at Spurs and had just signed Ossie Ardiles and Ricky Villa. He'd also wanted to sign Marangoni, but he couldn't because you were allowed only two overseas players in those days. Things didn't really work out at all for Claudio at Sunderland, but at the same time he contributed to a team which got us promoted from the Second Division.

Team-mate John Hawley added:

> Claudio was a lovely, lovely man and I found him absolutely superb. Even though things didn't come off for him on the pitch, he went back to Argentina and was voted as their Player of the Year by his fellow professionals. His skills weren't in question, but I think that he played on a different level from us. I can remember him saying at a team meeting, 'The ball is like a fire – it is too hot.' Football-wise it might have been better for him, but he enjoyed being at Sunderland. He made the most of it because he loved the experience, he was always open to learning and he coped well with the banter in the dressing-room when things weren't going for him.

In recent years the contributions from overseas internationals have been more transient. Sunderland have often had a poor return from their foreign legions, some of whom were not internationals. Others were, though, and the fact that they may have had decent pedigrees made little difference in the eyes of the club's fans.

Defender Jan Eriksson, who had won 35 caps for Sweden and scored against England in the 1992 European Championships, cost Sunderland £250,000 from Helsingborgs IF in January 1997. The following month he made his debut for Sunderland in a 1–0 defeat at Aston Villa, but he was booked, Savo Milosevic's winner took a deflection off him, he never reappeared in the first team and he went to play in America after a year with the club. The foreign influx reached fever-pitch during the 1999/2000 season. Danish international midfield player Carsten Fredgaard, signed from Lyngby for £1.8m, came on as a substitute in Sunderland's opening FA Premiership game at Chelsea – a 4–0 defeat – and never played first-team football for them again, subsequently going to West Bromwich Albion and Bolton on loan. Defender Thomas Helmer, who had been capped 68 times by Germany and arrived on a free transfer from Bayern Munich at the age of 34, fared little better. He made two FA Premiership appearances in August 1999 – as a substitute in a goalless draw at home to Arsenal and then in the starting line-up in a 2–1 defeat at Leeds United – and again that was it. In April 2000 Sunderland beat Wimbledon 2–1 at home, and striker Milton Nunez, who had won 29 caps for Honduras, came on as a substitute. He had been signed from Greek club PAOK Salonika for an initial £1.6m and any further fee was to be determined by appearances – but there were no more.

Slovakian international defender Stanislav Varga cost £650,000 from Slovan Bratislava during the summer of 2000, but played in just 21 League games and was at one time loaned out to West Bromwich. He then left for Celtic in the wake of relegation from the FA Premiership in 2003. Striker Lilian Laslandes had a good goalscoring record and seven caps with France to his name when he cost Sunderland £3.6m from Bordeaux during the summer of 2001. And although he managed 12 FA Premiership appearances during the first half of 2001/02, he failed to score and was eventually unloaded to Nice on a free transfer during the summer of 2003. Full-back Bernt Haas, a Switzerland international, cost £750,000 from Grasshoppers in August 2001 was sold to West Bromwich for £400,000 during the summer of 2003 after 27 League games for Sunderland, all of them in his first season with the club. American international midfield player Claudio Reyna cost £4.5m from Glasgow Rangers in December 2001 and played in 30 League games before joining Manchester City in 2003, having been sidelined by a serious injury. Cameroon international forward Patrick Mboma joined

Sunderland on loan from Parma in February 2002 and made just nine appearances, scoring once. Norwegian international striker Tore-Andre Flo was signed for a club record £8m from Rangers in August 2002 and scored four times in 29 games in the Premiership. He made one more appearance in 2003/04 before he was on his way to Italian club Siena. Defender Talal el Karkouri, a Moroccan international, joined Sunderland on loan from Paris St Germain during the transfer window in January 2003 and played in eight successive League games, all of which were lost. Many of these foreign imports had to go after relegation as manager Mick McCarthy battled valiantly to cut the wage bill he had inherited. In some cases the fees for which they departed were described as undisclosed, possibly because they were a lot less than those for which they had been bought.

All in all, Sunderland were not well served by many of their foreign imports. Some, in fact, were not even full internationals. French midfield player Eric Roy cost £200,000 from Marseille at the start of the 1999/2000 season, but played in only 24 League games in three seasons. Austrian goalkeeper Jurgen Macho made 22 League appearances between 2000 and 2003 after being signed from First Vienna. French defender Patrice Carteron was signed from St Etienne and made eight League appearances towards the end of the 2000/01 season, stopping only to make his mark with a goal in a 1–1 draw against Newcastle at the Stadium of Light. Young Argentinian midfielder Nicolas Medina never made a League appearance for the club in two seasons from 2001, but cost £3.5m from Argentinos Juniors during the summer of 2001. Other imports who failed to break into the first team early in the 21st century included Dutch defender Baki Mercimek, Danish defender Kim Heiselberg and Dutch midfield player Tom Peeters. Conversely, defender Stig-Inge Bjornebye was one of several players who came for a trial in Sunderland's reserves. It never worked out for him then, but he later did well with Norway and Liverpool.

The introduction of loan signings in the early 1970s had, of course, provided greater opportunities for short stays, and Sunderland's goalkeeping situation in 1985/86 underlined the point. Jim 'Seamus' McDonagh was in goal for the opening seven League games under Lawrie McMenemy's management. He was on loan from Notts County, he had spells with 11 different Football League clubs, he played League football for only nine of them and he had two periods with Bolton. A Yorkshireman from Rotherham, he also represented the Republic of Ireland 25 times. Then came Bob Bolder, for 29 games. He arrived on loan from Liverpool one month, he was signed the next month and he was loaned to Luton four months later. Next on the goalkeeping conveyor belt was Andy Dibble, who played in 12 games for Sunderland – on loan from Luton! He joined 13 different Football League clubs, he played League football for 12 of them and he had two stints with Luton and Middlesbrough. He also played in Scotland, for Aberdeen and Rangers, and collected three international caps with Wales along the way. And during Dibble's dabble with Sunderland, Scottish goalkeeper Cameron Duncan – who was not, however, a loan signing – added to the cosmopolitan flavour and the seemingly infinite variety by playing his only League game for the club. But even though he saved a penalty in a 1–1 draw at Grimsby Town in March 1986, Duncan was out for Dibble a week later. Four goalkeepers played 42 League games between them – and never played for Sunderland in any other season.

The following season, McMenemy brought in another much-travelled, on-loan goalkeeper, Bobby Mimms. Iain Hesford was given a mid-season break in December 1986, and Mimms made four appearances for Sunderland while on loan from Everton. He joined 12 different Football League clubs, he played League football for 11 of them and he had two spells at Rotherham United and Blackburn Rovers. Like Dibble, he had a loan spell at Aberdeen in 1990. And Hesford returned after another break at the start of Denis Smith's reign as manager on the way to the Third Division title in 1987/88. Steve Hardwick played in the first six League games of the season and made two Football League appearances while on loan from Oxford United before Hesford won back a regular place.

But probably the most intriguing of Sunderland's on-loan goalkeepers was Shay Given, who played in 17 games in early 1996 while on loan from Blackburn. He kept 12 clean sheets, five of them in succession, and played in a run of nine consecutive wins as Sunderland marched to the First Division championship in 1995/96. He took over from Alec Chamberlain and cemented a reputation as one of Sunderland's best loan signings ever. It was in 1996 that Given earned the first of more than 50 international caps as he established himself as the Republic of Ireland's first-choice goalkeeper, and the following year he returned to the North-East when Newcastle signed him for £1.6m.

Amsterdam-born midfield player Loek Ursem was a more unusual loan signing when he joined Sunderland from Stoke in the second half of the 1981/82 season. Ursem had previously been signed by the club's manager Alan Durban, but never made the starting line-up and was instead brought on as a substitute in four games, one of which was a goalless draw at Stoke.

As with permanent signings, there were occasional loan acquisitions who popped in and out of Sunderland while being more closely associated with other clubs. In September 1991, for example, Denis Smith signed much-travelled winger Peter Beagrie, who played in five games on loan from Everton. He made his debut against Middlesbrough, his home-town club and with whom he had started his career. And in 1994/95 Sunderland's manager Mick Buxton signed 31-year-old midfield player Ian Snodin on loan from Everton to ease an injury and suspension crisis. He started six successive games, but the irony was that he himself had a lot of injury problems even though he played nearly 500 matches during his career. He had missed virtually two seasons with Everton, he had more injury problems when they released him and he joined Oldham Athletic two months after his stint with Sunderland.

Other loan signings saw only minimal first-team action with Sunderland. Scottish defender Jamie Murray, who joined them on loan from Cambridge towards the end of the 1983/84 season, started one game at home to Spurs and was injured in it. Four years later, forward Dougie McGuire joined Sunderland on loan from Glasgow Celtic, started one game at York City and was also substituted.

But another of McMenemy's loan signings was historically significant – winger Tony Ford, who converted to full-back later in his lengthy career. Ford came on as a substitute for his home-town club Grimsby in a 1–1 draw at home to Sunderland in March 1986. The following week he made his debut for Sunderland as a substitute, scoring in a 1–1 draw at home to Bradford City. He went on to make nine appearances during his loan spell, which contributed marginally to his career tally of 931 – an all-time record for an outfield player.

Some players were destined for brief encounters by dint of special circumstances – those who represented Sunderland as guest players during wartime. And during the 1939–45 war there were two who were worthy of mention. Bill Nicholson will always be associated with Spurs, first as a player and then as a highly successful manager, most notably guiding them to the League and FA Cup Double in 1961. A Yorkshireman from Scarborough, he returned to the North during the war and was a guest player for Sunderland, Newcastle and Middlesbrough, later playing once for England in 1951 after returning to Spurs. He played four North League games and three FA Cup ties as a full-back during 1942/43 for Sunderland. Centre-forward Stan Mortensen, who went on to play 25 times for England and score a hat-trick for Blackpool in the 1952/53 FA Cup final when playing alongside Ernie Taylor, made one wartime appearance for Sunderland. Mortensen, originally from South Shields, scored once in it, too – a 5–4 victory over Middlesbrough in the Wartime Cup in February 1944.

There were naturally plenty of other players who might be termed 'one-match wonders', and Sunderland's retention of top-flight status for much of their history meant that a number of them were opting for quality of opposition as a substitute for quantity of appearances. Quite simply, they maximised their potential for 90 minutes of fame.

Maybe pride of place should go to right-half John Small, whose only League game of his career was for Sunderland in a 3–1 win over Manchester United at Old Trafford in March 1913, during the most successful season in the club's history. Frank Cuggy moved to centre-half in place of Charlie B. Thomson, who returned for the next match on Good Friday at the expense of Small. But although Small later joined Southampton, they were not in the League at that stage. Two other players, though, had less luck against Manchester City. Sunderland-born inside-right Tom Brown, who later played in Scotland, played his only League game for his home-town club in the opening match of the 1907/08 season and it resulted in a 5–2 defeat at home to City. And centre-forward Victor Staley's sole League appearance for Sunderland was in a 3–2 home defeat by City in January 1922. But he fared better at Roker Park than he did at Stoke, whom he joined later that year, because he never played a League game at all for them – or anyone else, for that matter.

Local left-back Andy York helped Sunderland to a 1–0 home win over Arsenal at Roker Park when Charlie Buchan scored against his future club, but it was not good enough for him to earn any more League appearances. York had stood in for the long-serving Ernie England, but was replaced for the return game a week later when Bert Hobson came in at right-back and another local lad, Bob Young, was switched to left-back. Centre-forward Fred Kirby, a local amateur, had played his only League game for Sunderland in a 3–0 defeat at Woolwich Arsenal in November 1911 when both George Holley and Buchan were missing. But they were back a week later, and that was it for Kirby, who was an England amateur international and won the FA Amateur Cup with Bishop Auckland. Left-winger Fred Gibson, a South African by birth, also played his only League game for Sunderland in North London – in a 5–2 defeat at Tottenham Hotspur in March 1910 when he deputised for Arthur Bridgett. He then spent the rest of his career in Scotland and the Midlands. Inside-left Clarence Gregory also played his only League game for Sunderland at Spurs – in a goalless draw in April 1921. Maybe the experience was what decided him to spend the rest of the career in his native Midlands and the South; he never got another chance with Sunderland, even though their line-ups were unsettled towards the end of the 1920/21 season. Inside-right Henry Logan, a Glaswegian, played his only League game for Sunderland in a 4–0 home win over Chelsea in

October 1909 when George Holley hit a hat-trick. He also played in an FA Cup tie that season in which Sunderland beat Bradford Park Avenue 3–1, but it did him little good because on both occasions they changed winning teams. Inside-left Harry Williams made his League debut for Sunderland in a 3–1 defeat at Chelsea in March 1921, but was dropped for the return fixture a week later and never played for the club again. His revenge was to score Chesterfield's first-ever League goal after they had been elected to the newly formed Third Division North in 1921/22, and then earn himself a move to Manchester United!

Other players made their bows in local derbies. Inside-left John Shaw, an amateur, made his only League appearance for Sunderland in a 2–1 defeat at Middlesbrough in front of a 24,000 gate in August 1906. Curiously, Joe Shaw, who scored 14 times in 31 League appearances for Sunderland, played alongside him at centre-forward. But six months later John Shaw moved to Clapton Orient. Inside-right Bob McCullough, another amateur, made his only League appearance anywhere when he played for Sunderland in a 3–1 defeat at Newcastle in February 1912. Similarly, Scottish centre-forward John Waugh, who eventually had another spell in the Football League with Gillingham after the 1914–18 war, played his only League game for Sunderland in a 2–1 defeat at Newcastle in front of a 38,000 crowd in December 1913.

Several Sunderland players made their only League appearances against Liverpool. Left-half Tom Kelly played the only League game of his career at home to them in a 2–1 defeat in September 1905 and was one of six players to occupy that position in the first nine games of the season. Left-back Peter Kelly turned out for Sunderland at home to Liverpool in a 4–1 defeat on New Year's Day, 1909, in what was his only game in League football. Right-half George Ardley played the only League game of his career for Sunderland at home to Liverpool in the final game of the 1919/20 season, but it ended in a 1–0 defeat. Local goalkeeper Keith Hird joined the club Sunderland in 1957 and had to wait until the final League game of the 1960/61 season – a 1–1 draw at home to Liverpool in front of 30,040 fans – for his only first-team appearance in nearly six years with them. James Boe, from Gateshead, fared worse at Everton when he deputised in goal for the younger Sunderland-born Leslie Scott in November 1914, and they lost 7–1: it was also the only League appearance of his career. Centre-half Richard Huntley helped his home-town club Sunderland to win the FA Youth Cup with a 2–0 win over Birmingham in the final in 1967, but played in only one League game for them – a 2–0 defeat at Everton in November 1968 when he stood in for Charlie Hurley. It was the only League appearance of his career.

Dundee-born left-back Duncan Stewart played his only League game for Sunderland in a 2–0 home win over Aston Villa in April 1923, but was not in the side for the return game, which finished the season. He was probably fated because he moved Southend United during the summer of 1924, played in their next League game at right-back and never played again for them either! Goalkeeper David Agnew, a Northern Ireland amateur international from Belfast, appeared for Sunderland in front of a crowd of 40,893 in a 3–3 draw at home to Villa in August 1950. He stayed with the club until the summer of 1953, but never played another League game.

Scottish left-winger Richard Bell played his only game for Sunderland in the final game of the 1936/37 season, a week before the club played in the FA Cup final, but they lost 3–0 at Leeds. Almost immediately he moved to West Ham but had only one League game for them – at inside-left in April 1939, when he was a goalscorer. Striker Ricardo Gabbiadini played his only League game for Sunderland when he came on as a substitute in a 2–0 defeat at Leeds in October 1989 – in a game in which his elder brother Marco was substituted. He had followed Marco and manager Denis Smith from York City, for whom he had also made just one League appearance as a substitute. He spent nearly three years at Sunderland and was sent out on loan four times.

For Peter Kelly, Tom Kelly, McCullough, Small, Boe, Staley, Ardley, Agnew and Huntley, playing one game for Sunderland was the full extent of their careers anywhere at Football League level. Other Sunderland players had to be content with the same amount of brief fame – right-back Matthew Scott in January 1894, left-back Joe Knowles in April 1897, left-half Ernest Bertram in March 1904, inside-forward James Hope in March 1909, right-back John Hastings in April 1909, centre-forward Josiah Kelsall in April 1914, England amateur international left-back John Morrison in December 1919, inside-forward John Finlay in September 1946, left-back Robert Craig in September 1949, inside-forward John Evans in September 1954, left-half Norman Wood in February 1955 and striker Sean Wharton in April 1989.

The large number of Sunderland's one-match wonders is rather strange because the club's high status for most of its history suggests that many of those players might have made the grade lower down the League ladder. One who did was wing-half Joe Kiernan, one of Sunderland's Scots from Coatbridge, who was at Roker Park for nearly four years. But he played in only one League game – a 4–2 win at Southampton in September 1962 – before moving on to Northampton Town during the summer of 1963. Kiernan then helped the Cobblers into the old First Division for the only season in their history, when they finished only two places and three points adrift of Sunderland in 1965/66!

There was something quirky about some of Sunderland's other one-match wonders. Left-winger John Lavery, for example, made his single League appearance for the club in a 2–1 defeat at Blackburn – on Christmas Day, 1897. And inside-forward Percy Whipp, a Glaswegian, made his only League appearance for them in a 1–1 draw at Bolton in September 1922 after manager Bob Kyle had made wholesale changes following a 5–1 defeat at Liverpool three days earlier, but he stayed with the club for only six months before opting to move to the recently formed Leeds United in a £750 deal.

With the advent of substitutes in the 1960s, some players appeared for the club for less than a full League game. Midfield player Nigel Walker came on as a substitute for Leighton James in a 3–0 home win over Watford in November 1983 in his second spell with Sunderland. He had previously been on trial at Roker Park after returning from America, but his second stint included a loan spell to Blackpool, for whom he scored a hat-trick on his debut four months after his brief League encounter at Sunderland. Scottish full-back Gary Ogilvie made his one League appearance as a substitute in a 1–1 draw at Chelsea in November 1988, but a month earlier he had earned double time by also coming on as a substitute in a Littlewoods Cup tie at West Ham as Sunderland went out 5–1 on aggregate. Local winger Richard Taylor made his only appearance for Sunderland in four years with the club – as a substitute for Dennis Tueart in a goalless draw at home to Blackpool in November 1971.

And when Sunderland went briefly Brazilian in 1999/2000, they signed giant forward Marcos di Guiseppe, who was also known as Bica. Born in São Paulo, he had played in Greece, Austria and Peru after leaving Brazil. He came on only as a substitute in a Worthington Cup 5–1 win over Walsall, replacing winger Neil Wainwright, but left after a two-week trial. The following month di Guiseppe emerged to have an extended trial – at Walsall! Again he came on only as a substitute – this time in their League derby at West Bromwich – and his appearance lasted just four minutes.

Then there were substitutes who never got onto the pitch at all. In 1974/75 midfield player Stan Ternent was twice a substitute in the early part of the season in a 1–0 defeat at West Bromwich and a 2–0 defeat at Cardiff City. While his playing career at Roker Park never took off, he did have a spell on the club's coaching staff soon afterwards. Gradually he embarked on a varied career in coaching and management, including a spell as No. 2 to his Sunderland team-mate and FA Cup hero Ian

Porterfield at Chelsea. He was reported to have been offered the manager's job at Sunderland when Denis Smith was sacked. And in March 1967, centre-half John Wile, who had been signed from Durham City, was Sunderland's substitute in a 3–0 defeat at Stoke. But he went on to have two spells with both Peterborough United and West Bromwich, initially as just a player. He then returned to London Road as player-manager in 1983 and had a stint as chief executive with Albion, for whom he had played exactly 500 League games.

The brevity of some stays was down to players being signed only on a temporary basis as trialists. Scottish left-back Alex Fotheringham had a month on trial with Sunderland from March 1899, and played in one League game – a 2–1 win at Bury – before returning to Inverness Caledonians. In October 1906 another Scot, left-winger John Law, joined Sunderland as an amateur one day, played in his only League game for the club in a 1–0 defeat at Bolton the day after, and left for Glasgow Rangers the following month. Owen Williams, a speedy left-winger, was born locally at Ryhope in 1896 and represented Sunderland Schools. While playing for Ryhope Colliery he had a trial with Sunderland and signed amateur forms with Manchester United, but neither club took up the option and he later moved to Easington Colliery. He moved into League football with Clapton Orient in the summer of 1919, and won two England caps four years later. In 1924 Williams returned to the North-East when Middlesbrough paid £3,000 for his services, and he enjoyed two promotions and one relegation with them, having also been rejected by them as a youngster. Eric Welsh was the first Carlisle United player to win a full international cap when he scored Northern Ireland's third goal in a 4–1 win over Wales at Ninian Park in March 1966. He had joined Carlisle from Exeter City the previous October and remains the winner of the most full international caps in the club's history – four. But it might have been different. Welsh admitted:

When I was playing for Linfield in the Irish League as an amateur, I was asked to go to Sunderland for a trial. I signed amateur forms for them and was heartbroken when I was told that the club had far too many junior players on its books and no longer required me. I was very downcast, but youth can shrug off such disappointments, so I went back to Linfield and Exeter signed me before many weeks elapsed.

Sunderland did not hold happy memories for the Welsh family as a whole, because Eric's younger brother Alan was an apprentice professional at Roker Park as a 16-year-old, but also failed to make the first-team grade. Scottish full-back Alan Hay joined Sunderland on a monthly contract during 1988/89 and made one League appearance at home to Ipswich Town. It was in March 1989 and Sunderland won 4–0, so does that make Hay one of the most successful players in the club's history even though he did not last the full match?

Other players stayed briefly with Sunderland in strange circumstances. Local inside-forward Ken Walshaw's career with the club was curious because he played two ties in the 1945/46 FA Cup. They lost at Bury when he scored and then at Birmingham, but he was never chosen for a League game for the club and left them after three years in 1947. Equally intriguingly, Dutch goalkeeper Eduard Zoetebier also made his debut for Sunderland at Bury and then played in a 2–0 defeat at Middlesbrough during the 1997/98 season, but both games were in the Coca-Cola Cup, and he too never made a League appearance for the club. Similarly, inside-forward Tommy White made his first three Sunderland appearances in FA Cup ties in 1946/47, two of them alongside Walshaw, and then played only twice in the League, scoring on his debut against Arsenal in September 1946. All five senior games in which he represented Sunderland were away games.

Then there were the good and the bad bits of business involving transfers. Left-back William Wood, who had cost nothing from Spen Juniors in 1948, was another Sunderland player whose only League game was against Aston Villa. It fell on 1 April 1950, and he was sold to Hull 15 months later for £5,000. Former Sunderland hero Raich Carter signed Wood, but he never played in a first-team game for City. Equally, striker David Bellion cost Sunderland nothing when he joined them from Cannes as a 19-year-old in August 2001, but two years later he brought in £1m when Manchester United snapped him up. Conversely, Geoff Butler, also a left-back, cost Sunderland £65,000 from Chelsea in January 1968, but he started only one League game for them and was a substitute in two others. New manager Alan Brown sold him eight months after he had arrived, in which time Butler's valuation had slumped by £40,000. Curiously, he moved to Norwich, against whom he had played for Sunderland in two FA Cup ties that had prompted the sacking of manager Ian McColl.

Scottish inside-forward George Whitelaw played in five games for Sunderland without scoring during 1958 and was said to have played with a smile on his face, which was ironic in the year in which the club was relegated for the first time. He would pretend to fall over while attempting a throw-in or tread the touchline as a tight-rope, and was supposed to have influenced a young Frank Worthington when his travels took him to Halifax the following year.

Winger Jamie Lawrence, who was to be associated with some eccentric hairstyles at various stages of his career, made just five appearances for Sunderland in 1993/94, but his recruitment was hardly conventional. Lawrence, who later became a Jamaican international, was 23 when he was signed by manager Terry Butcher and had never previously played League football, one reason being that he had just completed a prison sentence in Parkhurst Prison on the Isle of Wight for robbery with violence!

Then there were players who hastened their own exit from Sunderland after falling out of public favour. However long they had been at the club, for one reason or another they soon found themselves on their way out. Goalkeeper Walter 'Buns' Scott became the scapegoat for a disappointing start to what turned out to be the highly successful 1912/13 campaign. The directors insisted that he had been sacked for missing training, but it appeared that Scott had been the victim of what he called 'the hostility of a section of the crowd' at Roker Park. They had made him the fall guy for the poor start and it was claimed that 'a certain clique gathered round the goal and made use of offensive epithets towards him'. He was soon on his way after making 38 appearances for the club. Another goalkeeper, Peter Wakeham, who played 151 games for Sunderland, apparently made a V-sign to the fans during a game in 1961/62 and was on his way to Charlton Athletic at the end of the season, young Jim Montgomery being thrown in at the deep end in his place. Winger Terry Curran played for 13 different League clubs, and Sunderland were 11th on his travels when he was signed at the age of 31. He played in nine games for them during the 1986/87 season, but was released after making a gesture to the terraces when he was barracked during a reserve outing. Midfield player Lee Clark, from Wallsend, was Sunderland's record signing at £2.5m from Newcastle during the summer of 1997 and an ever-present in his first season with them. He became popular and played 83 games in two seasons, scoring 16 times, but then went to watch Newcastle lose 2–0 to Manchester United in the FA Cup final at Wembley, and was pictured wearing a T-shirt displaying a disparaging message about Sunderland's fans. Clark had made the mistake of accepting the shirt while talking to Newcastle fans before the final. He later apologised profusely, but the damage was done. He was transfer-listed and almost two months later joined Fulham, then managed by former Sunderland player Paul Bracewell, for £3m.

Other players stopped off briefly at Sunderland while making their names elsewhere, often on a series of travels. In 1976/77 striker Alan Foggon joined the select band to have played for each of the North-

East's big three clubs. He had helped Newcastle to win the Inter-Cities Fairs Cup and Middlesbrough to win promotion, but he played in 10 games without scoring as Sunderland plummeted towards relegation from the old First Division. Three other forwards – Lee Chapman, David Hodgson and Keith Bertschin – had short stints with Sunderland in the 1980s, but were more closely associated with other clubs during their careers. The same applied to centre-back Sam Allardyce in the 1980/81 season and goalkeeper Tony Coton during 1996/97, but both later spent a little more time with Sunderland as members of the coaching staff.

A little more remarkable was winger Ian Bowyer's contribution in 1981, when he played in 16 games for Sunderland. He joined them at the age of 29 from Nottingham Forest, for whom he had made than 200 appearances. But he did not last long and promptly returned to Forest at the start of 1982, and played in more than 200 games for them again, finally leaving them at the age of 36.

Then there are some footballers who are just in the wrong place at the wrong time, ending up with few appearances to their name because they effectively become understudies to team-mates who might have a greater pedigree or cost more in the transfer market. In Sunderland's case it often meant that local players struggled to break through and oust expensive buys, and certainly the concept of the understudy sprang up startlingly and starkly at various points in their history. And in post-war years the club needed to justify big-money signings in the wake of The Bank of England Team tag.

Busy inside-forward Frank Bee was from Nottingham, but joined Sunderland during the summer of 1947 and made his first-team debut at Blackburn on the final day of January 1948. But the following week Sunderland snapped up Len Shackleton from Newcastle, and the sting was that Bee was left out straightaway. He did return to play four times alongside Shackleton, scoring on the first occasion, but his days were numbered. After no more League appearances and a year out of the first-team limelight at Sunderland, Bee moved on – to Blackburn!

The 1950s produced another group of understudies whose first-team chances were limited. Wing-half Lyall 'Laurie' Bolton joined Sunderland in 1950 and left seven years later with just three appearances to his name because he had had to take a back seat behind George Aitken and England international Stan Anderson. Wing-half Bill Morrison was with the club from 1951 to 1958, but played in only 19 games, unable to oust Anderson on a regular basis. Right-winger Sam Kemp arrived in March 1952 and made just 19 appearances in almost five years because he was Northern Ireland international Billy Bingham's deputy. Centre-half John

Bone understudied Fred Hall, George Aitken and Ray Daniel, and managed just 11 games in seven years after joining Sunderland in 1951. Inside-forward John Maltby made 23 appearances in his five years at Roker Park from 1955 as he was forced to play second fiddle to Shackleton and Charlie Fleming. Left-winger Johnny Dillon joined Sunderland in 1959, made his debut as a 17-year-old and played in 23 games before moving on during the summer of 1962 after understudying Jack Overfield.

Centre-half Dickie Rooks found himself in a similar position. He was born in Sunderland and joined his home-town club on his 17th birthday, in May 1957, after finishing his apprenticeship as a joiner and carpenter. But four months later Sunderland signed Charlie Hurley, who became one of their all-time greats. Rooks did not make his League debut for the club until April 1961, but eventually moved to Middlesbrough in a £20,000 deal in 1965 – three years after he had first sought a transfer – after deputising for Hurley in just 40 games. And Rooks summed up the overall problem:

> My whole career at Roker Park was a constant fight for my place in the side. I was at a disadvantage, too, because I was the local boy who had cost nothing, while Charlie was a big-money signing from Millwall. I quickly got the feeling that, no matter how well I might play, Charlie would get the position if he was fit and available. I may have been wrong, but I had seen similar situations at other clubs when they would pay out big money for a player and seem to give him preference – seemingly to justify the decision to buy him. I'm not blaming Charlie for my troubles, but it was all very frustrating for me.

The trend continued in the 1960s. A little more than four years after joining Sunderland, wing-half Mel Slack scored on his debut in a 3–1 defeat at Stoke City in April 1965. He played in the next match and then left the club during the summer, having spent his time in the shadows of Martin Harvey and Jimmy McNab. Centre-forward Gary Moore had nearly five years on his home-town club Sunderland's books, but waited nearly two years for his League debut and made only 14 appearances for the club because Harry Hood, John O'Hare, Nick Sharkey and Neil Martin were among those ahead of him. Instead he made a name for himself in scouting circles, working twice in the England set-up and for Watford, Aston Villa, Leicester, Manchester United and Tottenham. Three players who joined Sunderland in 1964 struggled to become first-team regulars, although goalkeeper Derek Forster made a stunning

League debut for Sunderland against Leicester in front of 45,465 fans at Roker Park when he was aged just 15 years and 185 days. But Forster spent the rest of his nine years with the club understudying Jimmy Montgomery, playing just 19 games in all. Left-backs Jimmy Shoulder and Alan Black played second fiddle to Len Ashurst. Shoulder made just three appearances in a little more than five years, and Black made six in two. Local centre-forward Malcolm Moore was with Sunderland from 1965 to 1973, but played in only 12 games. He had to wait until April 1968 for his League debut, but players such as Martin and Billy Hughes always seemed to bar his way. Goalkeeper Trevor Swinburne became an apprentice with Sunderland in 1968, but it was four years later before he was given his League debut. He was with the club for nine years, but made just 11 appearances because he was another victim of Montgomery's long service.

As the game changed, there were fewer out-and-out understudies, although full-back Maurice Hepworth played only twice even though he was with Sunderland for five years from 1970. He could not dislodge the long-serving Cec Irwin. Scottish midfield player Tommy Gibb, a free-transfer signing from Newcastle during the summer of 1975, made only ten appearances for Sunderland in two years because, more often than not, England international Tony Towers stood in his way. Goalkeeper Mark Prudhoe joined Sunderland in 1980 at the start of a varied career, but played in only seven games in four years as a deputy to Chris Turner and Barry Siddall.

There were also Sunderland players whose main claims to fame coincided with successful Cup runs. Their circumstances were similar to those of winger Richard Bell, whose sole appearance was as Eddie Burbanks' deputy a week before the 1937 FA Cup final. But there had been an odd precedent when Sunderland reached the 1913 FA Cup final and George Holley was struggling to overcome an injury and illness. Inside-left Walter Tinsley, who made only ten appearances for Sunderland, had deputised for Holley in the build-up to the final against Aston Villa, but it was said that he was so overcome by nerves that he became ill and it was decided not to risk him. As a result, a half-fit Holley played and Sunderland lost, but Tinsley made amends by scoring a vital goal in a 1–1 draw against Villa four days later that almost clinched the League title.

When Sunderland reached the 1973 FA Cup final, defenders Ray Ellison and David Young were on the fringes of the team. Ellison played his only two games for the club soon after being signed for £10,000 from Newcastle in March 1973, but his limited chances made him something of a mystery man on the team photographs for the FA Cup final two months later. Young had arrived with Ron Guthrie from the Magpies two months earlier, but vied with Richie Pitt for a place in the starting line-up for the rest of the season. He ended up being the substitute against Leeds at Wembley, and moved on the following summer after making 40 appearances for Sunderland. Another rival for the same berth was John Tones, who played in the first two games of the Cup run against Notts County and was then largely forgotten. Tones played only ten games for the club, but had a career of contrasts. He had made his first-team debut as a goalscoring substitute in a 2–1 defeat at Lazio in the Anglo-Italian Cup in May 1970, but did not get a senior outing with Arsenal after he had joined them soon after the Wembley win.

Centre-half David Corner made the starting line-up at Wembley as an 18-year-old when Sunderland lost 1–0 to Norwich City in the 1984/85 League Cup final, but he had only three League games to his name. Corner had been substituted on his debut after Peter Davenport, later a Sunderland player, had scored a hat-trick for Nottingham Forest, and played in 45 games for the club before joining Leyton Orient in 1988. Striker Warren Hawke made 29 appearances for Sunderland between 1987 and 1993, mainly as a substitute, because of the form of Eric Gates and Marco Gabbiadini. But Hawke was a substitute at Wembley when Sunderland lost 2–0 to Liverpool in the 1992 FA Cup final and did get a run-out in place of Brian Atkinson.

Those players were lucky to get their limited chances when Sunderland were in the public eye more than usual, but there were the unlucky ones, particularly those such as John Hughes, Derek Ferguson, Jamie Murray and Claudio Reyna, whose careers at Roker Park were restricted by injuries. Left-winger Norman Clarke was especially unfortunate. He had arrived from Northern Ireland at the age of 19 following rave reviews that had attracted manager Alan Brown's attention, and soon played five games early in the 1962/63 season, but struggled to displace the established George Mulhall. And three years later he was forced to retire after picking up a cruciate knee injury while playing for the reserves in March 1964. A similar fate befell Scottish striker Harry Hood, who was a late developer because he went to a rugby-playing school and did not play football until he was 16. He spent only a brief time at Sunderland, between 1964 and 1966, even though he scored 10 goals in 34 appearances. He explained: 'I enjoyed my time with Sunderland, but manager George Hardwick was succeeded by Ian McColl, the one-time Scottish team manager, and things didn't go so well after that. I was unlucky with injuries and had to undergo a hernia operation. When I recovered, I couldn't get goals and was dropped.'

Naturally there were a few players on Sunderland's own doorstep who might have joined the club and yet escaped their grasp. The area was a conveyor belt of football talent, but the desire for big-name, out-of-town acquisitions meant that a lot of local lads slipped through the net and had only tenuous links with Roker Park. With some, though, it proved costly to miss out on their abilities because they later gained international recognition.

Jimmy Seed was from Blackhall in County Durham and played first for Whitburn, but was rejected by Sunderland after being on their books between 1914 and 1919. He had been gassed during the 1914–18 war after enlisting in the West Yorkshire Regiment and going out to Flanders. As a result, Seed never played a senior game for Sunderland, apart from one Victory League appearance, but he insisted that 'Those doctors don't know what they are talking about.' He then moved briefly to Mid-Rhondda before joining Tottenham and winning five England caps during his time with them. He won an FA Cup-winner's medal while with Spurs and captained Sheffield Wednesday to successive First Division titles in 1929 and 1930. Seed then served Charlton as a very successful secretary-manager for 23 years after a spell as a cartoonist. The Sam Bartram Gates were built by Charlton after their famed goalkeeper from the North-East had played his 500th League game in 1954, while the Jimmy Seed Stand stands as another memorial at the Valley. Seaham-born centre-half Tom Wilson joined Sunderland just before the 1914–18 war, but was kicked out after it because he was said to be overweight. But he joined Huddersfield Town from Seaham Colliery, staying with them throughout their successful period in the 1920s when they put their stamp on the League title three seasons in a row, and won the FA Cup and were beaten finalists on three other occasions. He also played once for England. Colin Bell was born at Hesleden in County Durham in 1946, represented Horden Schools and East Durham Schools before joining Horden Colliery. While with them, he had trials with Sunderland and Newcastle that came to nothing. He eventually joined Bury in 1963, and three years later moved to Manchester City, becoming one of their greatest players of all time. His strong running earned him the nickname Nijinsky, after the famous racehorse, and he went on to play 49 times for England between 1968 and 1976.

Others merely emulated Harry Hooper by returning to the North-East as prodigal sons. Left-back Tom Lilley was born at New Herrington and had played for three League clubs – Huddersfield, Nelson and Hartlepools United – before he finally moved to Roker Park at the age of 26. His stay there was brief. He waited a year for his first League game – a 3–3 draw at home to Portsmouth on the opening day of the 1927/28 season – but was then replaced by Bob Thomson, and the following year he was on the move again. After one game in two years with Sunderland, he joined St Mirren and then Fulham. Utility player Wilf Rostron was born in Sunderland, but joined Arsenal as a 16-year-old and did not move to Roker Park until nearly five years later, when he cost £40,000. He then made 87 League appearances for Sunderland, scoring 18 goals, 10 of them in the League during the 1978/79 season. His total included a hat-trick with two penalties in a 6–2 home win over Sheffield United as the Second Division promotion battle reached its peak, but Sunderland were beaten by Cardiff at Roker Park three days later and their chance was gone. In October 1979, though, Rostron moved back to the South when new manager Ken Knighton accepted an offer of £150,000 from Watford for him. Sunderland-born defender Nigel Saddington joined Doncaster Rovers as an 18-year-old. He temporarily slipped out of League football, but then manager Lawrie McMenemy took him to Roker in early 1986. Saddington stayed two years, making three appearances in the 1986/87 season, when Sunderland were relegated to the old Third Division for the first time, but then he was off again. He signed for Carlisle, but eventually he literally moved back to Roker Park because he bought one of the houses built on the site after it had made way for the Stadium of Light.

Perhaps the most curious tale of all concerned Len Shackleton's brother John, who was also on Sunderland's books in the late 1940s. During the 1939–45 war he had been a PT instructor and keen boxer, and suffered serious skull damage from which he nearly died. John had a plate inserted in his head, and after a season at Roker he failed his medical examination when the plate was discovered. He is understood to have lodged with Tommy Wright and named their landlady's pet goose Argus after Jack Anderson, who covered the club for the *Sunderland Echo!* An interest in boxing seemed to run in the Shackleton family, because Len once gave his hobby as refereeing amateur bouts.

All in all, there have been numerous cases of players who could count brief spells with Sunderland as part of their careers. Some took the money and ran – not only are they best forgotten, they are also easily forgotten. Others were unlucky for different reasons, and still others were simply in the wrong place at the wrong time. Their tenuous claims to fame often meant that in the fullness of time their names would surface only in the answers to obscure quiz questions set by people sporting anoraks.

11

EXTRA TIME

What do Len Shackleton, the Beatles, Stanley Matthews, Vera Lynn, Stan Anderson, Jimmy Tarbuck, Johnny Haynes, Max Miller, Billy Elliott, Joan Collins, Nat Lofthouse, Tom Finney, John Hanson, Duncan Edwards, Shirley Bassey and Didi have in common? The answer is that they all worked alongside former England and Sunderland winger Colin Grainger, who led a double life that merged the worlds of international sport and show business. Grainger, most recently a scout for Sheffield United, played alongside some great footballers with England and Sunderland, but he also became a professional singer and worked with some great entertainers, too. Didi was on the opposing side when Grainger sensationally scored twice in a 4–2 win at Wembley against the next world champions Brazil on his England debut in 1956. But the former winger had claims to fame when wearing his other hat too: 'I slept at Joan Collins' house before she made it really big in Hollywood because her father Joe was Winifred Atwell's agent and he got me on TV with her!'

Grainger, in fact, began his singing career while still playing football:

It started because I'd watched Al Jolson's films about 15 times, and I'd go down to my local club and they'd get me on stage to sing if the 'turn' didn't turn up. Then Nat Lofthouse got me up to do a cabaret spot when I was with England in Sweden, but in those days I couldn't do the singing full-time because of my football – I did it only in the summer. But when I was at Sunderland, I'd get on a train to go to King's Cross, visit Harry Secombe's singing teacher for half an hour – my record company, HMV, insisted on me going there – and catch a train back to Sunderland. It took me from 10am to 10pm for a half-hour singing lesson, and I used up all my football wages for the week to do it!

But Grainger has sung and recorded into his seventies, and added: 'I think I'm singing better than ever now, and every six weeks on a Friday I go to my local club and sing for my fellow OAPs. It's marvellous to go back to my roots where people appreciate me.'

Sunderland had other entertainers of various kinds in their playing ranks on occasions. Grainger was preceded by fellow wingers Billy Eden, who performed in a dance band, and Arthur Welsby, who played tenor horn in a brass band. Welsby made only three appearances for the club, but one of them was alongside Eden in the 1931/32 season. Inside-forward George Ainsley, who made his Sunderland debut the following season, was said to be a top-quality impersonator and did impressions of numerous show-business stars and politicians of the day. In 1937, Sunderland's first FA Cup-winning side included Patsy Gallacher, who was adept at leading the sing-songs, and Sandy McNab, who was a talented tap-dancer. Dave Watson, one of the club's 1973 FA Cup winners, once played on stage with rock-and-roll band Status Quo, while his fellow England international Chris Waddle invaded the pop charts when he and Glenn Hoddle performed the song 'Diamond Lights'.

It begs the question as to what other Sunderland players might have done with their lives off the pitch. They naturally became involved in a variety of roles – if they had the chance. It was not always given to them, though, because a high number died relatively young. They include some of the club's early pioneers – James Logan at 25 in 1896, Matthew Ferguson at 29 in 1902, Jimmy Millar at 36 in 1907, Arnie Davison at 46 in 1910, William Gibson at 43 in 1911, Ronald Brebner at 33 in 1914, Leigh Roose at 38 in 1916, Albert Milton at 32 in 1917, Sandy McAllister at 39 in 1918, Harry Low at 38 in 1920, Jimmy Leslie at 47 in 1920, English McConnell at 43 in 1928, Jack Bartley at 20 in 1929, George Payne at 45 in 1932, Jimmy Thorpe at 22 in 1936, Tom Wallace at 32 in 1939, Billy Ellis at 44 in 1939 and Percy Saunders at 25 in 1942. The deaths of some, such as goalkeepers Brebner and Thorpe, might be said to have been football-related, while others, such as Roose, Milton, McAllister and Saunders, were killed during active service. In post-war years Reg Wilkinson and David Wright both died at the age of 47 – Wilkinson during a match in 1946 and Wright in 1953. Equally tragic were the deaths of Keith Hird at 27 in 1967, Mel Holden at 26 in 1981, Jim Holton at 42 in 1993, Tim Gilbert at 36 in 1995 and Rob Hindmarch at 41 in 2002. In contrast, Joe Kasher was believed to be the oldest-ever former Sunderland player and the oldest surviving ex-professional footballer until his death in 1992, just six days short of his 98th birthday.

Other Sunderland players were notable all-round sportsmen, of which the footballer-cricketers probably provided the best examples. In the vanguard was double international Willie Watson, who played four times for England as a footballer and 23 times for them as a cricketer. His international football appearances coincided with his time as a wing-half with Sunderland in 1949 and 1950, while his cricket call-ups stretched from 1952 to 1959, during which time he hit two centuries, one of them saving England from defeat at Lord's against Australia in 1953. A graceful left-handed batsman, Watson played for Yorkshire and then Leicestershire, where he became assistant secretary, between 1939 and 1964 and scored more than 25,000 first-class runs. Maybe it was all in the sporting genes – his father William won three Football League titles and the FA Cup once while with Huddersfield Town.

Inside-forward Walter Keeton, who played 11 times for Sunderland in 1931, made two isolated appearances as an opening batsman for England in 1934 and 1939, the latter of which was at the Oval, where he also hit what remains the highest-individual score for Nottinghamshire of 312 not out. He hit 54 centuries in his career, and more than 2,000 runs in a season six times, continuing his top-class cricket career after having recovered from being knocked down by a lorry.

Talbot Lewis, who played in goal for Sunderland in the first four games of 1904/05 having started his career as a full-back, played cricket for Somerset between 1899 and 1914 and was also a top-grade billiards player. And in 1920 two other Sunderland footballers, half-back John Mitton and full-back John Morrison, also played for Somerset. Mitton, a Yorkshireman, played 82 games for Sunderland between 1920 and 1923 and once for Somerset, while Morrison's only appearance for Sunderland was in 1919. He played only once for Somerset, too, but he was a triple Blue in football, cricket and golf at Cambridge University, for whom he once hit an unbeaten 233 against the MCC. At one time he even turned his sporting attention to designing golf courses. In addition, two of Sunderland's England football internationals played county cricket – Raich Carter for Derbyshire against Worcestershire, Surrey and Northamptonshire in 1946, and Yorkshireman Mike Hellawell who was also a schoolboy sprint champion for Warwickshire against Oxford University in 1962, scoring 30 not out and 29 not out and taking 4 for 54.

Then there were Archie Jackson, a centre-half who made six appearances for Sunderland in 1923, and Archie Jackson, who played in eight Tests for Australia between 1929 and 1931, making 164 against England on his debut at Adelaide when he was only 19 and batting with Don Bradman. They were different people, but they were cousins! And if family matters are a sporting issue, then it should not be forgotten that Gary Owers, who made 320 appearances in midfield for Sunderland between 1987 and 1994, married British ice-skating champion Joanne Conway.

Sunderland also fielded several other footballers who excelled at other sporting pursuits. For example, Carter, John McPhee, Tommy

McLain, Don Gow, Colin Suggett, the renegade Tom McInally and Ken Willingham, who was also an England shinty international, were all very handy runners at various times. Nigel Walker and Andy Dibble did well at rugby union early in their careers, while Fred Gibson won a medal for shooting at Bisley, and Gerry Harrison played hockey and was the English Schools' under-15 javelin champion. Jackie Mordue was useful at fives, Jimmy Gorman at baseball, Suggett, George Mulhall and George Kinnell at basketball, Harry Threadgold at boxing and Eric Roy at tennis.

And when some Sunderland players could no longer play football, they often took up writing and talking about it. In the modern era a host of newspaper columnists and television pundits have climbed onto the media bandwagon in an ephemeral and unconvincing manner. But Len Shackleton and Trevor Ford were rival columnists, Ivor Broadis, John Colquhoun and Eric Gates also carved out media careers, and Ally McCoist has become such a famous face on television that his playing career has almost taken a back seat. He has also become a personality as a team captain on *A Question of Sport*, whose precursor *Quizball* brought one of Sunderland's most public thrashings during the 1966/67 season. Sunderland were drawn against Fulham in the first round of the football quiz programme, but their team of manager Ian McColl, players Len Ashurst and Gary Moore, and guest supporter Owen Brannigan lost 4–0 to Fulham's manager Vic Buckingham, England stars Johnny Haynes and George Cohen and comedian-cum club chairman Tommy Trinder.

Media fame, meanwhile, can provide the occasional embarrassment, as former Sunderland manager Peter Reid found when he ventured to Portugal as a television pundit for Euro 2004 and arrived at his hotel to find that his room had not been built! But it can also sustain a football personality in the spotlight, something which Charlie Buchan did better than anyone in Sunderland's history. When Buchan retired as a player in May 1928, he embarked on a career in journalism as the football and golf correspondent of the *Daily News* (later the *News Chronicle*), whose football annual he edited in the 1950s. He was also a commentator for BBC radio, but left his indelible stamp on the game in September 1951 when he and former Daily Mirror sports writers John Thompson and Joe Sarl jointly founded a magazine called *Charles Buchan's Football Monthly* 'with massive enthusiasm and slender capital'. As a result, Buchan became a household name to generations of football followers who may not have been fully aware of his illustrious playing background.

The new magazine cost 1s 6d (8p), and Stanley Matthews was pictured on the first front cover. Other well-known names featured in the inaugural issue included Joe Mercer, Joe Harvey, Henry Cockburn, Jimmy Dickinson and George Young. Co-editor John Thompson painted a picture of the magazine's evolution:

> In the early days there was one chair in the office of *Football Monthly*. We would perch around a trestle-table on orange boxes, courteously leaving the chair for any visitor tired from the trek up the steep stairs. The table was covered with a grey blanket and smelt of old apples, probably because Covent Garden was round the corner. Months before *Football Monthly* increased its assets, Charles Buchan arrived one morning carrying an absurdly expensive feather duster. Each day the old England captain would whisk it wildly over the walls and the tired strips of linoleum. He would look around as happily as if he had just scored against Scotland, but within seconds the dust would settle gracefully to await the next disturbance. Our office was in the Strand, and buses almost passed through the room, so it was difficult to keep it clean for long. The feather duster was our only extravagance. The winter was comfortless and draughts whistled around us. Charles Buchan would wrap newspapers round his legs to avoid frostbite, and the paper rustled when he moved. Placed furthest from the windows, co-editor Joe Sarl would peer with a kind of hopeless determination at typescripts and proofs, and at the end of the day he would walk towards the shining splendour of Mooney's Long Bar with the surprised look of a man seeing light at the end of the tunnel. We did find some incongruity in sitting on orange boxes to study an article from the Marquess of Londonderry, who had been converted to football by his friendship with miners in his father's pits. There was a dream-like quality in reading his description of how he had become a director of Arsenal – because of a conversation over dinner at Buckingham Palace with the Master of the Horse, who happened to be the club's chairman. After all, Buckingham Palace was just down the road from us, and for a moment the bare electric light bulb shone more brightly.

Buchan's brainchild eventually had a print run of 250,000. It was said to have been read by a judge's son in Yugoslavia, a boy in Brazil, a shoemaker in Alaska and a tugboat skipper who bought two copies so that he could send one to a youngster in hospital. Buchan died at the age of 68 at Beaulieu-sur-Mer while on holiday in the South of France in June 1960, but had lived to see the 100th edition of *Football Monthly* in November 1959, by which time its circulation had doubled to 120,000 in a little more than eight years. By its 10th anniversary in September 1961 sales had risen to more than 130,000. By this time Charles Buchan's

Publications Limited had moved to 161–166 Fleet Street from the Strand and they were producing 10 titles. In August 1953 the first edition of Charles Buchan's annual *Soccer Gift Book*, which was an immediate sell-out, had been published as a companion to *Football Monthly*.

The game's cognoscenti were quick to pay tribute to *Football Monthly*, at the same time underlining Buchan's stature. Joe Mercer once commented that 'The name Charles Buchan is automatically associated with all that is good in the game of football to people of my generation. Long may the magazine be a credit to his name and remain progressive, vital and interesting.' Stan Cullis added, '*Football Monthly* has consistently maintained a high standard, and I see it as a means of not only contributing a valuable service to its readers, but also of keeping the name of its founder, Charles Buchan, in the minds of the soccer public.' The magazine had authority, and feature writer Peter Morris once recalled:

Charlie was a stickler for his rights, but he always respected the rights of others. That perhaps developed the argumentative side of his character. Anyone who knew Charlie Buchan will testify to his powers in that direction. When in the mood, he could prove that black was white if he felt like doing so. The only way in which you could win was to argue against your own views, knowing that Charlie would almost certainly take the opposite line, so really agreeing with you.

Towards the end of the 1968/69 season *Football Monthly* decided to provide a trophy for the best player in the FA Cup final. Buchan had been on the losing side in two finals – in 1913 with Sunderland and in 1927 with Arsenal – and the citation for what was to be called *Football Monthly's* Wembley Award read: 'It will be decided on an after-match ballot among football writers covering the final, it will not necessarily go to a player on the winning side or to one of the goalscorers, and he will be judged as much on his sportsmanship and courage as on his ability and effort for his team.' The first winner was Leicester City's Allan Clarke, when his side were beaten 1–0 by Manchester City in 1969.

Some of the Sunderland players who ventured into journalism at the end of their careers had been brought up in a tough school of writing. The pen name Argus was long associated with reports on the club in the *Sunderland Echo*, and in the 1950s the journalist who was always on the case was Jack Anderson, whose style was to tell it as it really was. In those days players lived in dread of the *Echo's* Monday edition hitting the streets. Ivor Broadis, one of those who became a journalist, explained:

> Jack Anderson could tear you apart in one sentence and he had a go at everyone. No one was exempt from his vicious reporting style. But all the players feared Mondays the most. That was the edition in which he would write his considered report of the game from the previous Saturday and, believe me, it was always a case of 'no holds barred'. I can remember sitting in the big bath at Roker Park after training on a Monday morning and the players discussing who was going to be the one to go out and buy the lunchtime edition of the *Echo*. There were grown men ducking down and hiding beneath the water in fear of what was coming. That was Jack Anderson for you!'

And Len Shackleton painted a colourful picture of Anderson in his book Return of the Clown Prince, telling of when his younger brother John, who was then on the club's books, shared digs with winger Tommy Wright in Fulwell:

> Their landlady kept a goose at the digs. She put it in a pen in the back garden, and the plan was to fatten it ready for Christmas. Tommy and my brother nicknamed the goose Argus when the local reporter of that time was Jack Anderson, who was well noted for giving abrasive comments about some of the players. His Saturday-night sports column carried comments from the previous week's match, and on one particular occasion I remember finding Tommy fuming about Argus. His comments were to the effect that Tommy had only one way of beating a full-back – by kicking the ball past him and chasing round him – and wasn't capable of any greater variety of moves. Tommy was still fuming when we played our next game at Bolton, which was in front of a crowd of 40,000 or 50,000. Our goalkeeper Johnny Mapson kicked the ball out to Tommy at outside-right, and Tommy caught it! He took it like a rugby player, side-stepped the full-back and drop-kicked it over the bar! As he came back, he was chuntering to himself and any players with earshot: 'I'll show Jack Anderson. I'll show Argus that there is more than one way of beating the full-back!' On his way home to the digs with my brother, Tommy called into the local paper shop for that night's report on the match. He was still furious, and the first thing he did was to get hold of the goose Argus – after tripping over it! That seemed typical of Tommy. Basically he was a good lad, but a demonstrative character at times.

Other Sunderland players kept their links with football by venturing into different roles in the game. For example, Scottish international full-back Bob Smellie, a member of the Team of All Talents, became president of Queen's Park, while others became directors – John Auld at Newcastle United, Philip Bach at Middlesbrough and Dennis Tueart at Manchester City. Joe Devine, meanwhile, became a referee in his native Scotland. But numerous others kept alive their football passion by becoming managers, coaches and scouts. Sunderland can boast a reputation for having produced a high amount of managers who tried their luck in the English, Scottish and Irish leagues. At one stage the club was even reckoned to have earned the tag of the 'managers' factory' because they had six former players in charge of Football League clubs at the start of the 1972/73 season – Don Revie at Leeds United, Brian Clough at Derby County, Stan Anderson at Middlesbrough, Charlie Hurley at Reading, Len Ashurst at Hartlepool and George Mulhall at Halifax Town, while Billy Bingham was the national coach of Greece and Cec Irwin was the manager of then non-League Yeovil Town. In addition, all of them had been at Roker Park under Alan Brown's management.

Four people also combined playing and management careers at Sunderland. Bill Murray played 328 games between 1927 and 1936 and was then manager from 1939 to 1957; he played for no other English club and managed nobody else. Billy Elliott was a player at Roker from 1953 to 1958, making 212 appearances, but his management term was brief during the 1978/79 season. He then managed Darlington, and also had spells as a coach in Libya, where he looked after the national team, and in Germany, Belgium and Norway. Len Ashurst also coached a national team – Kuwait – and had a spell in Qatar after being sacked as Sunderland's manager after a little more than a season in 1984 and 1985. But his playing career at Roker had lasted much longer – from 1958 to 1970 – and he also turned his hand to management with Sheffield Wednesday, Cardiff City (twice), Hartlepool, Gillingham and Newport County (when they were in the League). Terry Butcher, who has also managed Coventry City and Motherwell, was Sunderland's only player-manager, although he played less and less during his 15 months in charge from August 1992.

Some other former Sunderland players took steps into management regularly. None was more successful than Brian Clough, who won the European Cup and the League title and served five clubs – Hartlepools United, Derby, Leeds, Brighton & Hove Albion and Nottingham Forest. Only two other former Sunderland players have managed five League clubs – Jimmy McGuigan at Crewe Alexandra, Grimsby Town, Chesterfield, Rotherham United and Stockport County, and Colin Todd at Middlesbrough, Bolton Wanderers, Derby, Swindon Town and Bradford City – while Raich Carter was in charge of four – Hull City, Leeds, Mansfield Town and Middlesbrough. Then there were Bobby Marshall at Stockport and Chesterfield, Bob Kelly at Stockport and Carlisle United, Warney Cresswell at Northampton Town – where his brother Frank and former Roker team-mate was his No. 2 – and Port Vale, Les McDowall at Oldham Athletic, Wrexham and Manchester City, Willie Watson at Halifax and Bradford City, Stan Anderson at Middlesbrough, Doncaster Rovers and Bolton, George Mulhall at Bradford City, Bolton and Halifax, Mick Docherty at Rochdale and Hartlepool United, Sam Allardyce at Blackpool, Notts County and Bolton, and Chris Turner at Leyton Orient, Hartlepool and Sheffield Wednesday.

Others got the chance to manage only one League club – Jack Poole at Mansfield, Bob Young at Norwich City (twice), Johnny Spuhler at Shrewsbury Town, Harry Martin at Mansfield, Bill Marsden at Doncaster, Ivor Broadis at Carlisle, Bill Robinson at Hartlepools, Charlie Hurley at Reading, Martin Harvey at Carlisle, Don Revie at Leeds, Doug Collins at Rochdale, Neil Martin at Walsall, Dickie Rooks at Scunthorpe United, Bryan 'Pop' Robson at Carlisle, Mick McGiven as team manager at Ipswich Town (when John Lyall became general manager), Vic Halom at Rochdale, Frank Worthington at Tranmere Rovers, Frank Gray at Darlington, John MacPhail at Hartlepool, Peter Daniel at Lincoln City, Gary Bennett at Darlington, Chris Waddle at Burnley, Peter Davenport at Macclesfield Town, John Cornforth at Exeter City and David Hodgson at Darlington (twice). But although Revie's only excursion into English League management was with Leeds, he did take charge of England before leaving to coach in the United Arab Emirates and Egypt. Bill Maxwell, meanwhile, made do with being the national coach of Belgium in the 1920s. Halom once tried something completely different –he stood as a General Election candidate in 1992 for the Liberal Democrats in Sunderland North.

A number of Sunderland players managed current League clubs when they were not in the League – Harold Buckle at Coventry, Ephraim Rhodes at Brentford, Bill Fullarton at Plymouth Argyle, Stan Ramsay at Shrewsbury, Harry Thompson, who was Headington United's player-manager before they became Oxford United, David Halliday, Joe McDonald and Cec Irwin at Yeovil, Bobby Gurney at Peterborough United, Ian Atkins at Colchester United and Ian Snodin at Doncaster. In contrast, others managed current non-League clubs when they were in the League – Jackie Mordue and Dickie Jackson at Durham City, James Hindmarsh and David Elliott at Newport, Ian Bowyer at Hereford

United and Paul Bracewell at Halifax. In some cases, though, they were also given management opportunities elsewhere – Buckle at Belfast United, Halliday at Leicester and Aberdeen, Gurney at Darlington and Hartlepools, Bracewell at Fulham and Atkins at Cambridge United, Northampton, Chester City, Carlisle, Oxford and Bristol Rovers.

Some players managed only League clubs in Scotland – George Livingston at Clydebank and Dumbarton, Billy Hogg at Raith Rovers, Jimmy Richardson at Ayr United and Cowdenbeath, George Anderson at Dundee, Alex Hastings at Kilmarnock, Harry Hood at Queen of the South and Albion Rovers, George Herd at Queen of the South, Joe Baker at Albion, John Hughes at Stranraer, Iain Munro at Raith, Hamilton Academicals and Dunfermline Athletic, and Ian Wallace at Dumbarton. In addition, Anderson was a director at Aberdeen, and Hughes had a spell as Scotland's youth coach. There have also been players who managed in England and Scotland – Jimmy Nicholl at Millwall and Raith (twice), Ralph Brand at Darlington and Albion, Bobby Moncur at Carlisle, Hartlepool, Plymouth and Hearts, and George Burley at Ayr, Colchester, Ipswich and Derby. Others managed league clubs only in Ireland – Bill Campbell at Linfield, Ken Chisholm at Glentoran, Ambrose Fogarty at Cork Hibernian, Cork Celtic, Drumcondra and Athlone Town, and Jim McDonagh at Derry City and Galway United.

Other players had more cosmopolitan and varied management experiences – Bobby McKay at Newport, Ballymena United and Dundee United, John McSeveney at Barnsley and Waterford City, Billy Bingham at Southport (when they were in the League), Plymouth, Linfield, Everton and Mansfield, and Ian Porterfield at Rotherham, Sheffield United, Aberdeen, Reading and Chelsea. McSeveney was also once Guyana's national coach, Bingham managed Northern Ireland, as well as having a spell as Blackpool's director of football and later becoming their vice-chairman. Porterfield had national coaching jobs in Zambia, Oman and Trinidad & Tobago before going out to the Far East. McSeveney was also Porterfield's assistant at Rotherham and Sheffield United.

Stan Ternent and John Wile may have made only the substitutes' bench as Sunderland players, but they too ventured into League management. Ternent has taken charge at Blackpool, Hull, Bury and Burnley, while Wile had a spell as Peterborough's manager.

When a lot of other Sunderland players left the game, they proved the point that England has remained a nation of shopkeepers. Those involved in various kinds of sports shops included Charlie Buchan, Walter Keeton, Joe Devine, Bert Davis, Willie Watson (with his brother

Albert), Johnny Crossan, Nicky Sharkey and Peter Daniel. Eddie Burbanks had had a sweet shop just a few yards down the road from Daniel in East Hull, while other shopkeepers almost overlapped generically rather than geographically in their enterprises. Stan Ramsay, Jimmy Connor, Raich Carter and Cec Irwin all had newsagencies or tobacconists, Ralph Brand was a newsagent and a grocer, while Len Shackleton had a confectionery and barber's shop and Jack Overfield had a confectionery and a tobacconist. Mike Hellawell was a greengrocer, while Sandy McNab and Cliff Whitelum merely worked in groceries, George Goddard was just a butcher's boy and Ted Purdon was a salesman in a store in Johannesburg. Alex Hastings, Johnny Spuhler and Ray Daniel ran post offices, and Hastings was also the manager of a bookshop in Edinburgh. John Auld was a cobbler, and something was certainly afoot when Billy Hughes took up shopkeeping because he owned a shoe shop in Sunderland called Billy Shughes! Ian Lawther and Tommy Urwin owned tailor's shops, David Wright had his own bakery business, Colin Waldron was a bookmaker and John Hawley has his own antiques business, while Dave Watson and Gordon Armstrong have also been involved in shop ventures. In addition, Sunderland's first manager Tom Watson also owned a tobacconist in Monkwearmouth station, while Overfield later had one of the most unusual occupations of all when he was no longer a shopkeeper – he studied poultry-keeping, and built up a six-acre chicken farm at Appleton Roebuck, near York.

The great Jim Baxter once said with sad irony, 'All the great players I've ever known have enjoyed a good drink.' It should not therefore be surprising that many Sunderland players became publicans at the end of their career. Centre-half Joe Smart, who played in the 1880s before Sunderland were a League club, was possibly the first when he became the landlord of the Aquatic Arms in Monkwearmouth. The club's first great goalscorer, Johnny Campbell, left the game with Newcastle in 1898 because he was in breach of their rules by becoming a licensee. Others known to have become publicans – in addition to Baxter himself, of course – include Willie Gibson, John Smith, William Fulton, Alf Common, Billy Hogg, Willie Clark, Charlie B. Thomson, Billy Cringan, Warney Cresswell, Alex Donaldson, Billy Grimshaw, Bill Marsden, Tom Scott, Bob Young, Bobby Marshall, William Simpson, Joe Devine, Albert McInroy, Sandy McNab, Ken Willingham, Tommy Reynolds, Arthur Wright, Joe Baker, John O'Hare, Bobby Kerr, John Hughes, Bob Lee, Jim Holton, Jim McDonagh, Micky Horswill and Iain Hesford. Players' public houses were dotted all over, but some were in intriguing locations – Joe Kasher at the Peel Park Hotel near Accrington Stanley's ground when they were a League club, and Billy Whitehurst at the Cricketers'

Arms outside Sheffield United's Bramall Lane. Others arguably went a touch up-market: Jimmy 'Daddy Long Legs' Watson, Jimmy Oakley, David Halliday, Alex Hastings, Jimmy Hamilton and Terry Curran became hoteliers at various times; Billy Hughes and Andy Kerr became club stewards; and Lee Chapman ran a wine bar. Also venturing into the trade were manager Alex Mackie, who became a licensee after a second financial scandal had hastened his retirement from football, and more recently assistant manager Viv Busby.

And if indeed it was often a case of 'Good health!' for Sunderland players when they left the game, then there are plenty of examples to prove it. Colin Nelson became a pharmacist, while still playing for the club, Derek Weddle became a chiropodist, Ian Hughes and Gary Moore worked for pharmaceutical companies, Leigh Roose trained as a doctor and bacteriologist, and Ronald Brebner trained as a dentist. Others became physiotherapists – Roger Wylde at Stockport, Jeff Clarke at Hearts and Joe Hinnigan at Chester – while Harry Bedford and David Willis had spells as masseurs to Derbyshire County Cricket Club. In addition, John Lathan studied as a physiotherapist, while Tommy Lloyd trained as a masseur.

It is also fitting that some Sunderland players have followed the lead of founders James Allan and John Grayston, who played a major role in recruiting Tom Watson, the manager of the Team of All Talents. They were schoolteachers, as were Ted Bell, Joe Shaw, Nigel Walker, Jack Huggins, Richie Pitt, Alan Spence and Norman Wood. Other players moved into heavy metal – James McMillan as a sculptor to the masonic trade, George Collin as a blacksmith and James Raine as the managing director of an iron-and-steel firm. Arthur Andrews, Walter Annan, Ernest 'Cliff' Thorley, Mick Henderson and Tony Norman became policemen, James Gillespie and Jimmy Gorman became cabinet-makers, Tom Ritchie and Barry Siddall became postmen, and Tommy Mitchinson and Ron Guthrie became milkmen. James 'Joe' Lane intriguingly worked in Hungary in the family printing business, while John Murray was employed in the calico printing trade. Others worked in jobs traditionally associated with the Sunderland area – Harold Buckle, Les McDowall, George Holley and Frank Cuggy in the shipyards, and Bob Kelly, Tom Wallace, Arthur Welsby, Peter Meechan, Harold Shaw, Jack Stelling, Evelyn Morrison and Harry Kirtley in the mining industry.

But the greatest memories surround events on the field and the lives and action of the people who created them. There are bound to be strong feelings in a game and an area where passions run high, and they have been an underlying theme in Sunderland's history at times. James

Hogg walked out on the club – and indeed football – in the 1920s after a personality clash with Bobby Marshall. Two other great forwards, Len Shackleton and Trevor Ford, always seemed to be at daggers drawn. Brian Clough never forgave Bob Stokoe for the remarks he made when he received the injury that finished his playing career there and then. In fact, one of Stokoe's FA Cup heroes of 1973 said, 'We used to hate him because he used to fight everyone in five-a-side in training. We didn't have a good relationship when he was manager, but he was his own man and we got on fine afterwards.' Then there were the myriad feelings from those who came into contact with Alan Brown during his two spells as manager. And there were the dressing-room factions that showed allegiance to either Charlie Hurley or Jim Baxter. And there was also the disagreement between manager Denis Smith and his assistant Viv Busby. They are not necessarily minuses on Sunderland's landscape, though: they must be understood in the context of people operating in a climate of highly charged emotions. They all cared in their individual ways.

Footballing passions give rise to moments of good humour, too. Striker Thomas Hauser arrived at Sunderland from Switzerland in 1989 and left for Holland three years later, but he was born about 30 miles inside the German border. He was nicknamed U-Boat by the Roker fans because his 65 appearances for the club included only 26 starts, so he was known as a German sub! Ivor Broadis, meanwhile, recalled a typical football anecdote:

We were on a tour of Turkey in 1950, a pretty far-flung place for an English football club to go in those days. It was another world for most of us, and I remember that there was this chap who used to walk around the streets near the hotel with half a grocer's shop on his back. He was loaded up with as much food, drink and provisions as he could carry and would go around shouting his wares. One thing he used to shout in English all the time was: 'Eggs and bread, eggs and bread!' With footballers being footballers, of course, a lot of the lads would mimic him and do it quite well. Then, towards the end of the tour, we were all invited to the Ambassador's house in Istanbul – well, it was more like a palace – and were told to be on our best behaviour. It was a cocktail party really, and we were all kitted out in club blazers and flannels. The Ambassador was anxious that all the players should sign the visitors' book on their way out, and, of course, we did as we were asked, and thought nothing more of it. The next morning, when we were having breakfast at the hotel, the manager Billy Murray came storming into the restaurant. He shouted: 'I've had the Ambassador on the phone this morning. Which of you bloody idiots signed his book Eggs and Bread?' We all burst out laughing, but Bill didn't think it was very funny. It had been Reg Scotson, the big, hairy right-half. Reg was a local lad and tough as old boots. Nothing scared him!

And on the pitch there have been numerous highs and lows as players have striven to do justice to a club of Sunderland's stature. They left lasting impressions on the adoring public, with moments to savour and moments to forget as the winter dramas unfolded year after year.

When, for example, centre-forward Ronnie Turnbull was asked how he felt about the prospect of making his League debut for the club at Roker Park in November 1947, he replied: 'I am terrified.' But his fears seemed to abate when the match got under way, because he scored all four goals in a 4–1 victory over Portsmouth! Striker John Hawley, a mere hat-trick hero on his Sunderland debut in comparison, also scored with a 40-yard shot against Arsenal goalkeeper Pat Jennings during his stay at Roker. He joked: 'They kept showing it on television, saying it was one of the best goals of the season. But all I could think was how stupid I had been to shoot from so far out!' Colin Grainger had been well aware of Ray Daniel's ability before they became Roker team-mates after playing against him for Sheffield United, and recalled another spectacular moment. It came in an FA Cup fifth-round tie in 1956 when Sunderland won a replay 1–0 at Roker Park. Grainger said, 'Ray scored from the halfway line. The ground was bobbly and wet, he just hit the ball on the half-volley and it few into the top corner. Our goalkeeper Ted Burgin said he should have had it, but we told him that two goalkeepers wouldn't have kept it out!'

There were the embarrassing moments too, such as the occasions on which Sunderland conceded two of the most bizarre goals ever. In April 1900 Manchester City's goalkeeper Charlie Williams provided a comic incident when he hit a goal-kick at Roker Park the full length of the field with the help of a strong wind behind him, and his opposite number, the long-serving Ned Doig, got a touch as he instinctively tried to keep the ball out, but he merely helped it into the net – and the goal, of course, stood. And Harry Threadgold may have had a reputation as a useful boxer as well as a goalkeeper, but it did him little good in his only season with Sunderland when they met Aston Villa at Villa Park in September 1952 because he was unsighted and failed to touch the ball as it bounced over his head and into the net from 35 yards out. The freakish aspect of the goal, though, was that Villa full-back Peter Aldis had scored it with his head. But maybe it was all summed up best during the worst League run in Sunderland's history in February 2003 when they lost 3–1 at home to Charlton Athletic with three own goals in eight first-half minutes – one from Stephen Wright and two from Michael Proctor.

In Sunderland's history there have been two Charlie Thomsons. Their spells with the clubs did not overlap, but it was still hard to distinguish between them because both were Scottish internationals and both were half-backs, and their playing records with the club were remarkably similar. Charlie Bellany Thomson made 236 League appearances for the club and scored six goals; Charlie Morgan Thomson made 237 League appearances for the club and scored seven. Charlie B. Thomson made 29 FA Cup appearances for the club, scoring twice; Charlie M. Thomson made 27 FA Cup appearances, scoring once. As a result, Charlie B. Thomson's full record was 265 appearances with eight goals, while Charlie M. Thomson's full record was 264 appearances with eight goals.

Scots, of course, were always associated with Sunderland's early days because they formed the backbone of the Team of All Talents which dominated the League championship in the 1890s. But they were still in evidence later on. The club's top-five leading goalscorers in 1965/66 were all Scots – Neil Martin, George Herd, John O'Hare, George Mulhall and Jim Baxter. Players always want to get off to good starts with new clubs. Winger John McSeveney said of his Sunderland bow in October 1951: 'I made my debut against Manchester United at Old Trafford, I was playing against Johnny Carey, we won 1–0 and I crossed the ball for Dickie Davis to score the winner.' But by 2004 McSeveney was still scouting in the game at the age of 73 – for Manchester United! Midfield man Calvin Palmer played only 42 games for Sunderland, but one at Roker Park in April 1968 was particularly significant for him. He took over as an emergency goalkeeper when Jim Montgomery was injured and helped his side to a 3–1 victory. Ironically, it was Sunderland's first home win for five months and it came against Stoke City, the club from which he had been signed in a £70,000 deal less than two months earlier! And Sunderland made the worst start of anyone in the 1990s, becoming the first League club to concede a goal in the decade. It came when Andy Payton scored for Hull against them at Boothferry Park on New Year's Day, 1990, in a 3–2 defeat – after the police had insisted on an early kick-off for safety reasons even though there were only 8,000-plus there in the end!

Amid it all, Sunderland's fans have been entertained by some great players, and they have never forgotten their all-time heroes. The opening of the Raich Carter Sports Centre in Hendon by Sir Trevor Brooking in 2001 proves it. And so does Charlie Hurley having Sunderland's training ground named after him, and being invited to dig up the centre spot at

Roker Park for it to be re-planted at the Stadium of Light.

It is unfortunate, though, that many of Sunderland's greatest English players, such as George Holley, Charlie Buchan, Raich Carter, Bobby Gurney, Len Shackleton, Stan Anderson and Brian Clough, received such sparse international recognition for different reasons. One example of an international that got away underlines the point. On 21 August 1935, Carter and Gurney played for England against Scotland at Hampden Park in what was described by the FA as a jubilee international match. It was in aid of the King's Jubilee Trust Fund, there was a gate of 56,316 with £4,000 receipts, and Scotland won 4–2, leading 4–0 after 50 minutes before England scored twice in the last 10 minutes. But it did not go into the record books, and the FA insisted that 'It was a one-off match and wasn't an official international.' The referee, in fact, was a Scot, and the inference is that the game was unofficial because England were scheduled to play an official match against Scotland later in the season in the Home International Championship. Identifying the England marksmen is not easy: even *The Times* did not mention their names in its match report, and the FA admitted that 'Our international committee minutes don't record the scorers.' But a newspaper cutting has been found that gives the scorers as Gurney and Bolton's Raymond Westwood. Apparently the most lasting recognition of the occasion was the presentation of a quaich – a Scottish drinking-cup or loving-cup – to each player. But the gift of a quaich to Raich and Bobby was poor fare in comparison with the lack of official acknowledgement of the status of the occasion. Gurney was capped only once by England, so he lost out on an official international appearance and an official goal, but he was said to be baffled rather annoyed about it. His son-in-law Michael Bates said:

> Bobby wasn't that sort of fellow. It seems silly and petty, but he wasn't bothered about it. He wouldn't make an issue of anything. He was gentle, very humble and didn't have a resentful streak in him. He just loved his football and was grateful that he could play it for £6 a week, compared with his father and brothers, who went down the pit.

In the early days, players knew where they stood in the grand scheme of football. In fact, they were virtual slaves before the maximum wage was abolished in 1961, and Stan Anderson illustrated the point:

> I used to get a couple of buses in every day for training. Being from Horden, I would get one so far and then change at Grangetown. On one particular day I was running between bus

stops, absolutely terrified of being late. I was in the first team, but just a young lad at the time, and you could not be late for training. We never saw the manager in those days, though. In fact, we would see Billy Murray only on Saturday afternoons. The trainers, as they called them back then, took charge of the sessions, with the manager normally in his office dressed in shirt, tie and suit. Well, as I was running for the bus this day, Mr Murray pulled up in a beautiful car – an MG Magnette, I think. He told me to get in and gave me a lift for the final couple of miles. I was terrified – too terrified to speak. Mr Murray was a decent man, but then it was like being in the Army and you did as you were told. I just sat there, amazed that I was being given a lift in the manager's car. It was no wonder that, when I did join the Army to do my National Service, I wasn't shocked by anything. Being in the Army was like being a player then – and being a player was like being in the Army. Simple, really!

The rapport between players and their public made up for a lot, though. By and large players were only too willing to join Sunderland because of the club's high esteem in so many different quarters. They wanted to be part of the club and they knew that they would always be extra-special to the many thousands of faithful fans if they did the business on the pitch. Winger Roy Greenwood, a Yorkshireman, summed it up: 'I made some good friends in the North-East and still go up there and meet them. I enjoyed it so much that I might have lived up there when I'd finished playing. Football is a religion to the fans, and they are the most passionate people I've ever played in front of.'

And there have been some special fans who have been proud to be associated with Sunderland. Singer Owen Brannigan was not Sunderland's only celebrity supporter, after all. There have been others, such as singer Alan Price and athlete Steve Cram, while Welsh comedian Stan Stennett was a lifelong friend of Trevor Ford and they were partners in a garage business long after the final whistle had been blown. Well-known Sunderland fans come from all walks of life. For example, it should not have happened to a vet, but it did. World-famous veterinary surgeon and author James Herriot became hooked on Sunderland as soon as he was old enough to be taken to his first game, after the 1914–18 war. And eventually the modest and totally unassuming Alf Wight would become a vice-president of the club he had supported for more than half a century. Alf, who died in 1995 aged 78, was born in Sunderland, in his own words 'just a Billy Clunas penalty-kick away from Roker Park!' Football always featured strongly in his life, so much so that he decided to write as James Herriot after taking the name from a Scotland and Birmingham City goalkeeper! He said:

> I was still struggling to write my first book at the time, and I can recall sitting at the table battling with it while keeping half an eye on the television because *Match of the Day* was on. I heard the commentator refer to the Birmingham goalkeeper Jim Herriot, and I thought to myself, 'That will do nicely as a name to write under,' so I went for it there and then! Actually, he was a Scot and many people always thought I was, too. But I was born in Roker, and Sunderland were in my blood from an early age. I watched the great Charlie Buchan, the majestic Raich Carter, Shack, Charlie Hurley...all of them. But probably my favourite player of all time was Carter. He could glide across the pitch, shoot with either foot and had the greatest body swerve you ever saw.

Sunderland supporters have often had to live in eternal hope, and no one has shared the degree of expectancy more than Jim Montgomery, the local-born goalkeeper whose reflexes arguably provided the greatest moment of all in the club's history at Wembley in 1973 and whose record-breaking 623 appearances will probably never be beaten. Monty recalled:

> I had some great times with Sunderland and played in many different teams while I was there. But the three teams that stand out most to me are those from 1964 when we were promoted, 1973 when we won the FA Cup and 1976 when we were promoted again. Each of those sides had great quality, yet, on each occasion that something was achieved, the club failed to build on it. Then, much later under Peter Reid, Sunderland finished seventh in the Premiership for two seasons in succession. Once again it was not built upon. This great club, which first returned to the top flight with that excellent team of 1963/64, really ought to have been living up there alongside football's big guns ever since. But it hasn't been the case. I was a Sunderland fan long before I ever played for them and that never leaves you. Maybe one day we will get back to the top of the tree and stay there.

As Alan Brown, the only person to manage the club twice, once said: 'Soccer is the biggest thing that happened in creation – bigger than any

"-ism" you can name.' And as long as that is deemed to be the case, Sunderland will remain at the forefront of football clubs whose allegiance must for ever be to those who really matter. The fans.